Green Households?

Domestic Consumers, Environment, and Sustainability

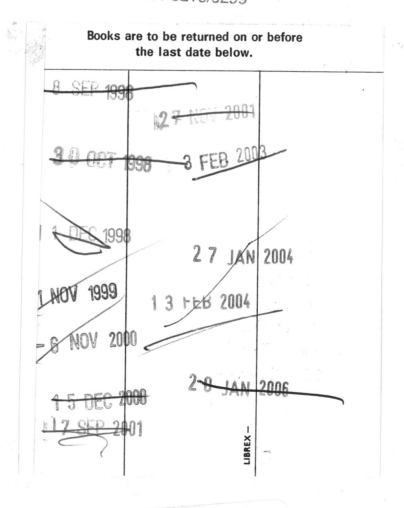

Green Households?

Domestic Consumers, Environment, and Sustainability

Edited by

Klaas Jan Noorman

and

Ton Schoot Uiterkamp

Earthscan Publications Ltd, London

First published in the UK in 1998 by
Earthscan Publications Ltd

Copyright © Klaas Jan Noorman and Ton Schoot Uiterkamp, 1998

A catalogue record for this book is available from the British Library

ISBN: 1 85383 482 3 (paperback)
ISBN: 1 85383 481 5 (hardback)

Typesetting and page design by the
International Institute for Applied Systems Analysis (IIASA)

Printed and bound by Biddles Ltd, Guildford and Kings Lynn

Cover design by Yvonne Booth

For a full list of publications, please contact
Earthscan Publications Ltd
120 Pentonville Road
London N1 9JN
Tel: 0171 278 0433
Fax: 0171 278 1142
email: earthinfo@earthscan.co.uk
http://www.earthscan.co.uk

Earthscan is an editorially independent subsidiary of Kogan Page Ltd and publishes in
association with WWF-UK and the International Institute for Environment and Development.

Contents

Preface

What could be more familiar than a household? Indeed, when something is widely recognized it becomes a "household" word, but paradoxically, this familiarity is not reflected in the attention given to households as an important socioeconomic sector with its corresponding environmental impacts. To date, much more attention has focused on the environmental impacts of industry, agriculture, and commerce, i.e., on the production side of the economy.

The generous grant awarded by NWO, the Dutch National Foundation for Scientific Research, has given a team of researchers at universities in the Netherlands the opportunity to conduct an interdisciplinary environmental research program on the vital yet relatively poorly studied household sector. The program, entitled HOMES (Household Metabolism Effectively Sustainable), is being conducted under the auspices of the NWO priority research program on sustainability and environmental quality. The HOMES program focuses on the diagnosis, evaluation, and changes in the rates of household metabolism in the Netherlands, i.e., the flows of energy and materials through households, and the production of waste. The program draws on a wide range of empirical research, using the examples of energy consumption, the use of domestic appliances (particularly "white goods" such as refrigerators and washing machines), and the use of the car.

This volume presents the findings of the first, diagnostic phase of the HOMES research, which consisted of a comprehensive investigation of past and present characteristics and trends of specific metabolic flows through households. The sustainability and environmental quality aspects of these flow patterns were investigated. This first phase of the program concluded with a joint HOMES/IIASA (International Institute of Applied Systems Analysis) workshop in Vienna in late 1995, at which working drafts of several chapters in this volume were presented.

Throughout the text, many of the data are expressed in Dutch guilders (Dfl). At the time of writing (October 1997), Dfl 100 = £32 = US$50.

The volume begins with an introduction by Professor Kerry Turner, followed by an exploration of the concept of household metabolism in the context of sustainability and environmental quality. The next eight chapters have been written from various disciplinary perspectives, ranging from the environmental sciences,

ix

geography and urban studies, to social psychology, economics, and public policy. Finally, we present an overall diagnosis and evaluation of household metabolism in the Netherlands in the past 50 years. The volume addresses what would constitute sustainable domestic consumption and lifestyles, and also how far there is to go to achieve this in an affluent, industrialized Western society.

We emphasize that the primary aim of the HOMES program is to address and explore the methodological issues surrounding relevant household–environment interactions. We hope that this volume will demonstrate the exciting and challenging aspects of this field of research and its relevance for all societies. We will strongly pursue work in this field and are looking forward to combining forces with related research activities elsewhere.

Klaas Jan Noorman
Ton Schoot Uiterkamp

HOMES Project Team
Center for Energy and
Environmental Studies
University of Groningen
Nijenborgh 4
9747 AG Groningen
The Netherlands

Acknowledgments

The HOMES program was made possible by grant support from NWO, the Dutch National Foundation for Scientific Research, through its priority program on sustainability and environmental quality. Financial support was also provided by the University of Groningen, Twente University, and Wageningen Agricultural University.

The authors are grateful for the general editorial and logistic contributions of Willeke Biemolt (IVEM), Ewa Delpos (IIASA), Linda Foith (IIASA), and Frances MacDermott (Earthscan).

We acknowledge especially the outstanding editorial work of Val Jones.

Finally, we thank Professor Kerry Turner for his thorough midterm review of the HOMES program, and for contributing the introduction to this volume.

Contributors

Wouter Biesiot (1951) has a PhD in physics, and since 1980 has been a staff member of the Center for Energy and Environmental Studies of the University of Groningen. As a senior lecturer at the Center, he is head of the energy and materials research unit. His major areas of research interest include dynamic energy analysis and materials substitution problems.

André G. Bus (1964) holds a bachelors degree in physical training and human geography. In 1994 he received a masters degree in technical planning at the University of Groningen, where he is currently employed as a research assistant. His PhD research focuses on sustainable urban renewal. His special interests include the principles of neighborhood design and building principles that reduce environmental degradation.

Albertine M.L. van Diepen (1966) graduated from the Institute of Social Geography, University of Amsterdam, and continued her studies as a postgraduate student in environmental policy. At the Netherlands Interdisciplinary Demographic Institute in The Hague, she worked on the interlinkages between demographic changes and environmental degradation. Since 1994 she has worked at the University of Groningen. Her special area of interest concerns the spatial implications of household developments and changing patterns of consumption. She joined the IIASA Population Project group in spring 1995.

Birgitta Gatersleben (1968) studied social and organizational psychology at the University of Leiden, where she graduated in 1993. Since February 1994 she has worked as a PhD student in the HOMES project at the Department of Psychology at the University of Groningen. Her main interest is in the social-psychological mechanisms underlying household consumer behavior in relation to environmental quality.

Peter Kooreman (1955) is professor of microeconomics at the University of Groningen. He holds a PhD from Tilburg University, Netherlands. He has (co-)authored various publications on household economic behavior, including *The Economics of Household Behaviour* (Macmillan, 1996).

Josee L. Ligteringen (1968) studied public administration at the University of Twente. As a research associate at the Center for Clean Technology and Environmental Policy at Twente, she participated in several projects in the area of environmental policy, including the evaluation of guidelines on the implementation of air quality policy (funded by the Dutch Directorate-General for the Environment); a review study of financial policy instruments in Dutch environmental policy (funded by the Evaluation Committee of the Directorate-General for the Environment); an international comparative study on decision making on waste facility siting (funded by the European Commission); and the evaluation of waste prevention projects in industry (funded by the Directorate-General for the Environment).

Vincent G.M. Linderhof (1968) studied econometrics at the University of Amsterdam (1993). He worked at the Netherlands Organization for Strategic Labor Market Research, before he started his PhD research at the University of Groningen in 1994. His research interests include the economic aspects of household metabolism.

Klaas Jan Noorman (1964), originally trained as a biologist, holds a MSc in environmental sciences from the University of Groningen (1990). From 1990 to 1994 he was affiliated as a research fellow at the Center for Energy and Environmental Studies at Groningen. During this period his major areas of research interest were natural capital accounting studies and dynamic energy analysis. In 1995 he received his PhD in environmental sciences from the University of Groningen. He has been coordinator of the HOMES research program since 1994.

A.J.M. (Ton) Schoot Uiterkamp (1944) has a PhD in biophysical chemistry from the University of Groningen. He was a staff member of UNESCO in Cairo, Egypt. He has held research positions at Yale and Harvard universities. He was staff member and department head at the Environmental Division of the Netherlands Organization for Applied Scientific Research (TNO). Since 1991 he has been professor of environmental sciences at the Center for Energy and Environmental Studies of the University of Groningen.

Jack van der Wal (1967) trained as an environmental scientist at the van Hall Institute (BE, 1989) and the University of Groningen (MSc, 1993). His PhD research at the Center for Energy and Environmental Studies at Groningen focuses on the physical flows of energy, water, and materials related to household consumption in the Netherlands.

Charles A.J. Vlek (1938) studied experimental and social psychology at the University of Leiden, where he obtained his PhD on the basis of "Psychological Studies in Probability and Decision Making" (1973). During his subsequent work at the Department of Psychology at Leiden, he spent study and research periods in Stockholm, Santa Barbara (California) and at Dartmouth College, Hanover (New Hampshire). He moved to the University of Groningen in 1976, to engage in experimental research in social psychology, combined with applied research in risk perception and decision making. He is currently professor of applied psychology, focusing on behavioral decision research. His special interests include risk perception and decision processes, human behavior as environmental exploitation/protection, and personal mobility and transportation as behavioral processes.

Henk Voogd (1950) holds a masters degree in human geography and urban planning from the University of Utrecht (1974), and a PhD from Eindhoven University of Technology (1982). His promoters were Henk Goudappel and Peter Nijkamp. In 1974–1978 he worked at the TNO Research Centre for Physical Planning in Delft. Between 1979 and 1985 he worked as associate professor of urban planning at Delft University of Technology. Since 1986 he has been professor of planning and urban geography at the University of Groningen. He has been visiting professor at the University of Reading (UK), the University of Washington (Seattle, USA), the University of Ghent (Belgium), and the University of Naples (Italy). He is (co-)author of several books on planning and planning methodology.

Harry C. Wilting (1957) is senior researcher at the Center for Energy and Environmental Studies (IVEM) of the University of Groningen. He holds an MSc in mathematics and computer science (1987), and has been associated with IVEM since 1990. He has a PhD in environmental sciences from the University of Groningen (1996). His thesis focused on the relations between economic activities and energy use, especially the energy requirements of household consumption. He is currently a member of the GreenHouse project team, which concentrates on options for the reduction of greenhouse gas emissions by means of changes in production structures and consumption patterns. His major area of research interest is energy analysis.

Household Metabolism and Sustainability
Some Introductory Remarks

R. Kerry Turner
CSERGE, University of East Anglia, and University College London

In recent decades, a pervasive feature of many Western societies has been the contrast between static or slow-growing populations, and the sharply increasing total number of households, the average size of which is diminishing (see van Diepen, Chapter 4). This trend has significant implications for the use of resources and the generation/disposal of waste, linked to the direct flows of resources through households and to the supply of resources necessary to support these flows. Household metabolism is therefore linked to a complex feedback process involving environmental, economic, social, psychological, and cultural factors and relationships. The diagnosis and evaluation of the household metabolism process in the Netherlands are the core objectives of the HOMES research program. The results of the diagnostic phase are reported in this volume. The HOMES project represents and excellent attempt to champion research that is both interdisciplinary in scope and likely to provide policy relevant findings.

The policy context today cannot be considered without recognition of the increasingly influential policy objective of sustainable economic development (see Noorman *et al.*, Chapter 1). Sustainable development as a concept is meant to encompass both wealth creation and quality of life/environment dimensions. It is clearly value-laden and its precise interpretation will differ according to which world view is adopted. Thus the notion of a sustainable household can be quantified in terms of material and energy flows over time, but will also be connected to attitudinal, social, and cultural factors and trends. The sustainable household concept is a very effective way of demonstrating the obligations that informed citizens in a sustainable society must fulfill. Household members will have to face up to the fact that modifications and/or changes in lifestyles are necessary. In this context, there is a need for information that will enable and inform individuals, and a set of incentives/regulations to steer behavioral responses.

Economists define sustainable development in terms of non-decreasing levels of utility, or income per capita, or real consumption per capita over time. In broad terms, it involves providing a bequest from the present generation to the next of an amount and quality of wealth that is at least equal to that inherited by the present generation. This requires a non-declining capital stock over time and is consistent with the criterion of intergenerational equity. The most widely publicized definition of sustainable development, credited to the World Commission on Environment and Development, also included an intragenerational equity criterion. Sustainability therefore requires a development process that allows for an increase in the well-being of the present generation, with particular emphasis on the welfare of the poorest members of society, while simultaneously avoiding uncompensated and "significant" costs, including environmental damage costs, on future generations. Such a cost liability would reduce the "opportunities" for future generations to achieve a comparable level of well-being. The sustainability approach is therefore based on a long-term perspective; it incorporates equity, as well as efficiency criteria, and it may also emphasize the need to maintain a "healthy" global ecological system.

A spectrum of overlapping sustainability positions, ranging from very "weak" to very "strong", can be distinguished, as illustrated in *Figure 1*. Weak sustainability requires the maintenance of the total capital stock, composed of manufactured or reproducible capital, human capital (the stock of knowledge and skills), and natural capital, exhaustible and renewable resources, together with environmental structures, functions and services through time, with the implicit assumption of infinite substitution possibilities between all forms of capital. The Hartwick rule is also used to buttress the weak sustainability position by regulating the intergenerational capital bequests. The rule states that the rent obtained from the exploitation of the natural capital stock by the current generation, should be reinvested in the form of reproducible capital, which would form the inheritance of future generations. This inheritance transfer should be at a level sufficient to guarantee non-declining real consumption and well-being through time.

The implicit assumption of capital substitutability underpins the further argument that extensive scope exists over time for the decoupling of economic activity and environmental impacts. The decoupling process is mediated by technical progress and innovation. While total decoupling is not possible, and with the important exception of cumulative pollution, society's use of resources can be made more efficient over time, i.e., the amount of resources used per unit of GNP goes down faster than GNP goes up and the aggregate environmental impact falls. From the weak sustainability perspective a key requirement for sustainability will be increased effective research and development, i.e., new knowledge properly embodied in people, technology, and institutions.

From the strong sustainability perspective the watchword is co-evolution, the idea that socioeconomic systems and environmental systems are now so

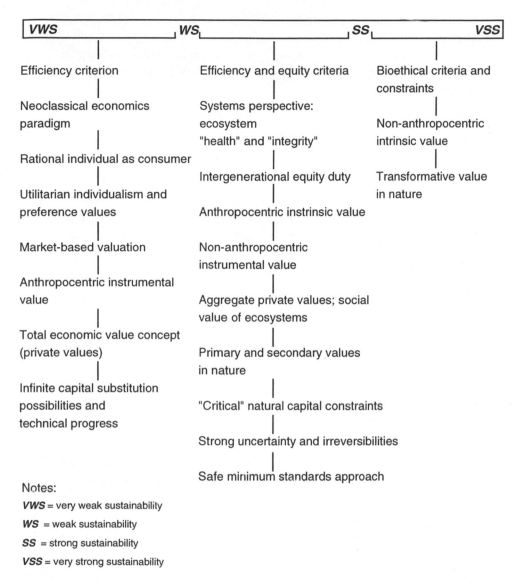

Figure 1. Spectrum of overlapping sustainability positions. Source: Adapted from Turner (1993).

interrelated, because of the sheer extent and pace of economic activity and change, that the components are now jointly determined in a continuous feedback process. The central assumption is that some elements of the natural capital stock cannot be substituted (except on a very limited basis) by man-made capital, and therefore there is a concern to avoid irreversible losses of environmental assets. Some of the functions and services of ecosystems, in combination with the abiotic environment, are essential to human survival. They are life-support services, e.g., biogeochemical cycles, and cannot be replaced. Other multifunctional ecological assets are at least essential to human well-being, if not exactly for human survival, including the landscape, space, and relative peace and quiet. We might therefore designate those ecological assets that are essential in either sense as being "critical natural capital". Supporters of the "deep ecology", very strong sustainability (VSS) position argue for a particular type of non-substitutability based on an ethical rejection of the trade-off between man-made and natural capital. The strong sustainability position is based on an ethical rejection of the trade-off between man-made and natural capital. The strong sustainability rule therefore requires that we at least protect critical natural capital and ensure that it is part of the capital bequest to future generations.

The combination of the risk of irreversible environmental losses and the high degree of uncertainty surrounding past and future rates of resource degradation and loss, as well as the full structural and functional value of ecosystems, leads the advocates of strong sustainability to adopt the precautionary principle. Conservation of natural capital and the application of a safe minimum standards approach are therefore important components of a strong sustainability strategy. The message is that environmental degradation and the loss of natural resources represent one the main ways in which today's generation is creating uncompensated future costs. Hence, the restoration and conservation of natural resources and the environment are crucial to achieving sustainable development.

A number of sustainability rules, which fall some way short of a blueprint, for the sustainable utilization of the natural capital stock can be outlined as follows:

- market and policy intervention failures related to resource pricing and property rights should be corrected;
- the regenerative capacity of renewable natural capital should be maintained, i.e., harvesting rates should not exceed regeneration rates; and cumulative pollution that could threaten waste assimilation capacities and life-support systems should be avoided wherever feasible;
- technological changes should be steered via an indicative planning system such that switches from non-renewable to renewable natural capital are fostered, and efficiency-increasing technical progress should dominate throughput-increasing technologies;
- resources should, wherever possible, be exploited, but at a rate equal to the creation of substitutes (including recycling); and
- the overall scale of economic activity must be limited so that it remains within the carrying capacity of the remaining natural capital. Given the uncertainties present, a precautionary approach should be adopted with a built-in safety margin.

The HOMES researchers have succeeded in identifying significant pressure points and potentially unsustainable trends in resource usage through the household metabolism concept. This analysis also demonstrates the different levels – local, national, and international – at which the global process of environmental change manifests itself. To take just one illustrative example, the rapid growth in the total number of households imposes a major burden on infrastructure support (space, basic utilities provision, transport links, etc.), on the economy, and on the environment. The increasing demands on water resources, which have capacity limits, represent a problem that can only be exacerbated by global climate change. The increasing number of households in coastal and other flood-prone areas poses additional environmental risks.

Particular pressure points/trends that can be highlighted include the household use of energy (for heating), domestic appliances, and the car, reflecting mobility/lifestyle changes. But it is important to differentiate between the household sector, individual households, and per capita levels. At the sectoral level, aggregate trends in resource use are continuing to rise. Resource efficiency gains, such as in domestic heating systems, electrical appliances, and the installation of building insulation, have been offset by the steep rise in the total number of households, family dilution (falling average size of households), and improved access to energy/water distribution systems (van der Wal and Noorman, Chapter 2).

Clearly, in a geographically small but densely populated country such as the Netherlands, the amount of "environmental space" per capita is an important aspect of sustainability. Analysis suggests that while population density has increased, the total amount of space available per person has inevitably fallen. But the amount of built-up area per head of population has increased significantly, and the capacity of neighborhoods to contribute to household welfare also seems to have declined (van Diepen, Chapter 5).

Bus and Voogd (Chapter 6) take a fresh look at existing urban neighborhoods and investigate whether the application of the principles of "ecological urban renewal" can rebuild the functional value of neighborhoods.

Within Dutch households, differences in income levels and age, together with spatial (rural/urban) location, account for significant differences in expenditures on durable consumer goods and in perceptions of what are the highest priority quality of life indicators. For example, in the survey conducted by Gatersleben and Vlek (Chapter 7), older respondents seem to value nature and the environment, personal privacy, safety, comfort, and aesthetics more highly than younger respondents. Middle-aged people consume most and have the most materialistic perceptions of welfare.

Economic theory would indicate that proper (i.e., efficient) resource pricing will significantly influence resource usage patterns and trends. This is confirmed for the Netherlands if one considers the aggregate resource usage trend increases for energy and water between the 1950s and 1980s. Over this period, the real prices for these goods actually fell, and those for fuel fluctuated (as car ownership more than doubled). But during the 1990s a reorientation of fiscal policy towards increased taxation on energy and waste has started to mitigate the problems arising from the trend towards the overconsumption of resources (Linderhof and Kooreman, Chapter 8).

The study of policy effects represents another key element in the eventual success of the HOMES program. In Chapter 9, Ligteringen highlights the concept of policy (intervention) failures, first analyzed in a series of studies funded by the OECD (Paris), covering transport, wetlands, and forestry sectors. The OECD work demonstrated that most policy failures were a combination of inefficiently targeted and/or uncoordinated policies, resulting in unintended negative or positive spillover effects.

This study in the Netherlands found that increased car ownership and use have been stimulated by the indirect effects of policies deployed in other sectors fiscal and welfare policy, and educational policy. The same positive stimulation effects also served to increase the use of domestic appliances. However, in the context of the use of energy for domestic heating, there was a much reduced policy spillover effect and, if anything, a net restraining impact was fostered by coordinated energy and environmental policy measures. Other positive policy effects were found in traffic/transport, public housing, and products policies.

References

Turner, R.K. (1993) Sustainability principles and practice, in: R.K. Turner (Ed.), *Sustainable Environmental Economics and Management*, Belhaven/Wiley, Chichester, ch. 1.

Chapter 1

Household Metabolism in the Context of Sustainability and Environmental Quality

K.J. Noorman, W. Biesiot, and A.J.M. Schoot Uiterkamp

Abstract

This chapter introduces the concept of household metabolism within the domains of sustainable development and environmental quality. It is argued that sustainable development refers to (value-laden) options for social development that pursue quality of life as well as quality of natural life-support systems. Both the natural and social sciences contribute to our understanding of the complex reality that is dealt with in sustainable development research. Since different normative perspectives on sustainable development lead to different development paths that vary considerably in their dynamics, various perspectives or "world views" are presented in this chapter. When designing development routes towards a more sustainable future, biophysical constraints are crucial. The metabolism concept is applied as a metaphor to relate the use of large amounts of materials and energy within human societies to pressure on the environment. The various aspects of sustainable development and environmental quality are brought together at the end of this chapter, where the HOMES (Household Metabolism Effectively Sustainable) research program is introduced.

1.1.   Introduction

The twentieth century has seen a sharp increase in the number of problems originating from new forms of human interaction with the environment. Most of these problems are associated with the over-exploitation of natural resources, the generation of waste, accelerated extinction of species, and the degradation of many ecological functions. This growing environmental awareness is symbolized in the phrases "sustainable development" (SD) and "environmental quality" (EQ), which became widely known after the publication of the Brundtland report *Our Common Future* (WCED, 1987).

Social responses to environmental problems have largely been restricted to fighting short-term symptoms and, at least until the 1980s, focused largely on the production side of economic activities. This focus gave rise to social and techno-logical responses such as clean(er) production aimed at mitigating and preventing the negative environmental impacts of industry and agriculture. Nevertheless, the scientific and public discussion concerning possible constraints on growth trends continues. Such constraints might be different in magnitude and in nature (phys-ical, technical, economic, social, cultural or institutional). Little is known about their combined influence, but it can hardly be ignored. It is increasingly being re-alized that the main driving forces underlying the environmental problems we are facing today have not changed over time: continuing population growth, combined with technical, economic and social development, have led to rising per capita consumption. Clearly, if the number and/or the affluence of consumers (expressed as consumption per capita) increase, so will their overall collective impact on the environment.

Only recently has attention shifted partly towards the consumption side of economic activities as a starting point for environmental protection. The notion that consumer activities (centered around households) can be linked through inte-gral chain management programs and life cycle analysis to the complex pattern of inputs and outputs of the economy (production/transport of goods and services), and thus to the associated environmental loadings, has been taken as a starting point for the interdisciplinary environmental research program HOMES (House-hold Metabolism Effectively Sustainable).[1] The HOMES program focuses on the interactions between human systems (at the level of households in the Netherlands) and the natural environment. The timescale is that of decades: the consumption patterns of the past five decades, and options for future decades up to 2050.

This introductory chapter positions the HOMES program within the domain of SD-related research. *Figure 1.1* illustrates the development of SD and EQ from concept to application, and the combination with the terms metabolism and households. First, Section 1.2 provides a brief overview of the growing awareness of environmental issues since the middle of this century leading to the coining of the term sustainable development.

Section 1.3 elaborates the concept of sustainable development. It is argued that, in essence, SD refers to (value-laden) options for social development that pursue quality of life as well as quality of natural life-support systems. Given the time-dependent sets of norms and values within and between societies, SD can be characterized as a dynamic and normative concept: different normative perspectives on SD lead to different development paths that vary considerably in their dynamics.

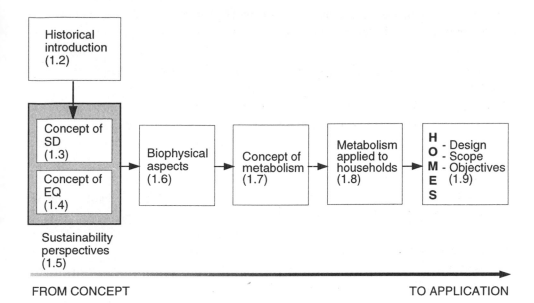

Figure 1.1. Outline of Chapter 1.

Some authors consider environmental quality issues as part of the more encompassing SD problem, while others treat them as two distinct concepts. It is therefore useful to discuss the concept of environmental quality separately; this is done in Section 1.4.

Sustainable development refers to system-wide, complex and long-term processes, including biophysical, economic, social, cultural, and institutional aspects. Scientific knowledge derived from various branches of the natural and social sciences (including their interdisciplinary connections) can contribute to our understanding of this "complex reality". Redirecting social behavior towards a more sustainable relationship with nature requires more than this, due to the existence of beliefs and values in social decision-making processes. Science can contribute here by exposing the implications of the various normative positions for SD routes. The latter are known as "world views" or "perspectives". Section 1.5 outlines some of these proposed perspectives.

When designing development routes towards a more sustainable future, consideration of biophysical constraints (such as the availability of natural resources, waste assimilation capacity, the functioning of atmospheric processes, etc.) is regarded as crucial. Section 1.6 deals with the biophysical constraints on SD, and Section 1.7 introduces the concept of metabolism as a metaphor to relate the use of large amounts of materials and energy within human societies to pressure on the environment. The concept of metabolism is also applied in Section 1.8 to household activities. Finally, the various aspects of SD and EQ are brought together in Section 1.9, where the HOMES program is introduced.

1.2.   Sustainable Development: An Historical Introduction

It was only in the 1960s that environmental issues received significant attention in society.[2] Before then, the adoption of the neoclassical economic paradigm, together with the rise of industrialization at the end of the nineteenth century induced the large-scale disregard of many environmental problems. Neoclassical theory emphasizes the role of the market, and the price mechanism is assumed to properly reflect the preferences of economic agents.   Since ideally relative scarcity is reflected in the price, the market is considered to take care of the optimal allocation of scarce factors of production (traditionally three factors of production are distinguished: capital, labor, and natural resources). However, the preferences for natural resources can be only partly reflected in the exchange relations in the market (see Dietz and van der Straaten, 1992). Consequently, the importance of the natural environment as a contributor to increasing welfare has received only limited attention in economic decision processes. The concept that natural resources are taken into account only as far as they are being traded in the marketplace is increasingly regarded as a shortcoming of neoclassical theory. Pigou (1952) was among the first to suggest a price correction (the so-called Pigouvian taxes) to internalize these negative externalities of economic activity (such as pollution or the exhaustion of natural resources) into economic decision making, in order to achieve the optimal allocation of scarce resources in the marketplace. Practical problems related to Pigouvian taxes include the difficulty in placing a value on environmental services in monetary terms, and in relating (future) environmental benefits to current financial costs.

Since the 1960s the emerging social awareness of environmental degradation has led to the recognition that the market-oriented neoclassical model can only partly deal with the complex dynamic interplay between economic activity aiming at increasing welfare levels, and the long-term impacts of these activities on the natural environment. Human societies and the physical environment interact strongly in many ways; the feedbacks within and among these systems are numerous, complicated, and are by no means yet fully understood. This complexity has led to the notion that the relationships between social activities, the physical resource requirements related to production and consumption processes, and the environmental impacts of these activities can not be studied within the domain of a single discipline. The application of the knowledge, models, concepts and tools of "traditional" disciplines has resulted in a number of interesting alternative approaches. Many of these approaches share the view that the (physical) environmental constraints imposed on economic activity should be taken as points of departure (Boulding, 1966; Kneese *et al.*, 1970; Georgescu-Roegen, 1971; Schumacher, 1973).

The Limits to Growth (Meadows *et al.*, 1972) was one of the first environmental reports to have a profound social impact. It considered the combined trends in population growth, industrialization, pollution, food production and the rate of exhaustion of natural resources, which seemed to be leading to levels that would be unsustainable in the future. Also in 1972, in response to the growing awareness of the interdependence of economic growth and environmental degradation, the UN Conference on Human Ecology, held in Stockholm, 1972, established the UN Environment Programme (UNEP). In spite of the increase in public awareness of environmental issues in the 1970s, however, few adequate policies were implemented to deal with them (van den Berg and van der Straaten, 1994).

The World Conservation Strategy, formulated in 1980, emphasized the ecological constraints on human activities and advocated the maintenance of essential ecological processes, life-support systems, and the preservation of genetic diversity to ensure the sustainable utilization of species and ecosystems (WCS/IUCN, 1980). The Brundtland report, *Our Common Future* (WCED, 1987), stated that existing patterns of economic growth were not ecologically sustainable, and that solutions for environmental problems had to be found. The WCED renewed interest in the concept of sustainable development as a yardstick for long-term environmental policies, describing it in broad terms: *"development that meets the needs of the present without compromising the ability of future generations to meet their own needs"*. Thus the Commission linked the current and future (basic and less urgent) needs of mankind to the environmental resource base. In this definition, sustainability issues are associated with social structures and the full range of human activities aimed at fulfilling human needs, and also with safeguarding the quality of life and the physical and biological environment.

Global environmental concerns led to the UN Conference on Environment and Development, held in Rio de Janeiro in 1992. The outcome of this conference, *Agenda 21*, outlined the global actions that would need to be taken to achieve a sustainable world within the next century. Since then many efforts have been made under this banner to achieve a more sustainable future.

The references cited in this section carry the long-term relationship between man and nature as a common characteristic, and provide broad introductions to the various views, concepts, methods and applications of the concept of sustainable development. As already noted by many authors, there are many definitions of sustainable development, each reflecting a different interpretation. In Sections 1.3 and 1.4 the concepts of sustainable development and environmental quality are discussed separately in more detail in order to underpin the starting point of the HOMES program.

1.3. The Concept of Sustainable Development

In essence, sustainable development concerns the (long-term) relationship between humans and nature. Many authors have offered definitions of sustainability (Pearce *et al.*, 1989; Pezzey, 1989) that differ widely in scope and focus. This indicates that the concept of SD lends itself much more easily to philosophical debate than to interpretation and implementation. Although the concept of SD has been generally accepted as a guiding principle in research, development planning, environmental management and public policy, there has been little consensus on the implementation of sustainable development due to the differences in stakes and interpretations.

Much of the confusion begins when interpreting the two components of the term "sustainable development". In this context, *sustainable* is generally associated with "the (long-run) ability to maintain or uphold" rather than "extending in duration". The second term, *development*, refers to a "process of change" rather than "growth" (which usually means "more of the same"). Although often used synonymously to convey the notion of "economic well-being", the terms growth and development have definite different meanings in current world affairs. Economic growth denotes the (quantitative) increase in economic production, often measured in terms of GDP or GNP per capita. Although some authors use the term "sustainable growth", many others believe that this is a contradiction in terms, since there can be no such thing as "sustainable growth in a physically finite world" (Daly and Cobb, 1989). Pezzey (1992) objects to this view, arguing that economic growth is fundamentally growth of the *value* of the output, which does not necessarily imply growth of physical requirements.

Economic development pursues improvements in the quality of life in general, and might be termed sustainable in the sense of "upholding" given above, in so far as such improvements do not lead to an increase in the amounts of natural capital consumed. Development suggests the presence of elements of qualitative change rather than purely quantitative growth. These qualitative changes can refer to different processes; they may concern the quality and composition of the output, or they could be interpreted as changes in the economy or society as a whole that are commendable from an ethical or a social perspective (see van den Bergh, 1991). As economic activity and the status of natural resources are strongly linked, development can also be seen as an evolutionary process with (nonlinear) feedbacks between a continuously changing economy and its corresponding environment. This broader interpretation can be found in the "Brundtland definition" of development: a coherent process of change with regard to the allocation of investments, the use of natural resources, technology and institutions.

The WCED is often credited as having been the catalyst for the renewed interest in the concept of sustainable development. The Commission acknowledged that the social, cultural, economic and technological development of human society had been made possible by biophysical inputs. From this one may argue that the concept

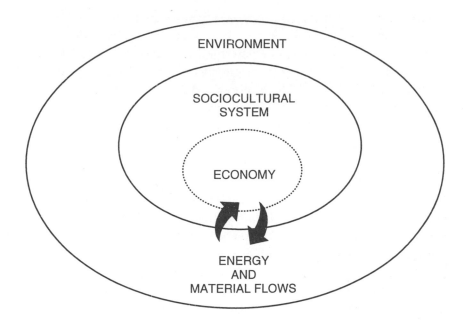

Figure 1.2. The economy–environment interface.

of sustainable development can be applied to at least three interrelated subsystems: the global ecosystem, the sociocultural system, and the economic system. This broader, more integrative interpretation led to the following definition:

> In essence, sustainable development is a process of change in which the exploitation of resources, the direction of investments, the orientation of technological development, and institutional change are all in harmony and enhance both the current and future potential to meet human needs and aspirations. (WCED, 1987)

Figure 1.2 illustrates the relations between these three subsystems. Within the economic subsystem, production and consumption activities take place in order to maximize welfare (utility). Welfare can be defined as the satisfaction of human needs and wants making use of scarce factors of production. The economy is embedded in the sociocultural subsystem, which consists of time-related sets of norms and values that determine the perspectives of an individual or a society on the interrelationship between the economic subsystem and the environment. The notion that norms and values are subject to change within and among human societies underlines the need to characterize the concept of sustainable development in dynamic and normative terms. This calls for continuous adjustment and reappraisal.

The natural environment provides the biophysical basis for increasing human welfare. The term "natural capital" is often used to summarize the wide range of natural services, and refers to all biosphere functions that directly or indirectly provide a service to humankind. Natural capital comprises the oceans, soil, atmospheric cycles, biomass, minerals, fossil energy, etc., that together form the basis of the global ecosystem. In general terms, natural capital can be subdivided into natural resource stocks (renewable and nonrenewable), and life-supporting environmental services such as waste assimilation, maintenance of atmospheric quality, and the preservation of biodiversity. Natural resource stocks provide the natural resource flows that form the inputs into production processes.

Some authors have attempted to classify the wide range of natural life-support functions. Stortenbeker (1990), for example, distinguished four "groups" of natural functions:

- *"carrying" functions*: the natural environment used as a substratum for cities, roads, railways, recreational facilities, etc.;
- *production functions*: the production of biomass, agricultural production, and the production of fossil fuels and minerals;
- *regulation functions*: natural purification and stabilizing functions; and
- *information functions*: the natural environment as a source of scientific information and a reservoir of genetic material; nature as a source of inspiration for education and re-creation.

The wider system perspective depicted in *Figure 1.2* acknowledges the fact that these three subsystems interact in complex ways, and suggests that the nesting requires a balanced development process. This led to the question of whether a hierarchy exists between the different "types of sustainability" that can be assigned to the nested subsystems. Baines (1989), for example, argued that ecological sustainability is an underlying principle for sustainable resource use and waste management, which should be the basis for a sustainable society.

The domain in which questions are asked and tools are adopted is determined by the extent to which the three subsystems are included in the process of problem definition. To some, besides environmental problems, sustainability involves a broader range of social issues such as poverty, the equitable distribution of wealth, equal job opportunities, peace, social security, etc. Others take a more restricted view of sustainable development, focusing on the long-term ecological viability of economic processes (see Opschoor, 1992).

In the sociocultural realm it appears that the multi-interpretive character of SD is related to ethical questions and different views concerning the relationships between humankind and nature, and between present and future generations. Various authors have presented different, partly overlapping sets of perspectives or world views on SD. Thus, to make the debate on SD more transparent, it is useful to distinguish these different world views, since the choice of any one perspective will ultimately determine the domain of questions that will be asked, and thus the tools that will be adopted to study the conditions for achieving a more sustainable future.

Two fundamentally different perspectives are discussed in more detail because they are intrinsically related to two key concepts of SD: "strong/weak sustainability" and "carrying capacity". First, the *anthropocentric perspective* takes the domain of human interests as its starting point. Second, the *ecocentric perspective*, widens the domain of interest to other, nonhuman species and ecosystems. Here the central theme is an anthropogenic assignment of rights to other parts of the "global village". While the first perspective can be criticized for neglecting nonhuman biodiversity and natural services in as far as they are not traded on the market, the latter can be criticized for creating unnecessary obstacles to social development, especially in developing countries (cf. Turner and Pearce, 1993).

The mainstream economic paradigm starts, inevitably, from the anthropocentric perspective. Within this paradigm, natural capital, as an economic asset like human-made capital (factories, infrastructure, dwellings) or human capital (knowledge, skills), has the potential to contribute to economic productivity and welfare (Barbier and Markandya, 1993). From this (utilitarian) viewpoint investments in maintaining the services and quality of the natural environment are only "economically efficient" if the returns, measured in terms of overall welfare, exceed the returns from alternative investments (in other economic assets) elsewhere in the economy. Such a narrowly defined cost–benefit approach regards natural capital only from the viewpoint of (market) economic efficiency and neglects non-marketable functions of the natural environment (potentially leading to irreversible losses of natural capital). At this point the differences between the anthropocentric and ecocentric viewpoints relate to the debate on weak and strong sustainability.

The key difference between weak and strong sustainability concerns the extent to which natural capital can be depleted, taking into account the possibilities for substitution between the various types of capital. The distinction between weak and strong sustainability is related to the stock conditions for SD (see below). When assuming that sustainable development implies that future generations should at least not be worse off in development terms than the present generation, weak sustainability starts from the assumption that natural capital, human-made capital and human capital are close substitutes. The weak sustainability rule advocates that at the aggregate of all three types of capital, total capital assets are constant over time. This implies that a single stock may decrease (or even be exhausted) as long as the sum of the capital assets is constant over time. According to the weak sustainability paradigm it is acceptable to run down natural capital assets as long as another type of capital (e.g., human-made capital) is built up instead. Strong sustainability assumes that critical natural capital stocks are non-substitutable and should therefore be preserved. Thus strong sustainability demands that each natural capital stock is kept essentially constant over time.[3] The anthropocentric perspective mainly carries weak sustainability characteristics, whereas the ecocentric perspective is mainly fuelled by strong sustainability considerations.[4]

Various concepts have been introduced to express nature's limited capacity to sustain and uphold social activities in the long run. For instance, the concept of carrying capacity is sometimes used to examine the increasing trade-off between human population growth and nature's ability to fulfill all necessary life-support functions at adequate levels. Sustainable development, then, refers to social development that does not exceed nature's carrying capacity (within the foreseeable future). The concept of carrying capacity is complex, and has been borrowed from population dynamics and ecology. Applied to the human species,[5] the concept of carrying capacity starts from the notion that humans are dependent on their natural environment in many ways, and that current and future human needs and wants can only be fulfilled within biophysical constraints. These constraints refer to nature's ability to assimilate "leaks" stemming from human-induced metabolic flows, to supply natural resource flows (within their regeneration margins), and to control and manage changes in biochemical cycles. Following Siebert (1982), Opschoor (1987) introduced the concept of "environmental utilization space" (EUS) as a metaphor to analyze the interactions between society and the wide range of environmental services that sustain social activities. These concepts emphasize the contribution of natural functions to the maintenance of human welfare, taking into account environmental quality considerations. The EUS concept has not always escaped the danger of being used as a pseudoscientific mechanism to limit human access to natural resources (cf. Buitenkamp *et al.*, 1992; WRR, 1994; *Milieu,* 1994).

1.4.   The Concept of Environmental Quality

The concept of environmental quality turns out to be as much value-laden as that of sustainable development. So, many interpretations concur. Some of them make a clear distinction between "sustainable development referring to social systems" and "environmental quality referring to natural systems", as if SD policies can be pursued more or less independently of EQ policies (or vice versa). Other interpretations assume an hierarchical relation between SD and EQ. Either SD is regarded as the dominant category that determines the margins left to the "natural environment", or EQ is considered as the main concept that can be quantified in such detail that the margins for SD routes can be established.

This description suggests a linear scale with the hierarchical positions corresponding to the two ends, and the "balanced position" in the middle of the scale. Priority of SD over EQ seems to correspond to the set of anthropocentric views that relates sustainability issues in varying degrees of exclusiveness to human interests. The reverse correlates with the extreme variants of the ecocentric view, which places values on the interests of nonhuman species and ecosystems to different degrees.

The first, utilitarian, view takes into account natural functions in so far as they are considered essential for the continuation of social processes and as far as they contribute to the maintenance of or increase in human welfare (here welfare refers to maximizing the net benefits of economic activity; see Opschoor and van der Ploeg, 1990). This implies that although some of the natural services as categorized by Stortenbeker (1990) definitely add to human welfare, they may not be essential for the continuation of vital social processes, and therefore are not considered to be of major interest within this perspective. For instance, the preservation of vulnerable nature reserves or endangered species might contribute considerably to human welfare, but is not directly essential for the continuation of social processes.

The utilitarian perspective is reflected in the role of natural assets as adopted in mainstream economic theory. Here environmental quality is measured only as a stock of environmental goods yielding a flow of services that ultimately contribute to maximizing the net benefits of economic activity. These services include the production of material and energy inputs for the economic system, the assimilation of waste, and the provision of amenity, life-support and general "ecological" functions (Barbier and Markandya, 1993). The utilitarian view acknowledges to some extent the fact that degradation of one or more elements of natural capital beyond some threshold might result in a breakdown of the complete natural system, and that certain biophysical constraints need to be conserved in order to guarantee nondeclining human welfare development.

In the ecocentric perspective, ethical, aesthetic, cultural and technical arguments are also seen as valid reasons for conserving natural capital in general, and for undertaking actions directed at the preservation of biological diversity. These considerations take into account the (future) quality of the natural environment for other species, and move away from the more narrowly defined domain of the anthropocentric perspective. Policies based on this perspective will vary according to the weight of the different categories of argument, ranging from "deep ecology" policies ("treading lightly on the Earth"), to "weak sustainability" type policies when the arguments are predominantly technical in nature (e.g., the potential usefulness of nature as a source of pharmaceutical products). An example can be found in the position of the WCED, which argues in favor of the preservation of biodiversity as a potential source of human welfare, not only on ethical and aesthetic grounds, but also on arguments that refer to agriculture, recreation and (pharmaceutical) industry (WCED, 1987). Within the concept of environmental quality, Opschoor and van der Ploeg (1990) distinguish two dimensions:

- *livability*, taking into account human health and experience of nature. Livability motives exceed basic sustainability conditions and include the possibility to enjoy cultural, aesthetic, or natural beauty; and
- *integrity*, taking into account the intrinsic value of biodiversity and the conditions under which these values can develop from an evolutionary perspective.

Since both of these dimensions can be described as dynamic and normative, analogous to SD, the concept of EQ can also be characterized as dynamic and normative.

Environmental quality is described by these authors as a measure of the extent to which the state of the natural environment corresponds to objectives concerning variables such as biodiversity, the presence and dimensions of ecosystems, concentrations of toxic substances in environmental compartments, and the disturbance of natural processes and biogeochemical cycles. This description seems to be in accordance with van Diepen and Voogd (1994), who describe quality in terms of the "degree of excellence", "property" or "attribute" of a geographical space.

This approach can accommodate the anthropogenic perspective as well as the ecocentric view, depending upon the relative weights given to "purely human-oriented" versus "purely non-human-oriented" aspects in the two dimensions. Such weight factors ultimately follow from the value system chosen, which also broadly determines the perspective on SD. This suggests that the issue of hierarchy is not related to the pair SD versus EQ, but to world views/perspectives versus the implications for SD and EQ (following livability and integrity considerations).

An important factor in the debate concerning the implementation of the concept of environmental quality is the lack of an integral understanding of the functioning and development of ecosystems and of the long-term impacts of human activities on the quality of the natural environment. For example, partial knowledge and wide margins of uncertainty forgo precision in prediction along the causal chains lines (process → emissions → dispersion → transformation → effects → consequences). The development potential of social as well as natural systems (and even more, interrelated social/natural systems) is thus only partially known and knowable. This leaves ample room for different sets of norms and values (combined into the world views or perspectives described in the next section) to guide corresponding development policies.

1.5.   Perspectives on Sustainable Development

Different world views reflect different ethical choices and concerns regarding the relation between humankind and the natural environment and regarding inter- and intra-generational responsibilities. These choices and concerns shape images of a society in which a wide range of social issues (such as social security, justice, and the (more) equitable distribution of available goods and services), and of issues concerning the natural environment are settled (and corresponding solutions are reached), in conformity with the underlying set of values and norms. Relatively "strong" knowledge derived from the natural and social sciences plays only a small but important part in this process of image building, as it leaves ample but finite room for various interpretations in the relatively wide uncertainty margins.

Various authors have proposed different world views in the SD debate (e.g., O'Riordan and Turner, 1983; de Vries, 1989; WRR, 1994). These world views reflect normative views on social progress, on the position of individuals in society, and on social perceptions of environmental problems. The boundaries between thcsc world views are not always sharp; there is often some overlap between them. Components of one view can be seen as rather trivial from the other perspectives. Nevertheless, each position is bound to be there, as all can find legitimacy in history, the present and/or future. So, scientific arguments alone are insufficient to reach consensus on any view. This implies that the designers of development strategies for a more sustainable future should build upon the contributions and insights of the various world views. Such a process might not necessarily only employ the standard consensus-seeking procedures of a democratic society, but could also resort to new methods that are more usable for decision making under large scientific uncertainties and high social stakes (e.g., Funtowicz and Ravetz, 1985).

Classification systems are based either on positions along a single dimension (like those presented by O'Riordan and Turner and also de Vries), or on positions in a multidimensional matrix (like the two-dimensional scheme of Schwarz and Thompson, 1990). Most of the one-dimensional systems are derived in a heuristic way (not explaining the nature of nor the rationale for the dimension chosen), while the two-dimensional schemes follow from high versus low value choices along axes that are chosen in a deliberate way (the choice of more intervals along an axis of course leads to more refined classification options).

O'Riordan and Turner (1983) distinguish four "basic world views", ranging from "cornucopian technocentrism" (which emphasizes the abundance of opportunities and supports market and technology-steered growth), through "accommodating technocentrism" (which promotes resource management guided growth), and "communalist ecocentrism" (which emphasizes environmental constraints on economic growth and decentralized socioeconomic systems), to the "deep ecology ecocentrism" (which adopts an extreme preservationist position based on notions of intrinsic value in nature and rights for nonhuman spccics); see also Archibugi *et al.* (1989).

Dc Vries (1989) presents four perspectives on sustainable development, each based on a specific image. These perspectives, each of which represents a different view and valuation of the "real world", range from the *technological perspective* of the *Technocrat–Adventurer*, with the prevailing image of "Spaceship Earth in its potential abundance", through the *resource-economic perspective* of the *Manager–Engineer*, with "Spaceship Earth in its physical finiteness" as the prevailing image, and the *environmentalist perspective* of the *Steward*, with the "Garden Earth" as an appropriate image, to the *ecological perspective* of the *Partner*, with "Earth goddess Gaia" as the central metaphor.

Schwarz and Thompson (1990) combine four "myths of nature" and the grid/group typology of social relationships to synthesize four "sociocultural–political" paradigms (see *Figure 1.3*). The myths of nature are based on different interpretations of ecosystem stability (derived from Holling, 1979; Timmerman, 1986). The typology of social relationships (derived from the cultural theory of

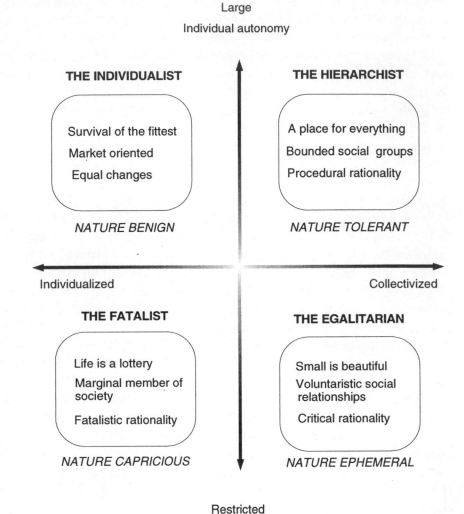

Large

Individual autonomy

THE INDIVIDUALIST

Survival of the fittest

Market oriented

Equal changes

NATURE BENIGN

THE HIERARCHIST

A place for everything

Bounded social groups

Procedural rationality

NATURE TOLERANT

Individualized

Collectivized

THE FATALIST

Life is a lottery

Marginal member of society

Fatalistic rationality

NATURE CAPRICIOUS

THE EGALITARIAN

Small is beautiful

Voluntaristic social relationships

Critical rationality

NATURE EPHEMERAL

Restricted

Individual autonomy

Figure 1.3. Four cultural perspectives and four ways of perceiving nature. Source: Schwarz and Thompson (1990.

Mary Douglas) is based on two "dimensions of sociality", i.e., the (lack of) desire of individuals to be part of a group (collectivism versus individualism), and the social prescriptions that individuals feel themselves subject to. They distinguish:

- the *hierarchist*, emphasizing bounded social groups with strong internal relationships, and viewing nature as tolerant but vulnerable to surpassing ultimate limits;

- the *egalitarian*, who strives for informal, horizontal social relationships and handles nature with great care from the viewpoint that ecosystems are very vulnerable;
- the *individualist*, who stresses the freedom and autonomy of individuals. The abundance of nature is taken for granted and is considered as an opportunity rather than as a threat; and
- the *fatalist*, whose individual ability to influence events is strongly restricted by prescriptions on his or her behavior. Nature is regarded as a lottery rather than as being controllable or manageable.

The presence of these different normative perspectives on the relations between humankind and nature turns out to be an essential element in the discussion on SD and EQ. Consequently, social actors will give different answers to questions relevant to the sustainability debate such as: "What is exactly meant by ecologically bound sustainable development?", "How do we define good environmental quality?", "How can we identify transition paths towards a more sustainable future", and "What indicators are required and acceptable to design successful development strategies?". Some of these questions might not be relevant within the domain of some perspectives. The fatalist, for instance, seems not to be interested in designing long-term strategies as he regards nature as not manageable, whereas the individualist dismisses long-term projections as superfluous since humankind will always find solutions to overcome possible problems (turning threats into manageable challenges). The positions of these actors do not fluctuate at random, but seem to be classifiable into a limited number of perspectives. This opens up the opportunity for scientific research to contribute to the communication between the various perspectives by identifying common characteristics at the level of diagnosing the environmental problems we face today, of evaluating these problems, and of implementing the changes required to maintain human activities within nature's "carrying capacity".[6] Communication between the various perspectives is regarded as essential in order to reach (new forms of) consensus on outlines of solutions that may initiate social changes towards a more sustainable future.

1.6. Biophysical Constraints on Sustainable Development

Key issues in the sustainability debate are covered by a wide range of academic disciplines and call for an interdisciplinary approach. In the search for a common denominator to investigate sustainability issues, physical aspects of the human society–environment interface can be taken as fruitful points of departure.

The dependence of welfare growth on natural resources is shown in *Figure 1.4*. Until the late eighteenth century the rate of use of natural resources (and of welfare growth) was strongly influenced by the rate at which solar energy could be collected. Once fossil fuel reserves began to be exploited, production was no

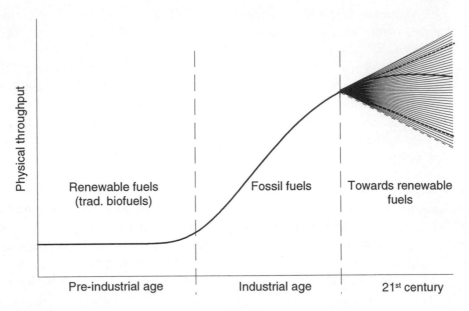

Figure 1.4. Developments in physical throughputs over time.

longer limited by the rate of natural processes nor by the need to employ animal and human power. This resulted in the accelerated growth of both welfare and the use of fossil fuels. Ayres and Kneese (1989) estimated that today, roughly 90% of social metabolism depends on the utilization of fossil fuels. Sustainable development goals demand simultaneously decreasing use of fossil energy and increasing use of renewable sources of energy, ultimately resulting in fossil fuel free social metabolism patterns.

The metabolism of an organism is determined by factors such as its structure, function, age, degree of organization and habitat. We therefore believe that the concept of metabolism is an appropriate and useful metaphor to describe the general biophysical interaction of humans with nature. Biophysical aspects and limitations ultimately delineate the research domain for academic disciplines studying SD issues. The biophysical constraints on SD are discussed in Section 1.7, and then the metabolism concept is introduced and applied to households.

The growing awareness that sustainable economic activity has to comply with ecological thresholds has initiated an ongoing debate on the extent to which natural resources can be used in production and consumption processes. It has been argued that different views of reality postulate different positions in the debate, so that exact choices are rather arbitrary. Although scientific knowledge of large-scale natural processes is fairly poor, ecological insights indicate that both the quality and quantity of natural resources and ecological processes are essential for their long-term continuation. This observation implies that although an exact judgment on the biophysical constraints on SD is beyond our reach, some general conditions for achieving SD can be formulated. Such conditions may be based on the growing understanding that the environmental impacts of economic activities can no longer be regarded as unintended (relatively small) negative externalities that occur at the periphery of the economy, but as unavoidable (and significant in magnitude) in safeguarding both human welfare, and the existence and functioning of nonhuman species and ecosystems.

In an effort to integrate physical principles and economic production and consumption processes, various authors have taken the laws of thermodynamics as a point of departure (Boulding, 1966; Ayres and Kneese, 1969; Georgescu-Roegen, 1971).[7] Although the application of thermodynamic principles to "real world" systems such as human societies requires caution and thought (Noorman, 1995), these principles may be useful in clarifying the physical functioning of economic activity. This can be illustrated by applying the law of conservation of matter and energy, which states that matter and energy are conserved in an isolated system, to the production of waste products in an economy.[8]

Daly (1990) formulated three rather straightforward conditions for the sustainable use of natural resources. These conditions hold that:

1. nonrenewable resources should not be depleted at rates higher than the development rate of renewable substitutes;
2. renewable resources should not be exploited at a rate higher than their regeneration level; and
3. the absorption and regeneration capacity of the natural environment should not be exceeded.

In addition to these three "Daly conditions", Biesiot and Mulder (1994) argue that an adequate supply of renewable resources needs to be built up in order to make a transition towards a more sustainable future. This additional condition implies that the first Daly condition is insufficient, in that it neglects the dynamics of a transition from a fossil fuel-based economy towards one based on renewables. The authors argue that the intended transformation requires a considerable investment of (depletable) natural resources, and thus requires thorough thinking on how to employ these resources in order to safeguard a transition to an economy based on renewables. The notion that a transition to a non-fossil fuel society would require the dissipation of huge quantities of nonrenewables has already been considered by Georgescu-Roegen (1971): "By using these resources too quickly, man throws away that part of solar energy that will still be reaching the earth for a long time after he has departed". To gain a better understanding of the relationship between household activities and their long-term environmental impacts, we propose the concept of metabolism as a metaphor. The origin of the concept, and the justification for using it as a means of inquiring into the interrelationship between social activities and their environmental impacts, are discussed further in the following section.

1.7.   The Concept of Metabolism

The concept of metabolism is rooted in the life sciences. In ecological science, metabolism refers to the material cycles and energy flows that determine the viability and continuation of organism–environment interactions. Organisms use flows of low-entropy (i.e., low degree of disorder) materials and energy for growth and maintenance, and convert them into high-entropy flows of waste materials and heat. These organisms are linked to others and to nonbiotic natural processes (such as solar influx) that are acting in reverse. The natural environment is thus characterized by "closed" and interacting mineral cycles.

The application of metabolism as a metaphor in the environmental sciences stresses the fact that human societies use large amounts of materials and energy in ways analogous to organisms. The resulting material flows in human societies should occur in "closed" cycles, just as in communities of other organisms in nature. Making the metabolism concept operational implies the design of metabolic models that describe the flows of materials and energy related to the services delivered. Furthermore, such models can be used to determine the associated environmental impacts and to predict some of the consequences of social and technological developments for these flows and impacts (Moll, 1993). Initially, the metabolism concept was applied to industrial processes only. Industrial metabolism is a field of study that investigates the application of energy and material flows by industrial systems, the transformation of these materials by means of energy into useful products, and the environmental implications of such processes. *Figure 1.5* shows a simplified scheme of the current social and environmental metabolism at a high level of aggregation. The metabolism concept can be extended to the concept of sustainability. Organisms are self-sustaining when they are in equilibrium with their environment. In such a case resources are metabolized in an optimal way: waste is converted into resources.

The metabolism concept as applied in the HOMES program specifically includes the dynamics of transition paths towards a more sustainable (end) state, i.e., a situation in which material cycles are closed and (renewable) energy use is optimized. Although the ultimate aim can be described as a climax situation in which all waste is converted into resources (and in which no evolutionary processes take place since at the system level all processes are optimized), the evolutionary routes towards such a climax situation are often characterized by the inefficient use of resources, quick turnover, and "trial and error" strategies. This, at first sight, inefficient utilization of resources marks the search for optimizing metabolic processes. A comparison of the Daly and Biesiot/Mulder criteria listed in Section 1.6, with the current social and environmental patterns of metabolism (*Figure 1.5*), shows that current consumption patterns are not sustainable (note 8 also illustrates this).

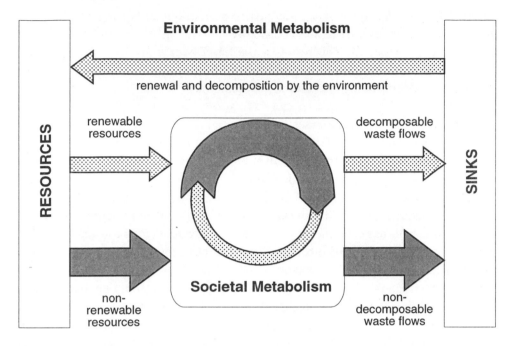

Figure 1.5. Social and environmental metabolism. Source: Moll (1993).

1.8.   The Concept of Metabolism Applied to Households: The HOMES Program

The increasing trade-off between human activities and the quality and sustainability of the natural environment is often attributed to the combined effects of population growth, increasing affluence and technological developments. Ehrlich and Holdren (1971) were the first to identify these three primary factors responsible for ongoing environmental decay, and formalized them in the so-called IPAT equation:

Impact = Population * Affluence * Technology.

Following the IPAT equation, it became common practice to express the environmental degradation originating from consumer activities in per capita terms, thereby ignoring the household as a social decision-making unit.

As the smallest consumer units, households consume a complex and changing mix of goods and services. The different lifestyles adopted by households affect the natural environment in different ways. To a large degree, individual consumers organized into households determine (both directly and indirectly) what kinds of goods and services are produced, how much is produced, and the ways in which they are produced (in fact, consumer organizations have been responsible for the "greening" of many products and services).

In our view, the above arguments justify a small but significant adaptation of the IPAT equation. Rather than emphasizing individuals, the focus should be on households and lifestyles. This results in the IHAT equation:

Impact = Households * Affluence * Technology.

The HOMES program focuses on household metabolism, which is related to lifestyle in many respects: lifestyles differ in structure and function, and therefore have different impacts on the metabolism of a household. Furthermore, the wide range of lifestyles and their dynamic features directly and indirectly influence the throughputs of energy flows and material cycles through the entire economy.

Developments in the field of energy analysis have resulted in a growing number of methods to determine the energy requirements for both production and consumption activities with increasing precision. For example, input–output energy analysis has been fruitfully applied to dynamically link the stocks and flows of energy at the level of a national economy (Noorman, 1995); and by combining input–output energy analysis and process analysis, Wilting (1994) has calculated the primary energy requirements of consumer products. Together with methodological developments in the last few years, an increasing body of relevant detailed statistics has become available, offering the possibility to relate financial expenditures of consumers to the "physical reality" of these expenditures.

By focusing on household metabolism, the HOMES program addresses the complex environmental problems of an important segment of Western society, typified by Dutch society. The term "household metabolism" refers both to the demand for resources, i.e., the direct flows of resources through households, and to the supply of resources, i.e., the materials and energy indirectly required to realize these flows (e.g., in mining, production of materials, construction of houses, and manufacturing goods). Household metabolism depends on a wide variety of factors – technical, economic, behavioral, spatial and administrative. Designing effective and socially acceptable policy instruments to reduce the rates of household metabolism (and their negative environmental impacts) requires a thorough understanding of the determinants of household consumption and their mutual relationships, as well as detailed information on possible differences between the "lifestyles" and resulting consumption patterns of different segments of the population.

Figure 1.6 gives an overview of the metabolic flows related to consumer patterns in households. Natural resources are extracted from the physical environment in order to produce goods and services to meet the (material) needs and wants and the (non-material) aspirations of the population. At present, only a small fraction of the total amount of natural capital that has been extracted is recycled. Recycling takes place both at the level of production and at the level of final demand

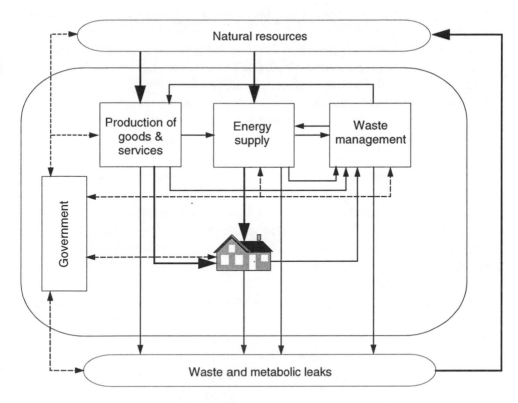

Figure 1.6. The concept of metabolism applied to households.

consumption (households). Reducing the throughput of flows of materials and energy by closing the relevant physical cycles is regarded as a necessary step towards a more sustainable future.

We believe that the focus on households in the Netherlands is justified, as it is a "model" Western society, densely populated and with intensive industrial, agricultural and transportation systems, and correspondingly strong environmental impacts. Households, the smallest social units, consume a complex and changing mix of goods and services. In recent decades the number of households in many Western societies has increased faster than the population.

There has been a steady increase in number of dwellings, which have been connected to a steadily rising number of goods and services provided by physical networks, such as drinking water and sewerage systems, electricity cables and gas pipelines, telephone lines and other information networks. The demand for goods and services has increased accordingly, as is reflected in the increase in household functions such as heating and washing.

1.9.   Scope and Objectives of the HOMES Program

The aim of the HOMES program is to develop and apply the concepts, operational approaches, methodologies, and instruments (e.g., models and scenarios) relevant for the *diagnosis* and *evaluation* of household metabolism in a complex Western society, in this case illustrated by the Netherlands. Since this type of household metabolism is not expected to be sustainable nor qualitatively acceptable, HOMES will also investigate the *changes* that will be necessary to accomplish a transition to household metabolism that does comply with these characteristics. Such a transition should result in a sustainable, adequate and equitable match between the supply of and demand for resources.

An historical perspective is created by considering the situation in the Netherlands over the period 1950–2050. The early years (1950–1970) represent the postwar reconstruction of the infrastructure and housing, and the later years (1970–1990) the penetration of consumer durables. For 1990 we use the detailed information that is available; data for the year 2015 are based on projections of trends in the period 1950–1990; and those for 2050 are based on prospective scenarios developed in the context of different normative approaches concerning sustainability and environmental quality. The year 2015 was chosen because this is the time horizon of most long-range economic forecasts and because detailed information on cleaner production and consumption processes is available. The final year, 2050, was selected to provide a long-term perspective in which conflicting patterns of demand and supply concerning natural and energy resources in the future can be studied (by the year 2050 it is likely that much tighter environmental quality standards will have been implemented and accepted).

Choices had to be made with regard to which household functions would be investigated. Three main functions or constituent components with different "time constants" and with different spatial and temporal characteristics were selected for specific case studies. These are, respectively: from the category infrastructure/housing, heating and mobility; from the category of durable household goods, white goods appliances; and from the category of nondurables, the consumption of water, gas and electricity. Together, these constitute the majority of material and energy flows (including waste production and handling) that make up household metabolism. The categories selected are investigated at the strategic, tactical and operational levels.

The total demand for natural resources is determined by the number of households (and their average size), by the consumption per household, and by the material and energy efficiency of consumption. The latter is a function not only of biophysical, technical, economic, spatial and behavioral aspects, but also of specific social institutions and administrative policy measures. Within the HOMES program these various aspects are covered by different scientific disciplines, each of which investigates different aspects of household metabolism using specific sets

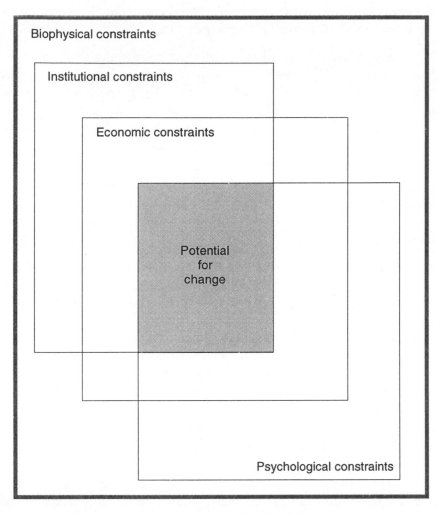

Figure 1.7. Different sets of constraints determine the potential for change.

of constraints. These different clusters of constraints put forward by the different disciplines ultimately determine the potential for changes in household metabolism along sustainability and environmental quality lines as established in the evaluation phase of the program (see *Figure 1.7*).

Population issues as such are not considered within the HOMES program, so the focus is on metabolic rates per household. Household metabolism is described in terms of stocks and flows. A distinction is made between the direct and indirect use of energy and materials per household, including the depreciation of consumer durables (e.g., heating appliances, white goods appliances, and cars). The emphasis is on the metabolism of (different segments of) households in the Netherlands. In a later phase, the household metabolism methodology could be applied to other countries. This yields *diagnostic* research questions such as:

- What relevant trends in household metabolism in the Netherlands can be identi-fied in recent decades, and what have been the impacts of household metabolism on environmental quality? To what extent have the observed trends been caused by changes in consumption per household and/or by changes in the energy and material intensities of consumption, due to e.g., technological developments, economic, spatial, behavioral and social changes, or administrative policy measures? As indicated, the program focuses on heating and mobility, white goods appliances and the consumption of water, gas and electricity.
- What conclusions about the future development of the use of resources for household consumption in the Netherlands can be derived by extrapolating these trends?

The distinction between the consumption and waste of resources is difficult to define *a priori*. From a technical viewpoint, the waste of resources is equivalent to the inefficient use of resources, but efficiency is directly related to the state of technology. Depending on the ethical and normative viewpoints chosen, the waste of resources can be regarded as being equivalent to the *unsustainable* use of resources.

The HOMES program specifically addresses the relationships between trends in consumption and the consequences for spatial and environmental quality, and for natural and sociocultural resources. We expect that the evaluation of the outcomes of the diagnostic phase of HOMES will show that for various normative settings, future demand for resources for household consumption will exceed the potential of a sustainable and qualitatively acceptable supply of resources. If so, "sustainable options" to reduce the rate of household metabolism will have to be (re)designed and ways of implementation identified. Depending on the various normative viewpoints, this yields research questions for the *change* phase of HOMES such as:

- What are the opportunities for and constraints on achieving substantial re-ductions in the future use of resources by households? By what technical, economical, spatial, behavioral and/or administrative policy options, instru-ments and methods could such reductions be achieved?
- What reductions in the use of resources by households can be (maximally) real-ized if the identified technical, behavioral, spatial, economic and administrative policy options, instruments and methods are (optimally) implemented?

In addressing these questions, two points should be noted. First, it can be ex-pected that options that aim to reduce future household metabolic rates by lowering material consumption levels will generally be more difficult to implement and will meet more public resistance than options that aim to reduce future material and energy demands by increasing the efficiency of service delivery. Therefore, the potential for demand reduction through efficiency optimization will be assessed first. If, as we expect, this reveals that efficiency-based options *alone* are insufficient to achieve a balance between demand and supply, then the potentials for and the constraints on achieving a reduction in the average level of material consumption will have to be considered. Second, an assessment of the amounts of energy and materials available to households in the Netherlands in the future obviously touches on the issue of global equity. A proportional and just distribution of the available global resources will result in strong additional constraints on future household metabolism rates. The similarities and differences between the results for the various normative approaches will be explored.

Notes

[1] HOMES is part of a larger program, the NWO (the Dutch National Foundation for Scientific Research) Priority Program on Sustainability and Environmental Quality, which aims to find and develop strategies for analyzing, solving and preventing environmental problems from a fundamental and long-term perspective.

[2] The interdependence of environmental conditions and social activities was already the subject of study of classical economists in the eighteenth century, and thus was not a new idea of the postwar period. Nevertheless, in this brief historical overview, 1950 was chosen as point of departure since the HOMES project covers the period 1950–2050. For further details of the changing views on the interrelationship between human (economic) activity and the natural environment, see Ponting (1992), Barbier (1989) and van den Bergh (1991).

[3] Strictly speaking, this leads to the paradox that natural capital stocks cannot be used at all by any generation because of the necessity to preserve them for use by future generations.

[4] Turner and Pearce (1993) argue that the strong sustainability paradigm remains anthropocentric although it allows for nonutilitarian values: the "fairness" in question refers to fairness between people. When taking into account non-instrumental values in nature and notions of rights and interests for non-human components of the biosphere, the authors use the term very strong (bioethics) sustainability.

[5] Daly (1991) remarks that there is some resistance to the application of the concept of carrying capacity to humans. For animals, carrying capacity can be considered almost entirely in terms of population, since per capita resource consumption is constant both over time and across individual members of the species (i.e., animals do not experience economic development, nor do they distinguish between rich and poor). Because of differences in standards of living, the unequal distribution of individual consumption levels, and different levels of technology, for humans we cannot speak of carrying capacity in terms of population alone.

[6] Moll (1993) further elaborated the notion that the boundaries between the various perspectives are rather vague and that elements of all perspectives can be found in development strategies. He proposed the "paradigm-independent" perspective of the environmental physiologist who facilitates the communication between the various perspectives by designing models that describe social and environmental metabolism.

[7] An overview of the application of physical laws to economic activity is given in Noorman (1995).
[8] Ayres and Kneese (1989) evaluated the mass of materials (including food and fuels) extracted commercially in the US in the period 1960–1975, and estimated that only 6% of the total mass annually accumulates in the economy in the form of durables. The other 94% are converted into waste residuals at a rate almost equal to the rate of extraction.

References

Archibugi, F., P. Nijkamp, and F.J. Soeteman (1989) The challenge of sustainable development. In: F. Archibugi and P. Nijkamp (Eds.), *Economy and Ecology: Towards Sustainable Development*, Kluwer, Dordrecht.

Ayres, R.U. and A.V. Kneese (1969) Production, consumption and externalities, *American Economic Review*, **59**:282–297.

Ayres, R.U. and A.V. Kneese (1989) Externalities: economics and thermodynamics. In F. Archibugi and P. Nijkamp (Eds.), *Economy and Ecology: Towards Sustainable Development*. Kluwer, Dordrecht.

Baines, J.T. (1989) An integrated framework for interpreting sustainable development: ecological principles and institutional arrangements for the sustainable development of natural and physical resources. In: J. Peet (Ed.), *Energy and the Ecological Economics of Sustainability*, Island Press, Washington, DC.

Barbier, E.B. (1989) *Economics, Natural Resource Scarcity and Development: Conventional and Alternative Views*. Earthscan, London.

Barbier, E.B. and A. Markandya (1993) Environmentally sustainable development: optimal economic conditions. In: E.B. Barbier (Ed.), *Economics and Ecology: New Frontiers and Sustainable Development*, Chapman & Hall, London.

Biesiot, W. and H.A.J. Mulder (1994) Energy constraints on sustainable development paths. In: P.B. Smith *et al.* (Eds.), *The World at the Crossroads*, Earthscan, London.

Boulding, K.E. (1966) The economics of the coming Spaceship Earth. In: H. Jarett (Ed.), *Environmental Quality in a Growing Economy*, Johns Hopkins University Press, Baltimore, MD, pp. 3–14.

Brown, L.R. *et al.* (1993) *State of the World 1993*, Earthscan, London.

Buitenkamp, M., H. Venner, and T. Wams (Eds.) (1992) *Actieplan Nederland Duurzaam*. Vereniging Milieudefensie, Milieuboek, Amsterdam.

Daly, H.E. (1990) Toward some operational principles of sustainable development. *Ecological Economics*, **2**:1–6.

Daly, H.E. (1991) Elements of environmental macroeconomics. In: R. Costanza (Ed.), *Ecological Economics. The Science and Management of Sustainability*, Columbia University Press, New York.

Daly, H.E. and J.B. Cobb (1989) *For the Common Good*, Green Print, London.

De Vries, H.J.M. (1989) *Sustainable Resource Use: An Enquiry into Modelling and Planning*. Thesis, Universiteitsdrukkerij Groningen.

Dietz, F.J. and J. Van der Straaten (1992) Rethinking environmental economics: Missing links between economic theory and environmental policy, *Journal of Economic Issues* (JEI), **XXVI**(1).

Ehrlich, P. and J. Holdren (1971) *Impact of population growth, Science*, **171**:1212–1217.

Funtowicz, S.O. and J.R. Ravetz (1985) Three types of risk assessment: a methodological analysis. In: V.T. Covello *et al.* (Eds.) *Environmental Impact Assessment, Technology Assessment and Risk Analysis*. Springer, Berlin.

Georgescu-Roegen, N. (1971) *The Entropy Law and the Economic Process*, Harvard University Press, Cambridge, MA.

Holling, C.S. (1979) Myths of ecological stability. In: G. Smart and W. Stanbury (Eds.), *Studies in Crisis Management*, Butterworth, Montreal .

Kneese, A.V., R.U. Ayres and R.C. d'Arche (1970) *Economics and the Environment: A Materials Balance Approach*, John Hopkins University Press, Baltimore, MD.

Meadows, D., J. Randers and W. Behrens III (1972) *The Limits to Growth*, Universe Books, New York.

Milieu, Tijdschrift voor Milieukunde (1994) Environmental utility space (special issue).

Moll, H.C. (1993) *Energy Counts and Materials Matter in Models for Sustainable Development: Dynamic Lifecycle Modelling as a Tool for Design and Evaluation of Long-term Environmental Strategies*. PhD Thesis, Groningen University.

Noorman, K.J. (1995) *Exploring Futures from an Energy Perspective: A Natural Capital Accounting Model Study of the Long-term Economic Development Potential of the Netherlands*. PhD Thesis, Groningen University.

Opschoor, J.B. (1987) *Duurzaamheid en verandering: over de ecologische inpasbaarheid van economische ontwikkelingen*. VU Press, Amsterdam.

Opschoor, J.B. (1989) *Na ons geen zondvloed. Voorwaarden voor duurzaam milieugebruik*, Kok/Agora, Kampen.

Opschoor, J.B. (Ed.) (1992) *Environment, Economy and Sustainable Development*. Wolters-Noordhof, Groningen.

Opschoor, J.B. and F. van der Ploeg (1990) Duurzaamheid en milieukwaliteit: hoofddoelstellingen van milieubeleid. In: CLTM (1990) *Het milieu: denkbeelden voor de 21ste eeuw*, Commissie Lange Termijn Milieubeleid, Kerckebosch, Zeist.

O'Riordan, T. and R.K. Turner (1983) *An Annotated Reader in Environmental Planning and Management*, Pergamon, Oxford.

Pearce, D., A. Markandya and E.B. Barbier (1989) *Blueprint for a Green Economy*, London.

Pezzey, J. (1989) *Economic Analysis of Sustainable Growth and Sustainable Development*. Environment Department Working Paper No. 15, World Bank, Washington, DC.

Pezzey, J. (1992) Sustainability: An interdisciplinary guide. *Environmental Values*, 1: 321–362.

Pigou, A.C. (1952) *The Economics of Welfare*, 4th edn, Macmillan, London.

Ponting, C. (1992) *A Green History of the World*, Sinclair-Stevenson, London.

RIVM (1992) *National Environmental Outlook 2, 1990–2010*. RIVM, Bilthoven.

Schumacher, E.F. (1973) *Small is Beautiful: Economics as if People Mattered*, Harper & Row, New York.

Schwarz, M. and M. Thompson (1990) *Divided We Stand: Redefining Politics, Technology and Social Choice*, Harvester Wheatsheaf, Hemel Hempstead, UK.

Siebert, H. (1982) Nature as a life support system: Renewable resources and environmental disruption, *Journal of Economics*, **42**(2):133–142.

Stortenbeker, C.W. (1990) Op weg naar het Paaseiland? De mens en zijn natuurlijk milieu. In: CLTM (1990) *Het milieu: denkbeelden voor de 21ste eeuw*, Commissie Lange Termijn Milieubeleid, Kerckebosch, Zeist.

Timmerman, P. (1986) *Mythology and Suprise in the Sustainable Development of the Biosphere*, Cambridge University Press, Cambridge.

Turner, R.K. and D.W. Pearce (1993) Sustainable economic development: Economic and ethical principles. In: E.B. Barbier (Ed.), *Economics and Ecology: New Frontiers and Sustainable Development*, Chapman & Hall, London.

Van den Bergh, J.C.J.M. (1991) Dynamic Models for Sustainable Development, Thesis, Tinbergen Institute, Amsterdam.

Van den Bergh, J.C.J.M. and J. van der Straaten (Eds.) (1994) *Toward Sustainable Development, Concepts, Methods, and Policy*, Island Press, Washington, DC.

Van Diepen, A. and H. Voogd (1994) Environmental quality and household behaviour. Paper presented at the Regional IGU Congress, Prague.

Wilting, H.C. (1994) *Energie Analyse Programma*. Handleiding versie 2.0. RuG, Center for Energy and Environmental Studies, University of Groningen.

WCED (1987) *Our Common Future*, World Commission on Environment and Development, Oxford University Press, Oxford.

WCS/IUCN (1980) *World Conservation Strategy: Living Resource Conservation for Sustainable Development*, World Conservation Strategy/International Union for the Conservation of Nature, Gland, Switzerland.

WRR (1994) *Duurzame risico's: een blijvend gegeven*, Wetenschappelijke Raad voor het Regeringsbeleid, SDU, The Hague.

Chapter 2

Analysis of Household Metabolic Flows

J. van der Wal and K.J. Noorman

Abstract

This chapter presents past trends of a number of metabolic flows related to house-hold consumption in the Netherlands. We describe and analyze both the direct and indirect demand for energy (i.e., energy embodied in goods and services), and the use of water and motor fuel. Following the principles of the concept of household metabolism, these input flows are related to the generation of waste residues. As an example of the environmental impacts of household consumption, we calculate the CO_2 emissions related to the total energy requirements of households. In addition to describing the metabolic flows through Dutch households, we identify some of the determinants of past changes in household consumption patterns.

2.1. Introduction

Consumption activities are associated with the exploitation of natural resources, the generation of waste, and the degradation of an increasing number of ecological functions. In order to achieve the objective of sustainability (including environmental quality aspects), harmonizing production and consumption patterns demands an analysis of past patterns of natural resource use associated with household consumption. In this chapter we describe and analyze historical trends in specific metabolic flows through households in the Netherlands, focusing on the physical resource flows related to the use of white goods appliances (e.g., washing machines, refrigerators, freezers), energy for heating, and motor fuel. Instead of taking into account the full range of natural resources required to meet consumer demand, we have translated the use of these resources into energy parameters. This approach builds partly on methodologies already fruitfully applied in previous studies (e.g., Biesiot and Moll, 1995; Wilting, 1996). Since household consumption patterns are

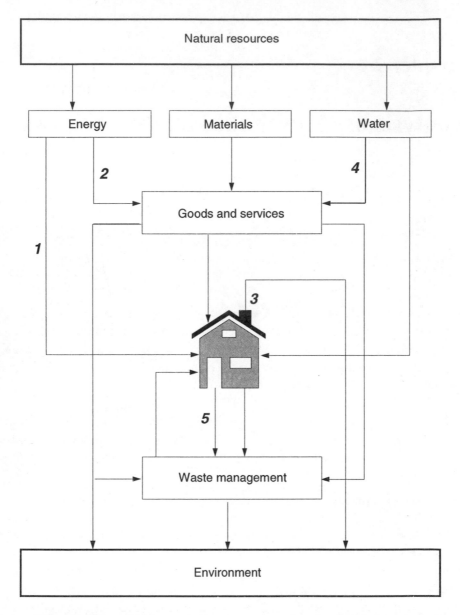

Figure 2.1. The household metabolism concept: the physical inputs and outputs related to households (flows 1–5 are described in the text).

also related to water use and the generation of waste, we also provide overviews of past developments in these specific metabolic flows.

Figure 2.1 (derived from *Figure 1.6*) places the household in the metabolism framework and summarizes the physical inputs and outputs related to household consumption. In the figure these physical flows are numbered as follows:

1. direct energy consumption, i.e., the energy consumed directly in or by households (natural gas, electricity, motor fuel);
2. indirect energy consumption, i.e., the energy embodied in consumer goods and services;
3. CO_2 emissions related to direct and indirect energy consumption;
4. domestic water consumption; and
5. solid waste flows from households.

Before discussing the patterns of domestic resource use in the past, we first briefly discuss a number of factors that have affected (and are still influencing) household metabolism in the Netherlands.

2.2. Determinants of Household Consumption Patterns in the Past

A broad range of factors have led to changes in household consumption patterns and related production activities. Opschoor (1989) described the effects of technical, economic, demographic, institutional and cultural developments (the so-called TEDIC complex), whose combined effects have been very influential indeed. The separate effects of these factors are discussed in the various chapters of this volume. In this section we briefly discuss a number of the determinants of household consumption of energy and water, and the production of waste. After describing the patterns of some economic indicators related to consumption at the macro level in the past, we assess the effects of demographic changes and family dilution on the use of energy and water and the generation of waste.

Although often criticized for not taking into account the environmental side-effects of economic activity, the gross national product (GNP) is generally taken as an indicator of "economic well-being". Over the period 1950–1995, the GNP in the Netherlands increased by 425%, an average of almost 4% per year (see *Figure 2.2*).[1] Between 1959 and 1974 the growth rate was nearly 6% per year. The first oil crisis in 1973 marked the beginning of a short period of slower growth, and the second oil crisis in 1979 gave rise to an economic recession with negative growth rates. Since 1982, the average GNP growth has been 2.1% per year.

The Dutch National Bureau on Statistics (CBS, National Accounts) compiles a consumption index reflecting changes in expenditures (see *Figure 2.2*). During the period considered, 1950–1995, the aggregate of all consumption expenditures increased fourfold. To assess the effects of the past increase in the number of households and of family dilution on consumption, the consumption indices per household and per capita are calculated from the aggregate consumption index.

Household consumption is directly related to disposable incomes and consumer prices. It appears that the average household income increased much faster than the average price level of consumer goods. Since 1959 the income–price ratio (in constant prices) at the household level has risen by 50% (CBS, several publications).

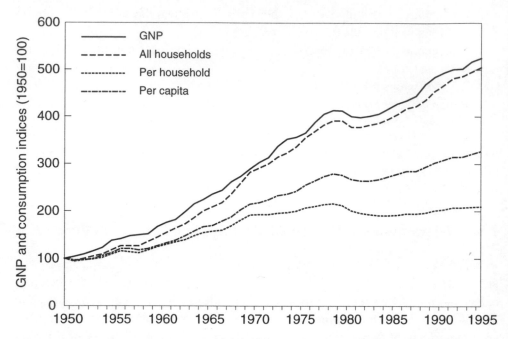

Figure 2.2. GNP and consumption indices, 1950–1995. Source: Adapted from CBS, National Accounts.

Besides these economic factors (these and other economic determinants are discussed in detail in Chapter 8), demographic changes have also affected household consumption patterns. Although discussed in Chapter 4, we briefly mention here the developments in the number and size of households. Between 1950 and 1997 the population of the Netherlands increased by 55%, from 10 million to 15.5 million, whereas the number of households increased by 140%, from 2.7 million to 6.5 million (see *Figure 4.4*). This divergence between the growth of the population and the number of households indicates that the average size of households decreased, from 3.7 in 1950 to 2.4 in 1995. This process is known as household dilution.

The scale effects of household size on the use of energy and water, and the generation of waste are shown in *Table 2.1*. The table shows the scale advantages of multi-person households in relation to the demand for natural gas and electricity; the energy demand per additional household member diminishes. To a lesser extent this scale effect is also visible in the generation of household waste. In contrast with energy demand, scale advantages do not occur in relation to water demand: the average water demand per household member is independent of household size, since most water is used for personal activities (showers/baths, toilets).

Table 2.1. Scale effects of household size on the use of energy and water and the generation of waste (one-person household = 100).

Household size	Households (%)		Water	Natural gas	Electricity	Regular waste
	1950	1995				
1	10	32	100	100	100	100
2	23	33	201	154	149	177
3	21	13	300	192	180	243
4	18	14	394	231	216	302
5	12	7	484	262	236	–
6+	16	2	–	292	252	–

Sources: Calculated from Weegink (1996a,b); VEWIN (1995); Landman and Veenstra (1995).

2.3. Energy Demand

This section presents time series data on household energy use in the period 1950–1995. A distinction is made between direct and indirect energy. Here we focus on direct energy use; time series data on indirect energy use are presented at the end of this section, and the subject is discussed in Chapter 3.

We distinguish three forms of energy used directly by households: *heat* for space heating, heating water, and cooking; *electricity* for lighting, cooling, washing, etc.; and *motor fuel* for transport. Ultimately we are interested in the amount of non-renewable primary energy sequestered from the Earth and the CO_2 emissions associated with household activities. The data on direct energy use are converted into primary energy terms using the energy requirement for energy (ERE) values for the different fuels.[2] We conclude this section by combining data on direct and indirect energy use to construct a time series of total primary energy use of the household sector in the period 1950–1995. Primary energy data and the CO_2 emission factors of the various fuel types are then combined to calculate the related CO_2 emissions.

2.3.1. Heat demand

Energy Carriers

Three activities determine the heat demand of households: space heating, heating water, and cooking. In 1950–1995 there were several shifts between the energy carriers used for these purposes. Four energy carriers can be distinguished: coal, oil, coal gas, and natural gas (*Figure 2.3*). In the 1950s coal was the most important, but was gradually overtaken by oil, which in turn was surpassed (in 1964) by coal as the most commonly used energy carrier. The situation changed radically in the mid-1960s, with the discovery and exploitation of the Slochteren natural gas

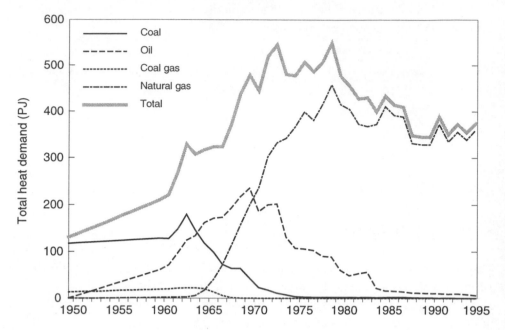

Figure 2.3. Heat demand (PJ) and the associated energy carriers, 1950–1995. Sources: Calculated from IEA and CBS, several publications.

field in the north of the Netherlands (estimated reserves in 1995 were still about 2000 billion m^3). Within a relatively short time natural gas became the major energy source for all sectors (including households) of the Dutch economy, and the contributions of coal and mineral oil gradually diminished. In the late 1960s the Dutch government decided to close down the coal mines in Limburg (in the southeast of the country), thus ending a long history of indigenous coal supply.

During the 1950s and 1960s coal gas (manufactured gas) was also used for heating in the residential sector, but since this required the existence of a grid, supplies were limited to urban areas. Another reason for the limited share of coal gas for heating was its price: compared with coal and mineral oil, coal gas was significantly more expensive, and was therefore only used for heating water and cooking. Supplies of coal gas for domestic use ended in 1969, and the existing gas grid was adapted and extended for the distribution of natural gas. Within a short time almost all households were connected to the natural gas grid; in 1950 about 57% of the total of 2.7 million households (i.e., 1.5 million households) were connected to the grid, compared with 96% (i.e., 6.2 million households) in 1995.

Developments in Heat Demand

The total energy used for residential heating in the Netherlands increased from 130 PJ (petajoules, or 10^{15} joules) in 1950 to 550 PJ in 1979, an average of more than

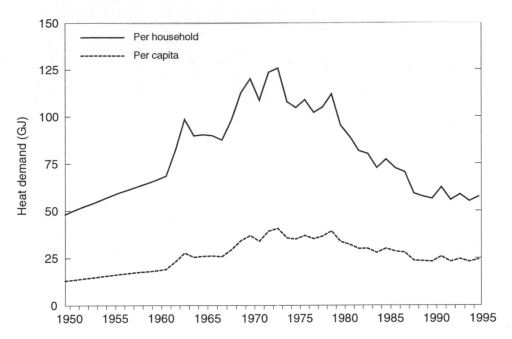

Figure 2.4. Heat demand (GJ) per household and per capita, 1950–1995. Sources: Author's own calculations.

5% per year. Following the 1979 oil crisis, however, when the Organization of Oil-Exporting Countries (OPEC) raised the (nominal) price of a barrel of oil to $23, many initiatives were introduced that aimed to reduce the consumption of primary energy in all sectors of the economy. Energy prices more than doubled, and so had a significant effect on the willingness of households to adopt energy-saving measures; by 1990 the direct energy demand for residential heating had fallen to 345 PJ, an average reduction of more than 4% per year (*Figure 2.3*). However, by 1995 the demand in the household sector had risen slightly again to 375 PJ.

Over the whole period 1950–1995 the household heat demand fluctuated considerably. After peaking just before the first oil crisis in 1973, household heat demand began to fall (see *Figure 2.4*). The decline was interrupted briefly in 1979 (due to a very cold winter), continued until 1990 (57 GJ per household), and since then has been relatively stable. Although an increasing number of individual central heating systems and water heaters came into use, efficiency improvements have resulted in significant reductions in the heat demand per household since the early 1970s. Since 1973 even the per capita heat demand has been decreasing.

Heat demand has always been dominated by space heating, followed by heating water and cooking. Data on the use of natural gas for these purposes have been available since 1980. *Table 2.2* shows the average natural gas demand per household; the amount used for space heating decreased strongly, whereas that for

Table 2.2. Natural gas demand (GJ) per household for space heating, heating water, and cooking.

	1980	1985	1990	1995
Space heating	87	68	56	51
Cooking	3	2	13	14
Heating water	10	8	2	2
Total	100	78	71	67

Source: Weegink (1996b).

heating water rose to 14 GJ per household per year. Although less natural gas was used for water heating after the second oil crisis, since 1985 it has increased again, due mainly to the higher capacity of water heaters. The amount of natural gas used for cooking has remained more or less constant, at about 2 GJ per household per year.

Determinants of Heat Demand

As noted above, the period 1950–1979 was characterized by a rapid turnover in the use of energy carriers and rising domestic heat consumption. Before 1963 natural gas consumption was of minor importance, but then grew in 1963–1979 as a result of both market-related developments and public policy incentives. These incentives (whose initial purpose was to encourage the rapid exploitation of Dutch natural gas reserves) were based partly on the assumption that the availability of (relatively cheap) nuclear power might reduce the price of natural gas. As soon as natural gas from the Slochteren field became available, the number of households connected to the gas grid increased quickly. The government invested heavily in the gas grid, and used price policy to stimulate consumption, by coupling the price to the most obvious substitutes (oil products). By allowing a delay in this price coupling in periods of increasing oil prices, the price of natural gas fell below that of oil. These policy incentives discouraged energy-saving, and probably also greatly increased the use of natural gas in the period considered.

Figure 2.5 shows the consumption and prices of natural gas in the period 1950–1995. The price fell rapidly when exploitation of the Slochteren field began. The two oil crises induced increases in the prices of fossil fuels and related products. The first energy crisis in 1973 had little impact on household natural gas consumption, but the government's energy-saving measures led to a fall in consumption over the period 1979–1985. When natural gas became available, the heating behavior of households changed: laborious coal stoves were used only between October and May, whereas gas fires could be used year round. Furthermore, once connected to the gas grid, more and more householders installed central heating systems, and so

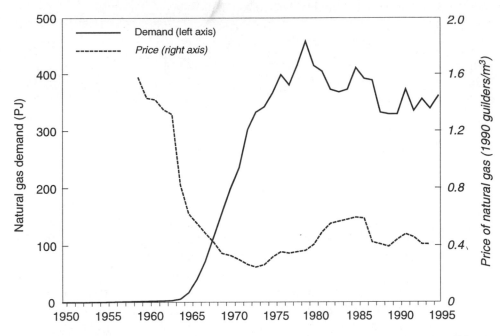

Figure 2.5. Natural gas demand by households (PJ) and real prices (1990 guilders), 1950–1995. Source: CBS, several publications.

could heat more rooms to a higher temperature. After 1965 all new homes were equipped with individual central heating systems, so that now 75% of all houses are heated by such systems.

The introduction of (natural) gas-fired boilers and geysers also led to the consumption of more hot water (for showers and bathing). Cooking on gas stoves became common, although this change in cooking behavior had relatively little impact on gas consumption, since much less gas is used for cooking than for space heating and heating water (Weegink, 1995b).

The availability of new heating systems and relatively low energy prices resulted in increasing residential heat demand until the late 1970s, when it peaked at 550 PJ. Despite the continued population growth and family dilution, the 1979 oil crisis marked the turning point in the pattern of rising natural gas consumption. The impacts of insulation and changing heating behavior on heat demand are shown in *Figures 2.3* and *2.4*. *Table 2.3* lists the main types of insulation that were installed in increasing numbers of homes. Double glazing is the most common, and is now found in 75% of all dwellings (Weegink, 1996b). By 1995 only 8% of the housing stock (485,000 dwellings) had no form of insulation.

Table 2.3. Insulation installed in dwellings (%).

Insulation	1978	1995
Double glazing	20	75
Wall	12	63
Roof	19	59
Floor	5	31
All kinds	10	23
None	65	8

Sources: Centrum voor Marketing Analyses (1979); Weegink (1995).

2.3.2. Electricity demand

Developments in Electricity Demand

Figure 2.6 shows the developments in household electricity demand over the period 1950–1995. Until 1980 residential electricity demand rose significantly at an average of 8% per year. After a short period of decreasing use in the early 1980s, since 1985 it has risen at an average rate of 3% per year. Notably, there were sharp increases in 1994 and 1995. Starting from the 1950 level of 2 GJ_{el},[3] electricity consumption per household rose to 11 GJ_{el} in 1995, the same level as in 1979 (*Figure 2.7*). Electricity consumption per capita increased from 0.5 GJ_{el} in 1950 to 4.6 GJ_{el} in 1995.

Determinants of Electricity Demand

In 1950 75% of Dutch households (2 million) were connected to the electricity grid, compared with almost all 6.5 million households in 1995. In the early 1950s, most electricity was used for lighting; few households owned a refrigerator, washing machine or other electrical appliances, due to the high prices of both the appliances and electricity. However, rapidly rising incomes and the decreasing real price of electricity in the period 1953–1973 stimulated purchases of domestic appliances (*Figure 2.6*).

Figure 2.8 shows the penetration rates of the washing machine, the refrigerator and the freezer. In a relatively short time, washing machines, refrigerators and TVs were being used in almost all households. Current penetration rates of the refrigerator and TV are beyond 100%, since some households possess more than one (van Ours, 1986). There are now well over 100 domestic electrical appliances (Weegink, 1996a), whose electricity consumption varies from low (toothbrushes, electric blankets, alarm clocks, etc.) to high (waterbeds, microwaves, water heaters, etc.).

Similar to natural gas consumption, the increase in real electricity prices in 1974–1981 also affected electricity use, although the impact was smaller than in

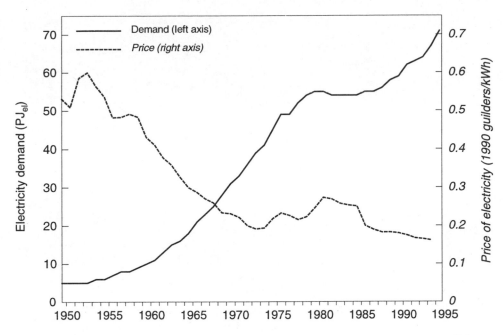

Figure 2.6. Electricity demand (PJ$_{el}$) of households and real prices (1990 guilders), 1950–1995. Source: CBS, several publications.

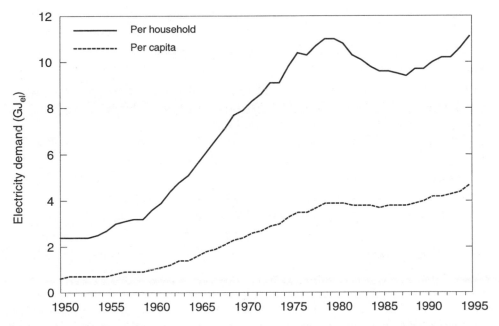

Figure 2.7. Electricity demand (GJ$_{el}$) per household and per capita, 1950–1995. Source: Author's own calculations.

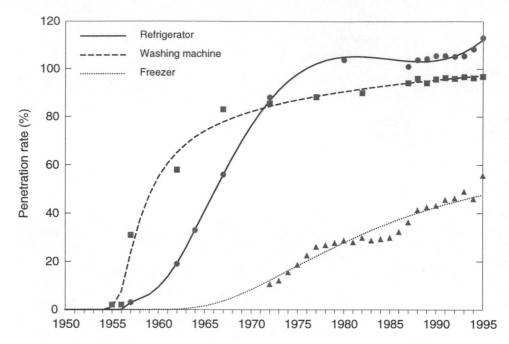

Figure 2.8. (Calculated) penetration rates of some consumer durables, 1950–1995. Source: After Bakker (1995).

the case of natural gas. Also analogous to the efficiency improvements in gas-fired appliances, rising electricity prices led to technological innovations to improve the efficiency of electrical appliances. Despite the ongoing population growth, household dilution, and the increasing penetration rates of existing appliances and a variety of new ones, the total electricity consumption of households fell slightly in the early 1980s. However, since 1985 the growth rate has accelerated again, mainly due to the introduction of new appliances.

The best known example of an efficiency improvement in an electrical appliance is that of the light bulb. Incandescent light bulbs can be replaced by compact fluorescent lamps, which consume around 84% less electricity than incandescent bulbs. Other examples of (significant) efficiency improvements are shown in *Table 2.4.* Note that the numbers are not corrected for intensity of use.

2.3.3.   Fuel demand

Developments in Mobility and Fuel Use

Over the past four decades personal mobility has steadily increased.[4] Between 1960 and 1995, the total motorized passenger kilometers[5] increased from 42 billion to 178 billion km (CBS, 1997), an average of more than 4% per year.

Table 2.4. Average annual electricity consumption (kWh) of some durable consumer goods (1995: the most efficient models commercially available).

	1975	1983	1989	1993	1995
Refrigerator	400	400	398	320	50
Freezer	–	550	490	380	50
Washing machine	500	275	245	236	220
Dishwasher	–	475	–	360	336
Central heating pump	500	450	331	290	–
Television[a]	200	112	92	88	–

[a] "Standby" state excluded.

Sources: Ansmink *et al.* (1987); Weegink (1995a).

Taking into account population growth, motorized km per capita increased from about 3700 km/year in the early 1960s to about 11,500 km/year in 1997. Along with the enormous increase in passenger traffic, the use of private cars increased enormously, and the share of passenger car kilometers (PCK) rose from 38% in 1960 to 82% in 1995. At the same time, the share of public transport decreased; the share of passenger train kilometers fell from 19% in 1960 to 8% in 1995, even though it rose in absolute terms.

The increase in motorized passenger transport corresponded to an increase in the demand for fuel. In the period 1960–1995 energy consumption for transport increased more than fivefold, from 51 to 280 PJ, the bulk of which was accounted for by motor fuel (231 PJ or 83% in 1995; see *Figure 2.9*).

Only some passenger transport can be allocated to households; business-related travel is not regarded as a household activity in this study. The distinction between private and business-related passenger transport can only be made with respect to passenger car transport (see *Figure 2.9*). Fuel consumption for private car use increased by almost 10% per year, from 10 PJ in 1960 to 196 PJ in 1993 (182 PJ in 1995). This indicates a rapid increase in the number of private cars, and in the distances driven. Between 1950 and 1995 the passenger car fleet increased from 140,000 (one car per 19 households or 72 inhabitants), to 5.6 million (one car per 1.1 household or 2.7 inhabitants). Growth was fastest in 1965–1980, but in the early 1980s it levelled off and is now even declining, although the number of cars is still rising in absolute terms. Due to the decreasing number of passengers per car, the gap between private passenger and private real car kilometers (RCK) closed slightly. The latter shows an explosive growth from 3 billion to 74 billion km. Although the average distance travelled by car has been fairly constant since 1975 (about 16,000 km), the reasons for driving these distances have changed (see *Table 2.5*). In the early 1960s passenger cars were used mostly for business purposes, whereas now they are used for a wide range of "miscellaneous" purposes, such as social contacts, shopping, etc. Commuter traffic now also accounts for an important part of the real car kilometers.

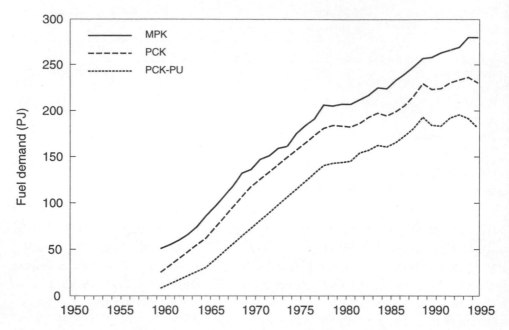

Figure 2.9. Fuel use for motorized passenger kilometers (MPK), passenger car kilometers (PCK) and passenger car kilometers for private use (PCK-PU), 1950–1995. Source: Author's own calculations.

Table 2.5. Reasons for private car use (%).

Year	Business	Commuting	Holidays	Miscellaneous
1960	66.8	8.0	5.9	19.3
1970	38.4	17.4	8.1	36.1
1980	21.6	29.5	10.1	38.8
1990	17.4	24.6	9.1	48.9
1995	21.1	24.6	7.5	46.8

Source: CBS, several publications.

Determinants of Fuel Demand

The number of real car kilometers driven is the main factor that determines the direct energy demand for passenger car transport. As indicated above, the number of kilometers driven increased due to the growth in the number of cars. Rising incomes allowed more households to purchase a car, and low fuel prices also encouraged increased mobility. Before the 1973 oil crisis the real average fuel price (gas oil, petrol and LPG) fell from about Dfl 2 per liter in 1957 to about Dfl 1.50 in 1972 (*Figure 2.10*; 1990 guilders; CBS, 1996), and fuel consumption increased accordingly (by 14% per year). After 1973 the average growth in fuel

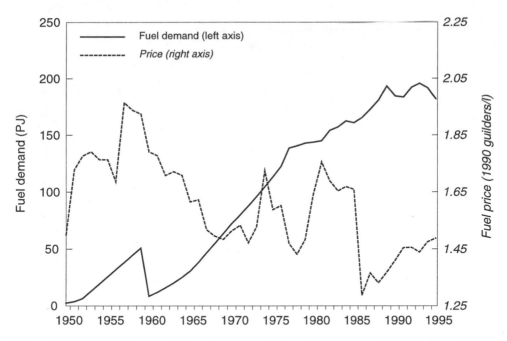

Figure 2.10. Fuel demand for private use (PJ) and average real fuel prices (1990 guilders) over time. Source: Author's own calculations.

consumption fell to 2% per year, while the price in real terms fluctuated between Dfl 1.29 and 1.75 per liter.

Besides price, two other factors influenced the use of motor fuel in 1968–1994: the weight of cars and the engine energy efficiency (see *Figure 2.11*). Between 1968 and 1994 the average weight of a new car increased from 839 kg to 1045 kg (CBS), due to the shift to larger, more solid cars. In the early 1980s (new) cars became lighter in weight, in response to the increasing fuel prices. The most recent increase in weight has been due to the inclusion of new features to increase safety and comfort, such as airbags, air conditioning, catalytic converters, etc.

The only factor that has offset increasing fuel consumption has been the development of more energy efficient engines. The average efficiency of a standard 1000 kg car improved by 1.6% per year between 1968 and 1994 (*Figure 2.11*). In absolute terms, the energy demand decreased from 3.6 to 2.4 MJ/km, but this was offset by a simultaneous increase in weight. Before 1980 the real energy use was constant at about 3 MJ/km; it then fell from 3 to 2.6 MJ/km in the period 1980–1984 as the average weight of new cars decreased significantly, and since 1985 has been more or less stable at 2.6–2.5 MJ/km. The effect of efficiency improvements is clearly visible in the fuel use of passenger cars (*Figure 2.9*; PCK), even though the data in the figure refer to entire car fleet. Taking into account the increasing weight

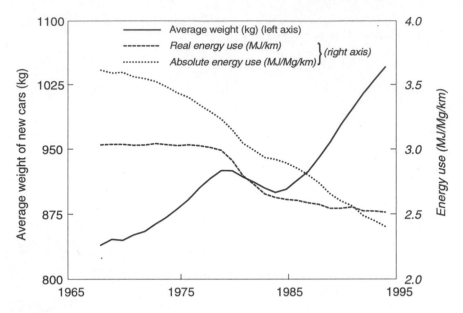

Figure 2.11. Average weight and energy efficiency of new cars sold in the Netherlands, 1965–1995. Source: Author's own calculations.

of new cars, the overall average efficiency improvements were 0.7% per year in the period 1968–1994.

2.3.4. Total direct (primary) energy consumption and related CO_2 emissions

From *Figure 2.12* it is apparent that most of the direct energy consumed by households is dominated by heat demand, although since the 1960s the shares of electricity and motor fuels have gradually increased. Direct energy demand peaked in 1979, after which it dropped until 1985 due to the reduced demand for natural gas for space heating. Since 1985, the direct energy demand of the household sector has risen again, due to the combined effects of the increased demand for electricity and for motor fuels. In 1995 direct heat (natural gas), electricity, and fuel consumption amounted to 374, 71, and 182 PJ, respectively; a total of 627 PJ. The share of the direct energy consumed by households accounted for about 22% of the total direct energy used in the Netherlands in 1995.

Although the post-1972 patterns in the prices of natural gas and electricity show many similarities, annual electricity consumption kept on rising (see *Figure 2.6*, whereas natural gas demand fell significantly (see *Figure 2.3*). Price effects have apparently played different roles here. Chapter 8 discusses the role of the price elasticities for natural gas and electricity. The installation of insulation has had a significant impact on the amounts of natural gas used for space heating.

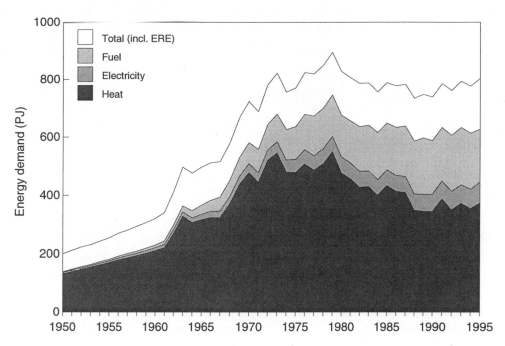

Figure 2.12. (Primary) residential heat, electricity and fuel demand (PJ), 1950–1995. Source: Author's own calculations.

The increased electricity demand has been due mainly to the many new electrical appliances that have become available in the last two decades. The increased fuel consumption has been due to the larger private car fleet; the intensity of use (per car) has remained more or less constant.

As mentioned earlier, we are also interested in the primary energy demand of households. Direct energy data are therefore converted into primary energy terms using the ERE values of the various fuels (*Table 2.6*; see note 2). It appears that the ERE values of refined oil and coke are considerably higher than that of natural gas. Over time, the ERE values of electricity decreased from 5.25 to 2.9 MJ/MJ because of changes in the mix of fossil fuels and efficiency improvements. Nevertheless, the current ERE values for electricity are still much higher than those of primary energy sources.

Figure 2.12 shows that the total direct *primary* energy requirements of households rose from 200 PJ in 1950 to 807 PJ in 1995; 45% and 28% higher, respectively, than direct energy use. The diminishing difference between direct energy use and direct primary energy use in the period 1950–1995 resulted from both the switch to natural gas, which has a relatively low ERE value compared with coke and mineral oil, and efficiency improvements in the electricity production sector.

The CO_2 emissions related to the direct primary energy used by households have changed as a result of the increasing share of natural gas, which has a relatively

Table 2.6. ERE values (MJ/MJ) and CO_2 emission coefficients (kg/GJ) of different energy carriers.

	ERE values (MJ/MJ)				CO_2 emission coefficient (kg/GJ)
	Extraction	Transport	Production	Total	
Coal	1.097	1.050	–	1.152	103.6
Coke	1.097	1.050	1.14	1.313	133.5
Crude oil	1.037	1.084	–	1.124	77.6
Refined oil	1.037	1.084	1.07	1.203	86.7
Natural gas	–	–	–	1.008	57.0

Sources: Noorman (1995); Wilting (1996); van der Wal (1992).

lower CO_2 emission coefficient (kg CO_2/GJ) than coal or oil products (see *Table 2.6*). CO_2 emissions related to electricity production have fallen from 435 to 184 kg CO_2/GJ_{el}. Between 1950 and 1995, CO_2 emissions related to the direct primary energy used by households increased from 20 to 52 Mt CO_2. As a result of the increased use of natural gas in the last few decades, however, the rate of growth of CO_2 emissions (160%) has lagged behind that of direct primary energy use (314%).

2.3.5. Indirect and total primary energy demand and related CO_2 emissions

In addition to direct energy, households also consume energy by purchasing goods and services. Production and consumption activities are closely related; since goods have to be produced before they can be consumed, the total energy consumption of an economy can be attributed to final demand consumption, including households (see Chapter 3). The indirect energy consumption of households can be determined by combining data on household expenditures and the energy intensities (MJ/Dfl) of the production sectors.

Using energy intensities (the amount of energy required for the production of a financial unit of output, MJ/Dfl) derived from input–output analysis and financial data from input–output tables, Wilting (1996) calculated the indirect energy use of households for the period 1969–1988 (see Chapter 3). A consistent set of input–output tables was not available for the whole of this period, so we have completed the 1950–1995 time series using the aggregated average annual energy intensities of household expenditures. These energy intensities are subject to changes due, for example, to technological developments, which we estimated using the total indigenous fuel use/GNP ratio (expressed in PJ/million Dfl) to indicate changes in the efficiency of energy use. We calculated that the indirect primary energy use of Dutch households increased from 313 to 1180 PJ between 1950 and 1995. Throughout this period, indirect primary energy use in the household sector exceeded direct primary energy use (see *Figure 2.13*).

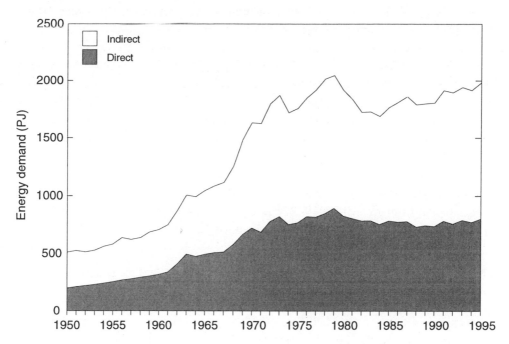

Figure 2.13. Developments in direct and indirect primary energy use of households, 1950–1995. Source: Author's own calculations.

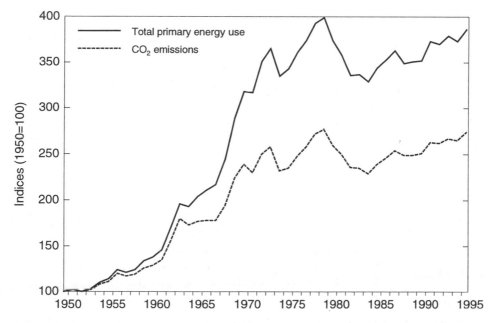

Figure 2.14. Indices of total (direct and indirect) residential primary energy use and CO_2 emissions, 1950–1995 (1950 = 100). Source: Author's own calculations.

Applying both process analysis and input–output analysis, van Engelenburg *et al.* (1991) calculated the direct and indirect energy requirements of a number of consumer durables over their entire life cycles. The indirect costs ranged from about 2500 MJ (dishwashers) to 4560 MJ (TVs). Taking into account the average lifetimes of such appliances, the annual indirect energy inputs of these appliances are 8–13% of total annual energy inputs.

The total primary energy demand of households (indirect plus direct) increased from 513 PJ in 1950 to 2047 PJ in 1979, after which it showed a decreasing trend until 1985 (see *Figure 2.13*), and then rose again, to 1983 PJ in 1995. *Figure 2.14* shows the indices of total primary energy use and the corresponding CO_2 emissions. The total CO_2 emissions that can be attributed to households amounted to about 47 billion kg (Mt) in 1950, 128 Mt in 1979, then fell to 111 Mt in 1985, and by 1995 had again risen to the 1979 level of 128 Mt.

2.4. Water Demand

Whereas in the 1950s and 1960s about 20% of households used surface water or groundwater directly, almost all households now use water supplied by the water companies. *Figure 2.15* shows that between 1950 and 1995, the total domestic water consumption almost tripled, from 266 million to 755 million m^3 per year. Since the water consumption per household remained fairly constant, at approximately 115 m^3 per year, the increasing demand in this sector can be attributed to the growing number of households, and the fairly constant demand per household to the smaller size of households. The latter is confirmed by the pattern of annual water consumption per capita, which increased gradually from 32 m^3 in 1950 to 49 m^3 in 1995; the latter corresponds to 134 liters per capita per day. In contrast with energy use, households are the major consumers of water, accounting for about 60% of the total.

Domestic water supplies are derived from various types of resources; see *Figure 2.16*. Although water supplies increased in absolute terms after 1973, the rate of increase slowed; the peak in 1976 was due to the very dry summer that year. Since 1950 most of the growing demand for water for domestic uses has been met from groundwater supplies.

In contrast with natural gas and, to lesser extent, electricity, the price of water does not affect residential water use. For a long time households paid a fixed tariff that was unrelated to the actual amount of water used. In the last decade, however, water meters have been installed in many households, although the price is so low that this has not affected consumption (the price elasticity of tap water is discussed in Chapter 8).

As noted in *Table 2.1*, water consumption per household increases proportionally with the number of household members. The tripling of the total water consumption of households can be attributed to: the increasing number of households

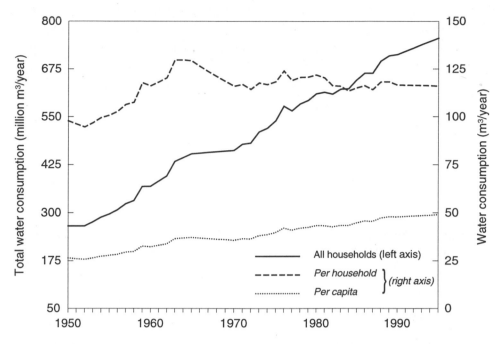

Figure 2.15. Water consumption of all households (VEWIN), per household and per capita, 1950–1995. Source: Author's own calculations.

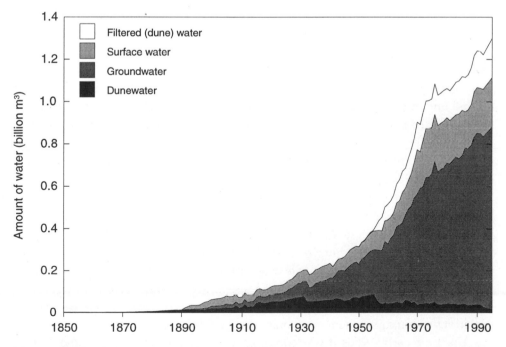

Figure 2.16. Sources of tap water, 1950–1995. Source: VEWIN, *Tap Water Statistics.*

Table 2.7. Domestic water consumption for various uses, 1965–1995 (liters per capita per day).

	1965	1973	1980	1992	1995
Bath/shower	25	27	29.3	47.5	47.3
Toilet	30	39	30.9	42.7	39.0
Washing machines	10	17	21.5	25.7	25.5
Dishwashers	10	10	11.9	9.5	5.8
Drinking/cooking	5	7	2.6	2.6	2.0
Other	5	4	11.3	6.9	9.4
Total	100	104	107.5	134.9	134.9

Source: VEWIN, several publications.

connected to the grid, population growth, and in particular, increased consumption per capita (due to the greater use of appliances such as washing machines, as well as toilets, baths/showers; van der Wal, 1994). Few homes in the Netherlands had such facilities in 1950, but since World War II all new houses have been fitted with sanitary facilities, so that the levels of penetration are now 100% or higher. The impacts of these changes on per capita water consumption are shown in *Table 2.7*. The combined consumption of water for these uses increased by 47 liters per capita per day in the period 1965–1995. However, less water is now used for drinking and cooking, probably as a result of the so-called "coca cola effect": many people now consume prepacked beverages rather than coffee, tea and water.

2.5.   Domestic Waste Production

Only limited data on solid waste are available, so that only general information on the amounts of waste generated by households, and the composition of waste flows are given here. This section summarizes the magnitude and composition of domestic solid waste flows since 1950. Since households consume a changing mix of goods and services, these waste flows have changed both qualitatively and quantitatively in recent years.

Solid waste can be divided into three categories: regular, non-recyclable waste; heavy volume waste; and recyclable (separated) waste. The latter can be divided into six subcategories: textiles, paper, glass, domestic chemical waste, organic waste, and refrigerators/white goods appliances. In the past there have been periods when recyclable or "useful" waste was collected separately, and periods when separate waste collection was hardly an issue. Most recently, economic as well as environmental concerns have influenced consumers' willingness to cooperate with initiatives encouraging them to separate their waste residues.

Until the early 1960s it was common for households to separate the various components of domestic waste. The "rag-and-bone" man collected clothes and textiles, the "peel" man collected organic wastes, and paper was also collected separately. Until 1980 waste separation was not given high priority, except for paper and textiles on a limited scale, and most domestic waste ended up in landfills. In the early 1980s, public policy initiatives inspired by environmental goals led to renewed efforts to encourage households to separate their waste. Collection systems were introduced first for glass, and then for chemical waste, textiles, organic matter and appliances.

2.5.1. Regular domestic waste

Between 1950 and 1992 in absolute terms, the total amount of regular domestic waste in the Netherlands increased from 1100 to 4700 kt (see *Figure 2.17*). The corresponding amounts per capita tripled, from 111 to 313 kg.

Domestic waste contains a large number of products and materials; organic waste, paper, plastics materials and glass together form approximately 85% of the total waste flow. Since 1971 the shares of both organic matter and paper have been stable at 47% and 26%, respectively. The share of synthetic materials increased slowly from 5% in 1971 to 9% in 1992. Due to the introduction of a glass collection system in 1980 the share of glass fell from 12% in 1981 to 4% in 1992 (Cornelissen, 1993, 1994). The remaining fraction (15%) is divided into 10 categories: iron and steel, non-ferrous metals, textiles, food waste, animal waste, ceramics, carpets, leather/rubber, wood, and special garbage (environmentally harmful products such as paint cans, batteries, cosmetics, and oil products). A significant proportion of regular waste consists of packaging materials: in 1992, 85% of all glass, 81% of synthetic materials, 66% of iron and steel, and 30% of paper in the regular waste flow were found to be packaging materials.

2.5.2. Separately collected waste

The total amounts of separated waste (paper, glass, textiles and domestic chemical waste) collected directly from households are shown in *Figure 2.17*. Since the reintroduction of collection systems in 1980, the total amount of separated waste collected increased from 450 kt to 1080 kt in 1992, corresponding to 32 and 71 kg per capita, respectively.

Separated waste can be reused or recycled at various stages in the production chain, either at the product level or as material inputs. If recycling is not feasible, incineration or disposal in landfills are the alternatives. In 1950–1960 the emphasis was on reuse and landfills, whereas after 1960 most household waste other than paper and textiles was disposed of in landfills. Since 1980 the reuse and recycling of products and materials has increased again.

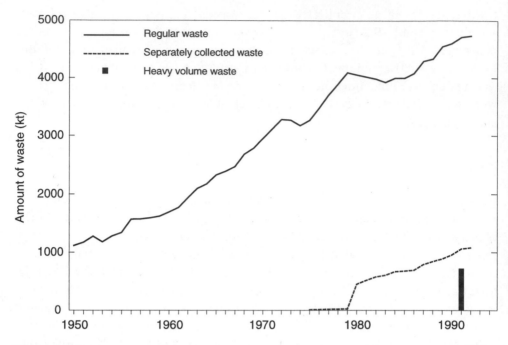

Figure 2.17. Amounts of regular waste, separated waste, and heavy volume waste generated by households, 1950–1992. Sources: Cornelissen (1994); Hanemaayer and Meiling (1994).

Table 2.8. Composition of the heavy volume waste generated by households, 1991.

Category	Amount (kt)
Building and demolition rubble	210
Garden waste	150
White and brown goods appliances	100
Home textiles	75
Furniture	75
Packaging materials	40
Miscellaneous	70
Total	720

Source: Hanemaayer and Meiling (1994).

2.5.3. Heavy volume waste

Heavy volume waste consists of a wide variety of products and materials. Data on the quantity and quality of this waste flow are scarce, although Hanemaayer and Meiling (1994) have published some data for 1991 (see *Table 2.8*). The

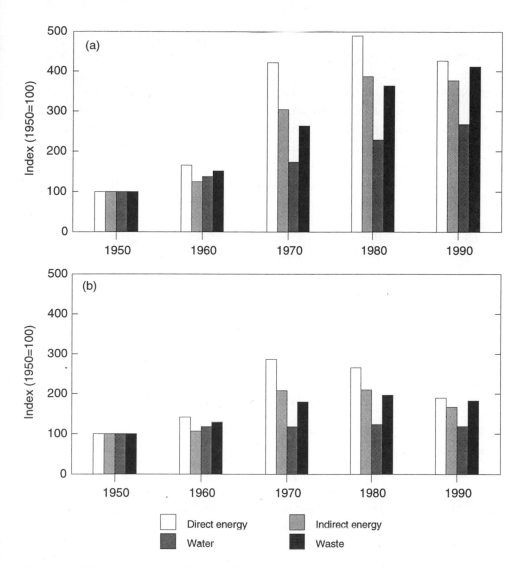

Figure 2.18. Four major physical flows though (a) the household sector, and (b) an average household (1950 = 100). Source: Author's own calculations.

amount of heavy volume waste is also shown in *Figure 2.17*. Former (1995) has studied developments in the number of discarded white goods appliances, taking into account changes in the lifetimes and the increasing penetration of these appliances, and the rising number of households. The number of washing machines and refrigerators disposed of each year increased from almost zero in the 1950s to about 400,000 at present.

2.6. Conclusions

Since World War II, households in the Netherlands have used steadily increasing amounts of natural resources. The consumption of natural resources (including energy) can be viewed from a number of levels: the household sector, the household itself, and per capita. At the sectoral level, the picture is dominated by the increasing use of natural resources (*Figure 2.18a*). Progress in some areas (e.g., the improved efficiency of domestic heating systems, electrical appliances, and insulation) has been offset by sharp increases in the number of households, population growth, household dilution, rising incomes and large-scale investments in distribution grids providing access to energy and water.

At the level of the average household significant progress has been made in reducing the energy demand for heating (*Figure 2.18b*). After doubling between 1960 and 1973, in 1992 the heat demand per household again returned to below the level of 1960. In contrast, the electricity consumption per household has risen due to the use of increasing numbers of electrical appliances. Water consumption per household has remained fairly constant, although per capita consumption has increased significantly. The amount of total waste (regular domestic waste and separated waste) generated shows a similar pattern, increasing almost fourfold, from 111 kg per capita in 1950 to 384 kg per capita in 1992. The relative changes in per capita consumption lie in between the presented data in *Figure 2.17a,b*) because the effects of population growth and household dilution have been filtered out.

Summary

- Household consumption and related natural resource use in general rose strongly during the period 1950–1995.
- The effect of population growth on energy use and waste production was strengthened by the household dilution process. Due to advantages of scale, large households are relatively more energy efficient and produce less waste per household member than small households.
- The demand for direct heat changed strongly during the period 1950–1995. In 1963–1969 coal, mineral oil and coal gas were substituted by natural gas. Subsequently heat demand increased rapidly until 1979 due to more widespread use of central heating systems and the rising demand for hot water. Since 1979, higher energy prices have led households to adopt various energy-saving measures (e.g., insulation), and the heat demand dropped.
- Except for the period 1980–1985, direct electricity use has increased sharply since 1950. Rising disposable incomes have meant that households could purchase more electrical appliances, and the penetration rates of refrigerators, washing machines, and TV sets increased from almost zero to (more than) 100%.

- The consumption of motor fuel has shown more or less the same trend as electricity use. Although the average annual distance travelled by car has been fairly constant since 1975, the number of cars has increased, and commuting now accounts for an important part of passenger transport.
- Total direct *primary* energy demand increased less strongly than the total direct
, energy demand due to the increasing share of natural gas in the energy demand structure, as well as efficiency improvements in the electricity production sector.
- As a result of rising consumption levels, the indirect energy requirements of households have also risen. Indirect primary energy use has always exceeded direct primary energy use.
- Domestic water consumption has increased more or less linearly since 1950, due largely to the more frequent use of toilets, baths/showers, and washing machines.
- Increasing household consumption levels have resulted in the generation of larger amounts of waste. Only a small proportion of all domestic waste is reused or recycled.

Notes

[1] In the period 1921–1939, GNP rose by only 65% (average annual growth 2.8%).
[2] The energy requirement for energy (ERE) is defined as: "the ratio of energy sequestered to deliver a unit of energy divided by the unit of energy" (IFIAS, 1974), or "the ERE value of an energy carrier gives the total amount of primary energy required for the production of the energy carrier" (Wilting, 1996).
[3] Since 1 W(att) = 1 J(oule)/s, 1 kWh = 3.6 MJ and 1 $GJ_{el} \approx 278$ kWh.
[4] Air travel is not considered here.
[5] Motorized passenger kilometers (MPK) are defined as the total amount of kilometers per capita travelled by motorized transport. Passenger car kilometers (PCK) are defined as the sum of kilometers per capita travelled by car, and passenger train kilometers are defined as the sum of kilometers per capita travelled by train. Real car kilometers (RCK) are the kilometers travelled by car, and are thus independent of the number of passengers. For example, a car carrying four passengers travelling a distance of 100 km results in 100 real car kilometers and 400 passenger car kilometers.

References

Ansmink, P., W. Fiechter, R. Lof, H. Miedema and P. Zijlema (1987) *Het elektriciteitsverbruik in huishoudens* (Electricity consumption of households), Report No. 28, University of Groningen, Center for Energy and Environmental Studies.

Bakker, J (1995) *Ontwikkelingen in het huishoudelijk elektriciteitsverbruik* (Developments in the electricity consumption of households), Report No. 24, Center for Energy and Environmental Studies, University of Groningen.

Biesiot, W. and H.C. Moll (Eds.) (1995) *Reduction of CO₂ emissions by Lifestyle Changes*, IVEM Research Report No. 80, Groningen-Utrecht.

CBS (several volumes) *Statistiek van de gasvoorziening in Nederland* (Statistics of gas demand in The Netherlands). Centraal Bureau voor de Statistiek, The Hague.

CBS (several volumes) *Statistiek van de elektriciteitsvoorziening in Nederland* (Statistics of electricity supply in The Netherlands), Centraal Bureau voor de Statistiek, The Hague.

CBS (several volumes) *Nederlandse Energiehuishouding* (Dutch energy statistics). Centraal Bureau voor de Statistiek, The Hague.

CBS (several volumes) *Energiestatistieken* (Energy statistics). Centraal Bureau voor de Statistiek, The Hague.

CBS (several volumes) *Maandstatistiek bevolking* (Monthly population statistics). Centraal Bureau voor de Statistiek, The Hague.

CBS (1995) *Vijfennegentig jaren statistiek in tijdreeksen* (95 years statistics in time series). Centraal Bureau voor de Statistiek, The Hague.

CBS (several volumes). *Statistiek van de motorvoertuigen* (Statistics on motor vehicles). Centraal Bureau voor de Statistiek, The Hague.

CBS (several volumes) *Statistiek van het personenvervoer* (Statistics on passenger transport). Centraal Bureau voor de Statistiek, The Hague.

CBS (several volumes) *Het bezit en gebruik van personenauto's* (Possession and use of private cars). Centraal Bureau voor de Statistiek, The Hague.

CBS (1996) *National accounts of the Netherlands*. Centraal Bureau voor de Statistiek, The Hague.

Centrum voor Marketing Analyses (1979) *Basisonderzoek Aardgas Kleinverbruik, BAK 1978* (Survey of natural gas consumption of small consumers). Nederlandse Gasunie and VEGIN, Amsterdam.

Cornelissen, A.A.J. (1993, 1994) *Fysisch onderzoek naar de samenstelling van het Nederlandse huishoudlijke afval* (An inquiry into the composition of household waste in the Netherlands). RIVM, Bilthoven.

Former, H. (1995) *Ontwikkelingen in huishoudelijk afval* (Developments in residential waste), Report No. 23, Center for Energy and Environmental Studies, University of Groningen.

Hanemaayer A.H. and K. Meiling (1994) *Informatiedocument grof huisvuil* (Information document on residential bulk waste). RIVM, Bilthoven.

IFIAS (1974) *Energy Analysis Workshop on Methodology and Conventions*, Report No. 6, International Federation of Institutes for Advanced Study, Guldsmedshyttan, Sweden.

IEA (several volumes) *Energy Statistics of OECD Countries*. International Energy Agency, Paris.

Landman, R. and W. Veenstra (1995) *Determinanten van de huishoudelijke afvalproduktie in Nederland* (Determinants of waste production in Dutch households), Report No. 10, Center for Energy and Environmental Studies, University of Groningen.

Noorman, K.J. (1995) *Exploring Futures from an Energy Perspective: A Natural Capital Accounting Model Study into the Long-term Economic Development Potential of the Netherlands*, thesis, University of Groningen.

Opschoor, J.B. (1989) *Na ons geen zondvloed: Voorwaarden voor duurzaam milieugebruik*, Kok/Agora, Kampen.

Van der Wal, J. (1992) *Elektriciteitsproduktie in relatie tot broeikaseffect en verzuring: van emissies tot milieuindex* (Electricity production related to the greenhouse effect: from emissions to environmental index), University of Groningen.

Van der Wal, J. (1994) *Direct and indirect water consumption of households in the Netherlands*, Working Paper, University of Groningen.

Van der Wal, J. (1995) Determinants of household energy consumption in the Netherlands. Paper presented at the International Energy Workshop at IIASA, Laxenburg.

Van Engelenburg, B.C.W., T.F.M. van Rossum, K. Blok, W. Biesiot, and H.C. Wilting (1991) *Energiegebruik en huishoudelijke consumptie*. Utrecht University, Dept. of Science, Technology and Society, and University of Groningen, Center for Energy and Environmental Studies.

Van Ours, J.C. (1986) *Gezinsconsumptie in Nederland, 1951–1980* (Household consumption in The Netherlands), thesis, Dept. of Economic Sciences, Erasmus University Rotterdam.

VEWIN (1995) *Het waterverbruik thuis* (Water use in the home), Rijswijk.

VEWIN (several volumes) *Leidingwaterstatistiek* (Tap water statistics), Rijswijk.

Weegink, R.J. (1996a) *Basisonderzoek Elektriciteitsverbruik Kleinverbruikers, BEK 1995* (Basic survey of electricity consumption of small consumers in 1995). EnergieNed, Arnhem.

Weegink, R.J. (1996b) *Basisonderzoek Aardgasverbruik Kleinverbruiker, BAK 1995* (Basic survey of natural gas demand of small consumers in 1995). EnergieNed, Arnhem.

Weegink, R.J. (1995a) *Basisonderzoek Elektriciteitsverbruik Kleinverbruikers, BEK 1994* (Basic survey of electricity consumption of small consumers in 1994). EnergieNed, Arnhem.

Weegink, R.J. (1995b) *Basisonderzoek Aardgasverbruik Kleinverbruikers, BAK 1994* (Basic survey of natural gas demand of small consumers in 1994). EnergieNed, Arnhem.

Wilting, H.C. (1996) *An Energy Perspective on Economic Activities*, thesis, University of Groningen.

Chapter 3

Household Energy Requirements

H.C. Wilting and W. Biesiot

Abstract

The concept of household metabolism refers to both the demand for natural resources and the supply of materials and energy indirectly required to realize these flows. This chapter concentrates on the direct and indirect energy requirements of households. From the household perspective, total energy use in a country can be allocated to household consumption (apart from imports and exports). Household energy requirements over a 20-year period (1969–1988) are investigated. Further, the energy requirements of households are examined in more detail on the basis of household characteristics for one year (1990).

3.1. Introduction

Households use energy for heating (natural gas), lighting (electricity) and transport (motor fuel). This so-called direct energy use is usually understood as the energy use of households (see Chapter 2). The energy directly used by households is a fraction of the energy used in an economy (typical OECD values range from 15 to 20% of total energy use). However, as discussed in Chapter 2, households also use energy in an indirect way. They purchase goods (food, clothes, etc.) and services (insurances, public transport, etc.) which are delivered by the economic production sectors. The energy directly used for the production and delivery of these goods and services can be considered as the indirect energy use of households. Assuming that the economy is based on this supply of goods and services, the total energy used in the production sectors can be allocated to households (apart from imports and exports). The sum of the direct and indirect energy used by households is referred to as the (total) energy requirements of households; see *Figure 3.1*. The direct energy requirements of households include both the energy used by households and the

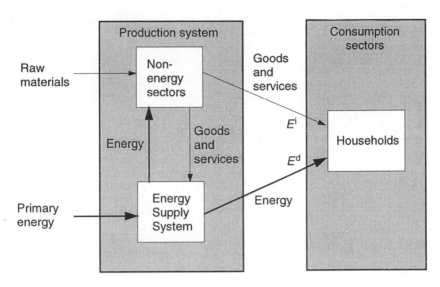

Figure 3.1. Direct (E^d) and indirect (E^i) energy requirements of households. Source: Wilting (1996).

energy used by the energy supply system needed for direct household use.[1] The energy used by the energy supply system is therefore divided among the direct and indirect energy requirements of households.

The approach described is generally applicable, but considering the availability of data, the energy requirements of households in the Netherlands are taken as an example. The energy requirements of households do not sum up to domestic energy use. The energy used by the economic production sectors is also destined for exports (for production and consumption) and investments, and in other countries, energy is used in the production of goods and services for households in the Netherlands. Therefore, in this chapter household energy requirements are examined in relation to other, direct and indirect, energy flows in the Dutch economy, including imports and exports.

In any given year, household energy requirements are the result of developments in previous years, so the latter have been investigated over a longer period. In view of the fact that a consistent set of data was available for the period 1969–1988, we have chosen this period for the calculations. At present, more than 6 million households (each with its own characteristics) determine the total household energy requirements in the Netherlands. Therefore, household energy requirements are also investigated at the level of households categorized according to income, size, etc.

The research described in this chapter has been carried out in the so-called lifestyles research project,[2] which focuses on the relation between lifestyles and CO_2 emissions. This relation can only be established indirectly, as illustrated by the

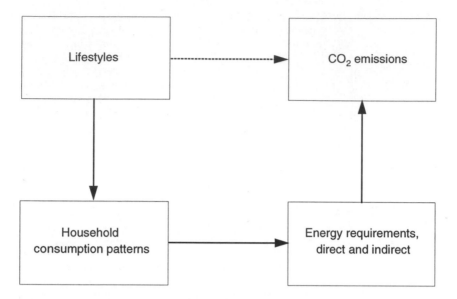

Figure 3.2. Design of the research program into the relation between lifestyles and CO_2 emissions via household consumption patterns and the corresponding energy requirements. Source: Noorman and Schoot Uiterkamp (1996).

dashed line in *Figure 3.2*. The lifestyle concept must first be shaped into patterns of household consumption, which can then be translated into energy terms, and the direct and indirect energy requirements can be ascertained. Finally, coupling of the energy data to CO_2 emission factors yields the required information.

The essence is the projection of the total primary energy use (in production, distribution and households) on behalf of household consumption on disaggregated household budget spending categories. This generates information on the relationship between household spending patterns and their effects (expressed as energy use and CO_2 emissions). The methodology can be regarded as a new development in the field of energy analysis and life cycle analysis, and is described in the next section (Vringer and Blok, 1995a; Biesiot and Moll, 1995).

3.2. Methodology

The (total) energy requirements of households are determined using methods from energy analysis. Energy analysis was developed in the early 1970s when interest in energy problems increased strongly (for overviews of the aims and methods of energy analysis, see Boustead and Hancock, 1979; Nieuwlaar, 1988; Wilting, 1996). Energy analysis considers the use of energy throughout the entire production and consumption chains (life cycles) of products. Energy requirements are expressed in terms of primary energy, i.e., energy in the form in which it appears in nature.

Thus, if a process uses electricity, the energy used in the production and distribution of the electricity is also taken into account, e.g., in the extraction, transport and combustion of coal. Energy analyses can be carried out from both technical (process analysis) and economic (input–output analysis) points of view.

Process analysis starts from a description in physical terms of the life cycle of a product. The energy used in different processes is determined in detail; for example, the energy used in the bakery, on the farm, and in the fertilizer plant contribute to the energy requirements of a loaf of bread. So, process analysis is an accurate but laborious method. Input–output analysis, which has its origins in economics, is based on input–output tables (see Leontief, 1941; Miller and Blair, 1985). An input–output table of an economy contains the transactions between economic sectors in financial units. Input–output tables contain only the direct transactions between economic sectors, but the indirect deliveries between sectors can be determined using a mathematical formalism. In the example of the loaf of bread, the deliveries of the fertilizer plant and agriculture are indirect deliveries to the bakery. The energy requirements of the bakery are determined by combining the financial data on the (direct and indirect) deliveries to the bakery with data on energy use in the economic sectors. Input–output analysis is a rapid method of calculation, but is less detailed due to the use of aggregated data in input–output tables. The bakery, for example, belongs to the flour-processing industry, which also produces biscuits. A combination of elements of process analysis and input–output analysis results in a so-called hybrid analysis, which builds on the advantages of both methods.

Household energy requirements are determined in two ways. The first approach uses input–output tables to determine household energy requirements. The combination of economic input–output data and energy statistics delivers, by means of input–output energy analysis techniques (Bullard and Herendeen, 1975; Wilting, 1996), data on the energy intensity of (about 60) production sectors. The energy intensity of a sector gives the total amount of energy required for the production of a single financial unit of output. By combining these sectoral energy intensities with household consumption data (also derived from input–output tables), household energy requirements are calculated.

The second way to determine the energy requirements of households in more detail is based on a hybrid method (van Engelenburg *et al.*, 1994). Energy analysis is used to determine the energy intensity of a range of (over 100) basic materials used in the delivery and consumption of goods and services. These data, combined with the sectoral energy intensities (calculated with input–output analysis), are used in a simplified life cycle analysis (LCA) of goods and services corresponding to the categories in household budget spending surveys. The results of the analysis are contained in the Energy Analysis Program (EAP), a software program designed for this purpose (Wilting *et al.*, 1995). This enables also re-analysis of the data set for other parameter values (material recycling schemes, new technologies, etc.). The

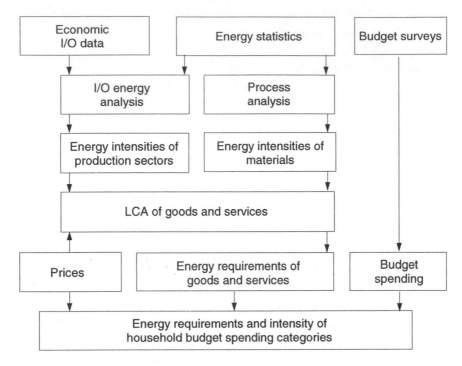

Figure 3.3. Flowchart of the methodology for calculating energy parameters of budget spending categories. Source: Noorman and Schoot Uiterkamp (1996).

EAP consists of a common database of basic data on the energy requirements of materials, economic sectors, forms of transport, etc. With this program the energy requirements of goods and services can be calculated relatively quickly, and are then used in combination with price information and data on spending in some 350 household budget categories in order to yield information regarding the energy requirements and energy intensities of these categories.

Figure 3.3 shows a flow chart of the methodology for assessing energy requirements and intensities. The methodology requires reliable and compatible statistical data on energy production and consumption, economic input–output matrices, household budget survey data, and information on the prices of goods and services. Few countries have collected such data sets (Bruggink, 1995).

3.3. Household Energy Requirements in Relation to Energy Use in the Netherlands

Since the Netherlands has an open economy, domestic energy use is not equal to household energy use. Energy use in the production sectors is destined not only

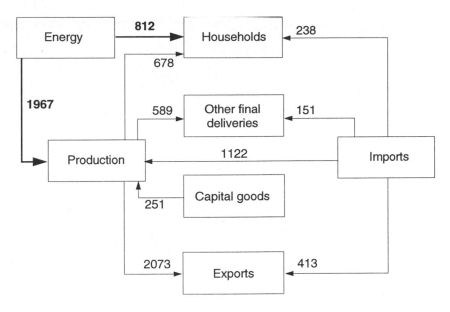

Figure 3.4. Direct (thick) and indirect (thin) energy flows (in PJ) in the Netherlands in 1990. Source: Wilting (1996).

for household consumption, but also for exports and other final deliveries like government consumption[3] and investments. On the other hand, energy is also used in the production of household consumption goods in foreign countries. This section sketches household energy requirements in relation to the other flows of energy embodied in goods and services, in order to gain insight into the relevance of household energy requirements in total energy use in the Netherlands.

Figure 3.4 shows the energy requirements of households in relation to other direct and indirect energy flows in the Netherlands for 1990. The indirect energy flows are calculated using the energy intensities of the production sectors (calculated with input–output analysis) and monetary flows in the economy. The direct energy flows are based on direct energy use data. All flows are converted to primary energy with Energy Requirement for Energy (ERE) values for the different fuels. The ERE value of a fuel is the ratio of the energy sequestered to deliver a unit of energy, divided by the unit of energy (IFIAS, 1974). In computing indirect energy flows, no differences in technology at home and abroad are assumed.

Figure 3.4 shows the relevance of the approach: the aggregated indirect flow of energy into Dutch households is larger than the aggregated direct flow, so that both should be taken into account in identifying energy reduction options. Further, exports are very important for the Dutch economy in terms of embodied energy.

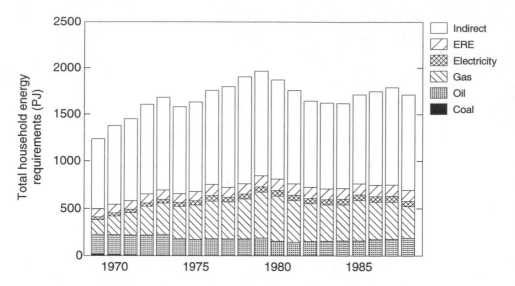

Figure 3.5. Direct (specified per energy carrier) and indirect energy requirements of Dutch households in 1969–1988. Source: Wilting (1996).

3.4. Household Energy Requirements in the Period 1969–1988

In this section we examine a time series in order to analyze the changes in household energy requirements in the period 1969–1988. The calculations are carried out by means of the input–output method. The energy flows that accompany the consumption of goods and services by households are calculated for the chosen period using the energy intensities of the production sectors.

Figure 3.5 shows the historical trends in the direct and indirect energy requirements of households in the Netherlands. The indirect energy requirements turn out to be higher than the direct energy requirements. In 1969–1988, the share of direct energy in total energy requirements fluctuated between 0.39 and 0.44. Both direct and indirect energy requirements rose during the 1970s, with a slight fall in 1974 following the first oil crisis. During the 1980s direct energy requirements remained at the same level. The indirect energy requirements increased slightly in the period 1984–1988. In 1988, the total energy requirements had returned to the level of 1973.

Figure 3.5 also shows direct energy use of households per energy carrier. The energy required for the production and distribution of energy carriers, calculated with ERE values, is included in the direct energy, although it is indirect from the household's perspective. Natural gas, which is used mainly for heating, has a large share in the direct energy use of households. The figure also shows a shift from oil products to gas and electricity. Direct electricity use doubled in the period 1969–1988. Indirect energy use is not shown per energy carrier, since the division

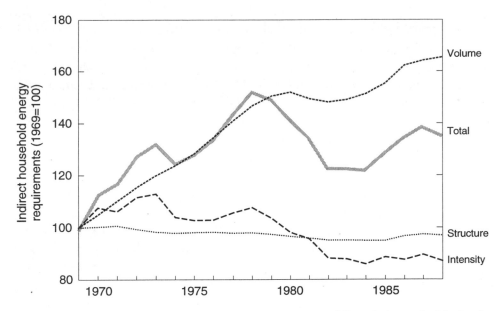

Figure 3.6. Index of indirect energy requirements of Dutch households in the period 1969–1988, as well as indices showing changes in the volume and structure of consumption, and in energy intensity. Source: Wilting (1996).

is rather uncertain due to the lack of a reliable data series. Part of indirect energy use takes place abroad with possibly a quite different fuel mix. Besides, the output of production sectors is rather heterogeneous and only a part, with possibly a fuel mix deviating from the average, is aimed at households.

Changes in direct household energy requirements result from factors such as the number of dwellings, the number of appliances, the specific energy use of those appliances, etc., although this chapter does not go into these factors (see Chapter 2). Here, we examine the changes in the indirect energy requirements of households resulting from changes in either the energy intensities of the production sectors or in the consumption patterns of households. Changes in consumption patterns concern changes in either the volume or the structure of consumption. The structure of consumption is defined here as the share of each production sector in total household consumption.

Figure 3.6 shows the trends in indirect energy requirements of households since the base year 1969. The figure also shows the relation between energy requirements and changes in the energy intensities of production sectors, and in the volume and structure of household consumption, respectively. For each of these three factors, the figure shows the changes in energy requirements resulting from changes in the relevant factor only. This is done by keeping the values of the other two factors at their base year values. The combined effects of the three factors are not shown.

In the 1970s the increase in indirect household energy requirements seems to have resulted from a growth in the volume of consumption. Due to the economic recession following the second oil crisis, this growth levelled off. This effect in combination with a fall in energy intensities of the production sectors led to a decrease in indirect energy requirements. The decrease in energy intensities seems to have been due to a combination of a delayed effect of the 1973 oil crisis, and an effect of the 1979 oil crisis (Wilting, 1996). The decrease in energy intensities corresponds to a rise in energy prices in the periods following both oil crises. After 1984 the volume of consumption increased again, and so did indirect energy requirements. Changes in the structure of consumption patterns (i.e., shifts in purchases from one production sector to another) had little effect on the indirect energy requirements of households.

These results correspond to those of Vringer and Blok (1995b), who investigated a longer time period, 1948–1992, using data on household expenditure from budget surveys and the system of National Accounts to calculate the energy requirements of households in the Netherlands. Improvements in the energy efficiency of production sectors were neglected. For all years in the time series, the energy intensities of 1990 were used. So, the time series reflects the changes in energy requirements which can only be assigned to changes in household consumption patterns. Over the whole period considered, the total primary energy requirements of households increased, due mainly to a rise in household consumption. Changes in consumption patterns had little effect. Van der Wal and Noorman have confirmed these findings in another approach that also accounts for technological developments (see Chapter 2).

Figure 3.5 showed the energy requirements of all households, in an effort to focus on the volume trends in energy flows. In contrast, *Figure 3.7* summarizes the trends in energy requirements per household. Between 1969 and 1988, the number of households grew from 3.9 million to 5.9 million, and the average household size fell from 3.25 to 2.45. The total energy requirements per household in the 1980s were about 20% lower than in the 1970s, but almost the same as in 1969. Possible explanations have been given above. The direct energy requirements per household decreased strongly after 1979 as a result of the decline in natural gas use.

Figure 3.8 shows the trend in energy requirements of all households as a result of the rising trend in the number of households and the declining trend in energy requirements per household.

Vringer and Blok (1995b) also translated the expenditures on the main consumption categories (derived from the National Accounts) into energy terms. *Figure 3.9* shows the corresponding trends in energy requirements per household. All parameters increased over the period considered, except the energy requirements for food and clothing/footwear. This seems to have been caused by the decrease in household size.

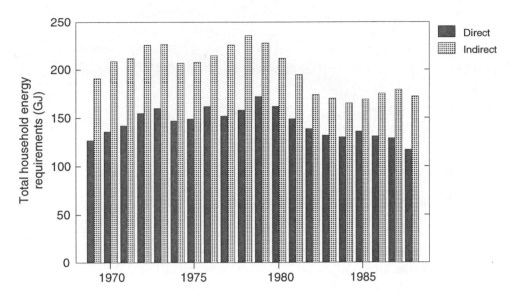

Figure 3.7. Direct and indirect energy requirements per household, 1969–1988.
Source: Wilting (1996).

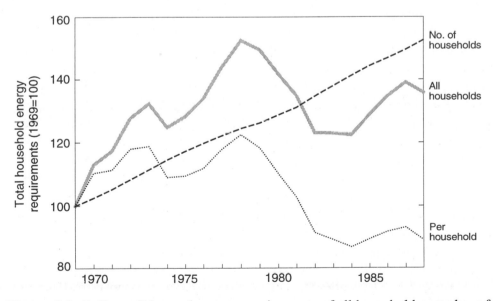

Figure 3.8. Indices of the total energy requirements of all households, number of
households and total energy requirements per household 1969–1988 (1969 = 100).
Source: Wilting (1996).

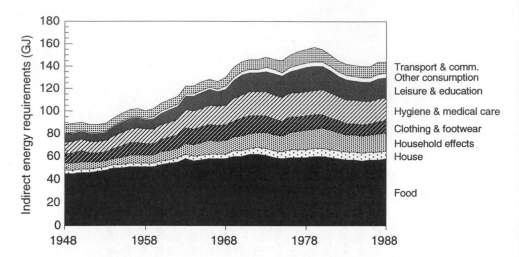

Figure 3.9. Indirect energy requirements of an average Dutch household divided into main consumption categories. Source: Vringer and Blok (1995b).

3.5. Energy Requirements of Individual Households

The energy requirements of an individual household are determined by the energy requirements of the separate expenditures of that household. Since the expenditures of individual households differ, as do the energy requirements of different consumption items, so the energy requirements per household will also differ. Differences in expenditure result from differences in relatively invariable quantities such as income, family phase, and household size. Moreover, differences may result from other characteristics such as chosen lifestyle. This section examines more closely household energy requirements for one year (1990).

Household energy requirements are calculated by means of the energy intensities of consumption items (determined with the EAP program) in combination with budget survey consumption data. The energy intensities for about 350 items from all consumption categories (food, housing, clothing, etc.) have been determined. Not all consumption categories can be fully analyzed with EAP. Expenditures on items such as holidays, medical care and a large part of transport are more difficult to analyze with the hybrid method. However, almost 70% of the indirect energy requirements of households are covered in the EAP analyses.

Table 3.1 shows the distribution of expenditures and energy requirements over the main spending categories for an Dutch average household in 1990. There are appreciable differences in energy intensities at the level of the main consumption categories. Such differences are also found between and within more disaggregated categories, which indicates the relevance of this approach for (public) policy.

Table 3.1. Total expenditures (Dfl), energy intensities (MJ/Dfl) and energy requirements (GJ) for the main consumption categories of an average household in the Netherlands in 1990.

	Total household expenditures		Energy intensity	Household energy requirements	
	Dfl	%	MJ/Dfl	GJ	%
Food	7,408	18.8	4.86	36.0	15.4
House	7,532	19.1	1.20	9.0	3.9
Household effects	3,690	9.4	5.23	19.3	8.3
Clothing and footwear	2,816	7.1	3.06	8.6	3.7
Hygiene	1,515	3.8	3.06	4.6	2.0
Medical care	4,046	10.3	2.45	9.9	4.2
Education and recreation	5,893	14.9	3.96	23.3	10.0
Transport and communication	3,958	10.0	3.04	12.0	5.1
Total non-energy expenditures	**36,859**	**93.4**	**3.33**	**122.7**	**52.6**
Petrol	980	2.5	22.39	21.9	9.4
Heating	1,043	2.6	58.01	60.5	25.9
Electricity	567	1.4	49.43	28.0	12.0
Total energy expenditures	**2,590**	**6.6**	**42.61**	**110.4**	**47.3**
Total expenditures analyzed	**39,449**	**100.0**	**5.91**	**233.2**	**100.0**
Expenditures not analyzed	658				
Total expenditures	40,107		5.91	233.2	

Source: Derived from Biesiot and Moll (1995).

Figure 3.10 shows the results in a graphical form; there are clearly high and low energy intensity spending categories in household consumption.

The total expenditures, and the corresponding energy requirements of a household depend on the income of that household. Vringer and Blok (1995a) calculated the energy requirements for different income classes. The group of about 3000 households in the budget surveys has been split into deciles, and values for the average energy requirements and some percentile values have been determined; see *Figure 3.11*. There is an almost linear relationship between expenditures and energy requirements. Apparently, the more a household can afford to spend, the higher the resulting energy requirements will be, while the energy intensity of these expenditures decreases slightly over the income/expenditure range. The elasticity of energy requirements related to expenditure level is calculated to be about 0.8. The square symbols on the 50 percentile line (median) indicate the weighted mean expenditures through which the line has been drawn. The relative deviation of the 50 percentile line shows little variation with expenditure. The variation of the main consumption category spending within household expenditure is shown in *Figure 3.12*. The categories petrol, transport, recreation, medical care, clothing/footwear, and household effects show strong positive correlations with household expenditure.

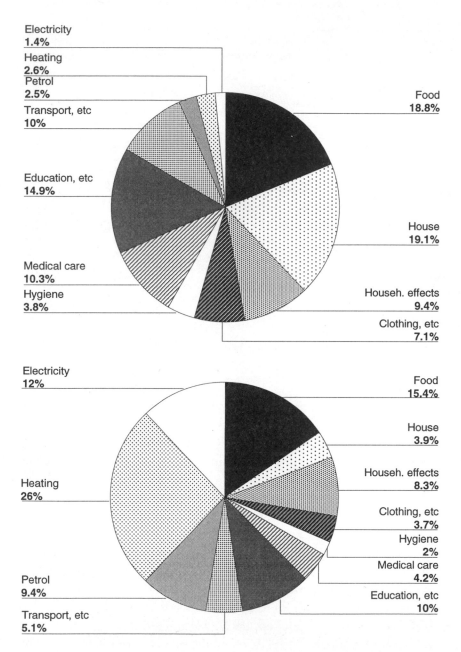

Figure 3.10. Relative shares of the main household consumption categories in money (top) and in energy terms (bottom). Source: Derived from Biesiot and Moll (1995).

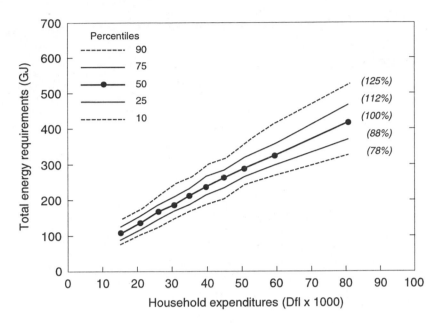

Figure 3.11. Total energy requirements versus household expenditures. Source: Vringer and Blok (1995a).

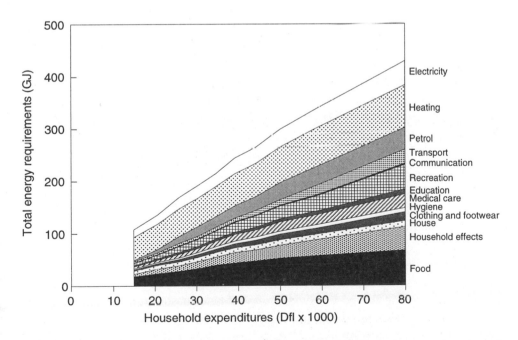

Figure 3.12. Total energy requirements of the main consumption categories plotted versus household expenditures. Source: Vringer and Blok (1995a).

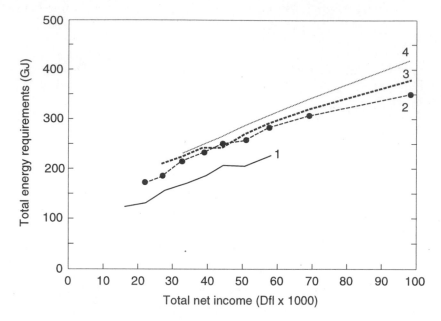

Figure 3.13. Total energy requirements versus net household income for households with one to four members. Source: Vringer and Blok (1995a).

The calculations of Vringer and Blok (1995a) also show differences in the energy requirements per income group. The energy requirements of the majority of households are within ±25% of the average value. This figure can be regarded as an estimate of the short-term household energy reduction potential.

Significant differences have been found between the energy requirements of single- and multi-person households,[4] as illustrated in *Figure 3.13*. These differences can be assigned mainly to the main consumption categories food, electricity, heating, and household effects. The differences within the various multi-person household groups are not significant. For households with two or more members there appears to be no correlation between household size and total energy requirements, apart from the income effect. This result does not correspond to the findings of van der Wal and Noorman (Chapter 2), who found a correlation between direct energy requirements and household size.

Schneider (1994) examined differences in expenditures that are not related to the relatively invariable quantities mentioned above. The investigation concerned the expenditures of groups of households that were similar in terms of family phase, income and size; see *Table 3.2*. For all groups of households, three types of spending patterns were found: large expenditures on mobility (purchasing a car and fuel), households effects (furnishings), or recreation (especially holidays). Households with large expenditures on mobility generally have high energy requirements. The

Table 3.2. Average energy requirements of consumption styles of five household types.

Segment	1 Young couples	2 Older couples	3 Young families	4 Older families	5 Singles
Arithmetic average	270	272	275	337	145
Group with average expenditures	272	270	265	329	148
High expenditure on mobility	330	330	338	394	210
High expenditure on household effects	265	277	283	360	140
High expenditure on recreation	253	328	256	309	133
Group with highest energy requirements	330 (mobility)	330 (mobility)	338 (mobility)	394 (mobility)	210 (mobility)
Group with lowest energy requirements	251 (moderate food)	244 (moderate household effects)	256 (extreme recreation)	309 (extreme recreation)	128 (moderate household effects)
Energy requirement per person	135	136	73	88	146
Energy intensity (MJ/Dfl)	6.1	6.7	6.5	6.5	7.8

Source: Schneider (1994).

investigations were based on expenditures in just one year; longitudinal research is required to answer questions about the stability of spending patterns over time.

3.6. Conclusions

In the period 1969–1988, the volume of household consumption in the Netherlands rose strongly, due partly to a 50% increase in the number of households. The energy requirements of all households increased by about 30% in this period. So, energy efficiency improvements in production and consumption processes partly compensated for the volume growth of consumption. The decline in household size has played a role, in that the energy requirements per household decreased by about 10% over the period considered.

The total primary energy requirements of all 6.13 million households in the Netherlands in 1990 were about 1650 PJ.[5] The energy requirements per household amounted to 270 GJ, about 55% of which concerns indirect energy use. This shows the importance of the indirect energy requirements of households. There are large differences in the energy requirements of individual households, arising from characteristics such as income, household size, etc.; even households with similar characteristics show appreciable differences in their energy requirements.

The methodology developed in the lifestyles project has been found to be a valuable tool for analyzing not only household consumption at a disaggregated level, but also the scope and content of options for changes in household consumption that would be in line with strategies aiming to reduce fossil fuel use and the related CO_2 emissions.

Summary

- The indirect energy requirements of households are larger than the direct energy requirements. This shows the relevance of the approach followed here.
- The development of total energy requirements of households in the 1970s and 1980s is a combined effect of the growth in the volume of household consumption and the decrease in the energy intensities of the various production sectors. Energy efficiency improvements only partly compensated for the volume growth.
- There are appreciable differences in energy intensities within and among household consumption categories.
- There is an almost linear relationship between household expenditures and energy requirements.
- Households with similar characteristics, such as income, size, etc., show differences in energy requirements due to differences in spending patterns.

Notes

[1] Although the direct energy use of the energy supply system (e.g., for the production and distribution of the electricity used by households) is used only indirectly by households, it is directly related to the direct energy use of households. Thus, in order to express all flows in primary energy units, it is therefore included in the direct energy requirements of households,

[2] The term lifestyles has been adopted for the research program "Reduction of CO_2 Emissions by Lifestyle Changes", carried out by the Center for Energy and Environmental Studies of the University of Groningen, in collaboration with the Department of Science, Technology and Society of Utrecht University, with financial support from the Dutch National Research Program on Air Pollution and Climate Change, 1992–1995. Participants in this and previous programs include: K. Blok, B. van Engelenburg, J. Potting and K. Vringer (Dept. of Science, Technology and Society of Utrecht University); K. de Paauw and A. Perrels (Business unit Policy Studies of the Dutch Energy Research Foundation); H. Schneider and T. Schmidt (CEA Consultancy, Rotterdam); and W. Biesiot, R. Kok, K.J. Kramer, H.C. Moll, K.J. Noorman and H.C. Wilting (Center for Energy and Environmental Studies, University of Groningen).

[3] In fact, government consumption, which is based on taxes, can partly be assigned to households. But since households have no direct influence on government con-

[4] This is in agreement with the results of various HOMES research lines; see other chapters in this volume.

[5] Household energy requirements determined with the input–output method are little higher than those determined with the hybrid method. The figure given is based on a thorough comparison of both outcomes and the assumptions made in the calculations (Wilting, 1996).

References

Biesiot, W. and H.C. Moll (Eds.) (1995) *Reduction of CO_2 Emissions by Lifestyle Changes: Final Report to the NRP Global Air Pollution and Climate Change*, Research Report No. 80, Center for Energy and Environmental Studies (University of Groningen) and Dept. of Science, Technology and Society (Utrecht University).

Boustead, I. and G.F. Hancock (1979) *Handbook of Industrial Energy Analysis*, Ellis Horwood, Chichester.

Bruggink, J.J.C. (Ed.) (1995) *Energy Demand, Lifestyle Changes and Technology Development*, report presented at the World Energy Council 16th Congress, "Energy for our Common World", Tokyo, Japan.

Bullard, C.W. and R.A. Herendeen A (1975) The energy cost of goods and services, *Energy Policy*, 3:484–493.

IFIAS (1974) *Energy Analysis: Workshop on Methodology and Conventions*, Report No. 6, International Federation of Institutes for Advanced Study, Stockholm.

Leontief, W.W. (1941) *The Structure of the American Economy, 1919–1929*, Oxford University Press, New York.

Miller, R.E. and P.D. Blair (1985) *Input–Output Analysis: Foundations and Extensions*, Prentice-Hall, New York.

Nieuwlaar, E. (1988) *Developments in Energy Analysis*, PhD thesis, Utrecht University.

Noorman, K.J. and A.J.M. Schoot Uiterkamp (Eds.) (1996) Proc. 1st Int. HOMES/IIASA Workshop, November 1995, University of Groningen.

Schneider, H. (1994) *Op zoek naar energie-extensieve leefstijlen: bestedingspatronen en energiebeslag van Nederlandse huishoudens*, Report No. 9346, Communicatie- en Adviesbureau (CEΛ), Rotterdam.

Van Engelenburg, B.C.W., T.F.M. van Rossum, K. Blok and K. Vringer (1994) Calculating the energy requirements of household purchases: a practical step by step method, *Energy Policy*, 22:648–656.

Vringer, K. and K. Blok (1995a) The direct and indirect energy requirements of households in the Netherlands, *Energy Policy*, 23:893–910.

Vringer, K. and K. Blok (1995b) *Consumption and Energy Requirements: Time Series for Households in the Netherlands from 1948 to 1992*, Research Report No. 95016, Dept. of Science, Technology and Society, Utrecht University.

Wilting, H.C., W. Biesiot and H.C. Moll (1995) *EAP: Energie Analyse Programma: handleiding versie 2.0*, Research Report No. 76, Center for Energy and Environmental Studies, University of Groningen.

Wilting, H.C. (1996) *An Energy Perspective on Economic Activities*, PhD thesis, University of Groningen.

Chapter 4

Developments in Household Composition in Europe

A.M.L. van Diepen

Abstract

This chapter presents some important characteristics of the concept of a household. Not all European countries follow the United Nations definition of a household as a socioeconomic unit consisting of individuals who live together occupying all or part of a dwelling. After describing empirical household developments in Europe, we evaluate the situation in the Netherlands in this broader geographical context. The various methods that are used to assess, model, and project future changes in household size and composition are briefly presented. The scope for further research relating to the household, such as household metabolism, is evident.

4.1.   Introduction

The processes of household formation and dissolution have recently become a rising topic of research. The characteristics of households are of interest both for policy and for commercial purposes (Keilman *et al.*, 1988; van Imhoff and Keilman, 1991; van Diepen and van Ginneken, 1994; van Ginneken and van Diepen, 1994). When mapping out strategies for the future, planning agencies with responsibility for providing housing, social services, energy supplies, etc., have to anticipate future changes in household structure. As units of consumption with budgets to spend, households are of great interest to both entrepreneurs and commercial agencies.

Households are not uniform entities. With the growing complexity of society, the variety of types of households has increased, as well as public groups. Households vary according to many different characteristics, such as size and composition, income and consumption behavior, habits, attitudes, and preferences.

Every household can be regarded as a special and unique entity with individual characteristics.

Information is needed on the variety of households and their particular attributes and distribution. It has become increasingly difficult to adequately address the wide variety of households for policy or for commercial purposes, even though the need to approach households from a particular angle has increased. Households have become of "target groups" of various policies, so that information is needed on the types of households, their common characteristics, and behavioral patterns. The segmentation of households according to particular points of view is therefore gaining interest in research. In this chapter we attempt to provide a general classification of households, according to size and composition.

4.2. Concepts of the Household

Traditionally, a household has been perceived as a family household, the primary unit in which individuals are socialized and interact with each other, and can be considered as the molecular units of a population (UN, 1981). As a sociodemographic unit, a household can be described according to its composition, reflecting the mutual relationships among its members. The family has always been the basis for classifying households; thus there are family households, one-person and non-family households.

Traditional family life was considered an appropriate approach for understanding and assessing population developments in general. Changes in the structure of the family have long been part of the domain of demographers, who are primarily interested in quantitative aspects of changes in populations. A population is regarded as a pool of individuals, distinguished by age and sex and sometimes by marital status. The population size is the outcome of the interplay of three components: mortality, fertility, and migration. Based on these three components, several population characteristics are used as the main descriptors that determine the population size and its structure, e.g., growth rate, sex structure, age structure, and marital structure. These demographic characteristics are also the basic ingredients in processes of household formation and dissolution, since changes in the size and structure of the population have direct impacts on the number of households. Therefore, when dealing with household developments and the formation of people into households, demographic factors are important; a household is often categorized according to the demographic characteristics of its members, e.g., sex, age, and marital status.

However, the traditional family household based on marriage has lost its dominant position. The family life cycle (i.e., the different family living circumstances of an individual over the course of a lifetime) is not as clear-cut and predictable as it used to be. The lives of individuals between cradle and grave can lead along many different paths. Family dissolution by divorce and family formation by cohabitation have become widespread phenomena throughout Europe. This wider variety of living arrangements has received increasing attention in household research, and is reflected in the classifications that are now used to describe households: couples with or without children, married or unmarried, and single parents with children. The traditional concept of the family no longer provides an adequate description of the groupings of individuals into social units. Households share the same language, norms, and values, and are above all social units and expressions of the ways in which people choose to arrange their personal lives. Whereas the concept of a household is closely related to demographic events as rooted in family life, concepts of kinship and social coherence or identity are not included in the definition of a household. Within Europe, only in Portugal, Spain, and Italy are the definitions of a household still based on the kinship relations between members. These countries provide statistics on families rather than on households.

Most European countries have followed the definition of the UN (1980) which does not consider family structure, but starts from the definition of a household as a socioeconomic unit consisting of individuals who live together occupying all or part of a dwelling. Two key concepts in this definition are: first, households are "housekeeping" units, sharing resources to provide household members with food and other essentials for living, and second, households are "housing" units, occupying all or part of a dwelling. A Habitat inventory of worldwide household projections (Doblhammer-Reiter, 1993) showed that most European countries have followed both dimensions of this definition for census purposes, but some have accepted only one part of the UN approach. In the Netherlands, the definition is based on the dimension of a household as a housekeeping unit, whereas in Denmark, Finland, Luxembourg, Norway, Sweden, and Switzerland a private household is defined exclusively as a housing unit. At the time of writing, the definitions used for census purposes in France and Greece were not known.

A household is an economic unit in that the income earned by its members is usually shared. This income enables the household to meet the needs and wants of its members, and is therefore an important discriminatory factor. Income-based characteristics are also commonly used to refer to particular types of households, e.g., "wage-earner households", "welfare-mother households", and "double-income households". With the spread of industrialization and urbanization, the traditional form of the family, i.e., the extended family with several generations within one household, became less necessary as the most appropriate organization of family life to support the acquisition of a household income. With the emergence of the welfare state, there was less need for people to live together with relatives, and increasing affluence meant that more people could live on their own. Households are also spatial entities, with a clear spatial connotation; without an address a household can not be established. Geographers focus on the relationship between spatial settings and specific household characteristics, and have attempted to identify the behavioral characteristics of different types of households in specific environmental settings (van Diepen and Ennen, 1996).

With regard to the house and housekeeping, a household is directly subjected to external influences such as policy interventions from various perspectives, including housing policy, tax and income policies, and migration policies (see Chapter 9). Thus a household is established within a legislative and institutional context as well, which limits the opportunities for and constraints on household formation. Setting up a household is not only the result of sociodemographic and economic behavior, i.e., the desirability and affordability of establishing a household, but is also bounded by legal rules (Schmid, 1988).

Hence, households are linked with sociodemographic, economic and legislative developments. Without reference to kinship relations, the term "household" is a rather neutral concept. It involves individuals sharing some moments or attributes of consumption of some kind. The emphasis is on the household as an operational unit.

4.3. Household Developments in Europe

Despite the interest in the processes of household formation and dissolution, little information for international comparisons of households within Europe is available. The best documented countries are those in northern Europe, whereas data for southern and eastern Europe countries are often lacking. Most of the data on households originate from population censuses, which are conducted every five or ten years. Among the 12 member states of the European Community in 1991, three do not conduct general population censuses, but rely on data collected by other means. In the Netherlands, for example, data are obtained from sources such as population statistics, the Labor Force Sample Survey and the Housing Demand Survey.

Because the definitions used in different countries are often not fully comparable, caution is needed when making cross-national comparisons of developments in the household sector. We also have to keep in mind that each country has its own historical peculiarities and circumstances. The commencement of trends, and their role in any event, may be different for the various countries, and their influence on the current situation, may not be identical. Nevertheless, recent changes in the composition and distribution of households in several European countries show some similarities, although they may differ in magnitude. In this section we present some official statistics on households in Europe, collected by UNCHS (Habitat). We then describe changes in the number and distribution of households by size since 1960.

Between 1960 and 1990, the population of Europe (excluding the former Soviet Union) increased by 18%, from about 430 million (UN, 1993) to more than 500 million. In the same period the number of households increased at about double

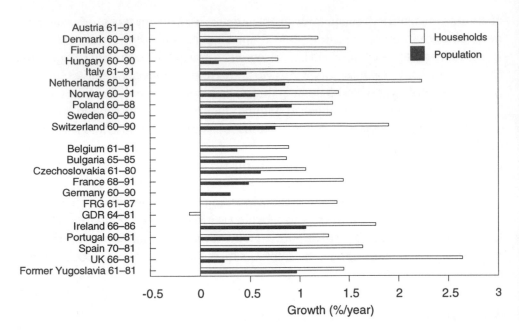

Figure 4.1. Annual average growth of the population and the number of households in Europe, 1960–1991.

this rate. *Figure 4.1* shows the population and household growth rates for two groups of European countries. For the first group of ten countries (top), the data on the number of households cover a period of about 30 years, and for the second group the data cover about 20 years. Note that the first years of observation are not all the same. The figure shows the annual (geometrically) average percentage changes in population and the number of households calculated for the period of observation.

The number of households grew twice as fast as the population in most countries, except for Poland, Ireland, Spain, and the former Yugoslavia, where population growth was relatively high compared with household development. The UK is a rather unusual case in that the number of households increased relatively rapidly. The Netherlands scored high on both the population growth and the increase of the number of households. Data on contemporary Germany are somewhat ambiguous, since information on households is still separated according to the former West (FRG) and East (GDR) Germany, whereas the population data are for both parts together. Opposite to the trends throughout the rest of Europe, in the former GDR the number of households fell dramatically; between 1964 and 1981 the household growth rate was negative, due to a decrease in the proportion of small households and an increase in the proportion of larger households. Despite the rise during the 1970s the number of households did not reach the level observed in 1964.

Apparently, the correlation between population and household growth over time has become weaker and more equivocal. The increase in the number of households has turned out to be less correlated with population growth exclusively, so that the average household size has declined. This implies that in all countries there has been an overall shift from larger to smaller households.

Figures 4.2 and *4.3* illustrate the shifts in the distributions of one- and five-person households, respectively, in 21 European countries. Note that the numbers and years of observation are not the same, so the lengths of the lines vary. For the countries of southern and eastern Europe insufficient data are available for a time series up to the 1990s; for some countries the data cover only short periods.

Figure 4.2 shows that in all countries the proportion of one-person households increased steadily, although the size of the share varied, from 8–20% in 1960, to 18–40% in the late 1980s. The trend is more obvious and the level is noticeably higher in northern and western European countries than in southern and eastern European countries. The largest shifts occurred in Sweden, Switzerland, and the Netherlands, where the proportion of one-person households doubled.

The proportion of two-person households increased steadily by 5% or more per year between 1960 and 1991; again, only the GDR showed a reverse trend. The shares of two-person households of the different countries are not as dispersed as those of one-person households; indeed the trends are quite similar. The trends in the proportion of three-person households in European countries are more or less the same, and at the same level, increasing from 18–23% in 1960, to 14–20% in the late 1980s.

Households consisting of five or more persons have become less common over the last few decades, and the trend is clearly decreasing (see *Figure 4.3*). In the early 1960s these large households represented 13–35% of the total, falling to 4–12% 30 years later. Only in Poland has the share remained constant at 18%, and in France the share has risen recently. Among the countries of northern and western Europe, Ireland is an exception, with a large share of large households, although this decreased to one-third of all households in 1986. In 1981 (more recent data are not available) the former Yugoslavia, Spain and Portugal also had large shares of large households.

In the early 1960s in most of the 21 countries, at least 40% of all households consisted of one or two persons. These percentages were lowest in Italy, Portugal and the former Yugoslavia where less than 30% of households were small. In Ireland, Poland, and the Netherlands, which could be considered predominantly Catholic, like the southern European countries, the shares of one- and two-person households were relatively low: 33, 35 and 36%, respectively. Only the former GDR showed an extreme score of more than 50% small households at that time.

By the late 1980s there had been a general increase in the proportion of one- and two-person households. From the 13 countries that generated data on household distribution, Ireland and Poland showed the smallest shares of small households,

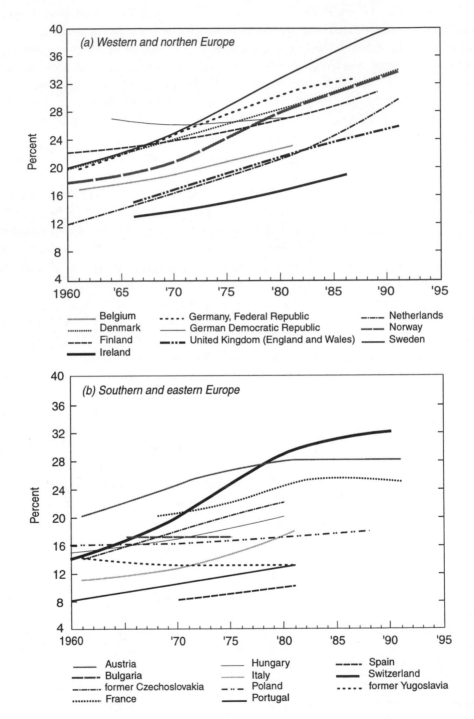

Figure 4.2. Proportion of one-person households within the total number of households in Europe, 1960–1991.

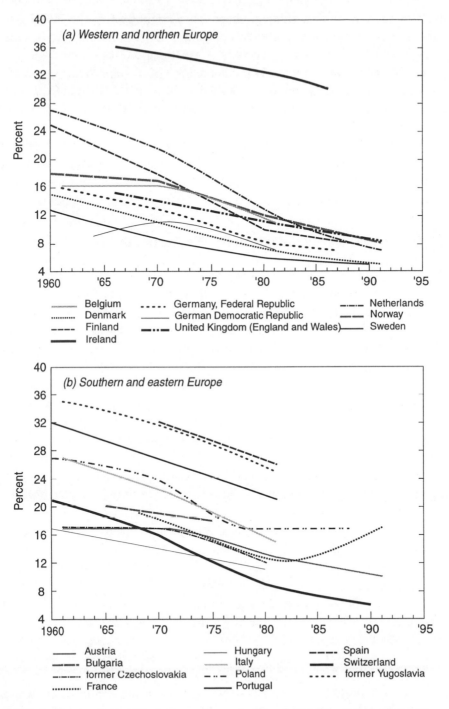

Figure 4.3. Proportion of five-person households within the total number of households in Europe, 1960–1991.

amounting to 40% of the total by the late 1980s. In Ireland most households still have at least five members, although there was a slight decrease to 30% by 1986. Ireland therefore still has the highest proportion of large households in Europe. In 1991 the proportions of small households in Austria and France were 56 and 55%, respectively. In the Netherlands, Switzerland, the UK, former West Germany, and the Scandinavian countries, the shares exceeded 60% in 1990, and in Sweden even reached a share of 71% small households. Simultaneously, the proportion of large households fell to less than 10% in all these countries.

The largest shifts in household size, by more than 20% over the 30 year period, occurred in the Scandinavian countries, Switzerland, and the Netherlands. The case of the Netherlands is the most remarkable, in that the relatively small share of small households changed to a relatively large share of small households.

4.4.   Household Developments in the Netherlands

Within Europe, the Netherlands has experienced extreme changes in the number and composition of households. This section describes and analyses this process in more detail. If data are available, we start our analysis in the year 1950.

For Dutch government statistics, the term household was introduced in the 1947 census. Households were defined as "all groups of two or more persons living together, regardless the nature of their mutual relationship" (Ploegmakers and van Leeuwen, 1994). Kinship or marriage was not relevant in this ample definition, and people living alone were excluded. The family was usually the basis of analysis. Since 1960 the household has been used as the point of departure in CBS inventories; a household is defined as a housekeeping unit, consisting of a group of two or more persons who live together under one roof, share a living room, and have at least one meal together daily. People living alone are regarded as a separate category, whether or not they share a dwelling, if they do not share a living room and meals with others.

The demographic structure of the Netherlands has changed considerably since World War II; the population increased from about 10 million in 1950 to 15 million in 1994. In contrast with the first half of the century, after 1950 the growth rates of the population and the number of households started to diverge (Latten, 1993; see *Figure 4.4*). In 1950 there were about 2.5 million households, compared with more than 6 million in 1995; recent projections indicate that there will be 7.3 million households by the year 2010 (CBS, 1996).

The average household size has fallen progressively, from about four members in 1950, to only 2.4 in 1994. This process of diminishing household size, often referred to as household dilution, can also be seen in the composition of house-holds. *Figure 4.5* shows the distribution of household sizes at five points in time between 1947 and 1992. One- and two-person households have become the largest

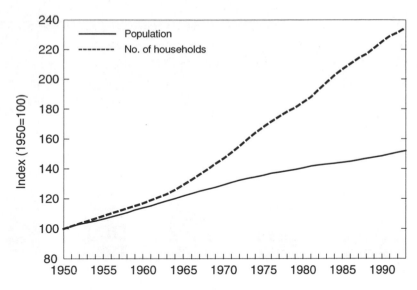

Figure 4.4. Population and numbers of households in the Netherlands, 1950–1993 (1950 = 100). Sources: CBS (1989, 1995).

household categories. In particular, the proportion of one-person households increased from about 10% in 1947 to 30% in 1992. With reference to the total population size, more than 12% of the Dutch population now lives alone, perhaps not always by design or desire, but as a result of being widowed or divorced. The proportion of two-person households also increased from 23% in 1947 to 31% in 1992; they now represent about two-thirds of all Dutch households.

The shares of three- and four-person households were more or less constant between 1947 and 1992, declining by 5 and 2%, respectively, to about 16% each in 1992. The share of larger households with more than five members also fell from 27% in 1947 to 6% in 1992. Six-person households now represent only 1% of the household sector.

We now examine the driving forces behind the household dilution process, using a crude quantitative analytical approach to identify the explanatory factors, by comparing the population growth and the increase in the number of households (see *Figure 4.4*). If the number of households had grown at the same rate as the population, an extra 1 million households would have been formed between 1960 and 1992, rather than the 3.1 million observed. Thus, only one-third of the household changes between 1960 and 1992 can be explained by population growth. Such a rough calculation, however, does not take into account other factors such as the impact of the changing population age structure on the process of household formation. Lower fertility and mortality rates have resulted in a changing age structure. In 1960, for example, 29% of the population was aged less than 15,

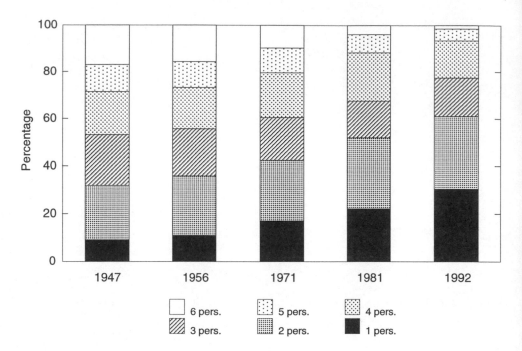

Figure 4.5. Distribution of households in the Netherlands according to size, 1947–1992. Sources: CBS (1989, 1993).

compared with 18% in 1992. Changes in household size therefore need to be decomposed into changes in the age structure as well.

The impact of age structure changes can be isolated by applying the 1960 age-specific headship rates on the 1992 population age structure. Headship rates are defined here as the proportion of the population that are heads of households, distinguished by sex and age. For this calculation, six age cohorts are distinguished, subdivided by sex. The results are interpreted as the impacts of shifts in sizes of the age cohorts on the number of households by equal rates of people per age cohort heading a household. Application of this headship rate approach leads to a 60.2% increase in the number of households between 1960 and 1992. As population growth accounts for 34% of the household changes (32.5 divided by the total household increase), 29% of the household changes can be attributed to shifts in the age structure (60.2% minus 32.5% population growth, divided by the total household increase). The enlargement of some age cohorts contributed in particular to the increase in the number of households. For example, the 25–34 year age group represented 13% of the total population in 1960, and 17% in 1992. At this age, people are most likely to change their household situation.

The residual 37% household changes represents the changes in the headship rates themselves, implying that more people in each age group were heads of

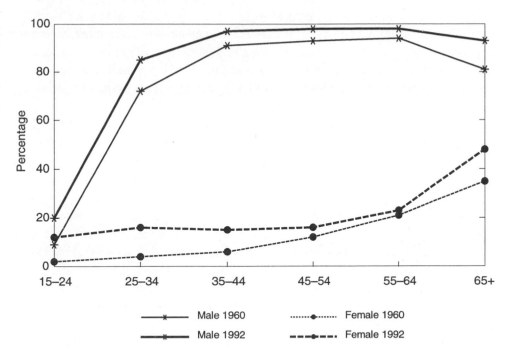

Figure 4.6. Headship rates by age and sex in the Netherlands, 1960 and 1992. Sources: UN (1987, 1993).

households. Between 1960 and 1992 there was an overall increase in headship rates, as shown in *Figure 4.6*. For both men and women aged under 45 and over 65 years, headship rates rose significantly, reflecting changes in the household formation process toward more independent lifestyles. Social changes such as young people leaving the parental home at an earlier age, couples separating, and older people not entering old people's homes until later ages have led to the formation of extra households. Prinz (1991) found similar results from calculations of the decomposition of household changes for three industrialized countries, Austria, Canada, and Norway.

4.5. Understanding Household Developments

The changes in households described above reflect large shifts in the ways people arrange their daily lives. Several attempts have been made to postulate a theory for understanding these processes of household formation and dissolution in society, but two views dominate the discussion.

First, the framework known as the "second demographic transition" emphasizes the changes in society toward individualism (van der Kaa, 1987; Lesthaeghe, 1983). In this view demographic changes are recognized as reflecting social transformations, i.e., changes in social values, priorities and lifestyles. Self-fulfilment, personal development, and independence have become more important in people's lives. The decreasing importance of religious and political institutions, and less conditioned social networks have led to more individual freedom, as reflected in the new and changing forms of living arrangements in the industrialized world.

Second, in a well-known economic approach, Becker (1981) based his understanding of household formation and dissolution on the notion of the household as a productive entity, creating joint income. According to Becker, if adults expect to benefit from a mutual exchange of talents, e.g., earning money or taking care of the home, which together are necessary for establishing a household, they will prefer marriage or cohabitation. If the benefits the partners expect from being a couple exceed those they expect from remaining single or getting a divorce, they will consider it worthwhile to form a communal household. In mutual exchange and completion, the members together are responsible for establishing and maintaining the household, and performing all the necessary household functions. In this context, it is assumed that the cost–benefit balance of the household situation is most profitable for every (adult) member.

Several attempts have been made to identify the driving forces behind the processes of household formation and dissolution, which are predominantly demographic in origin. The results of some of the efforts to explain the changes in the number and size of households are discussed below.

4.5.1. Demographic factors

The decline in average household size is directly linked to two concurrent demographic developments: first, women are having fewer children, and second, the age structure of the population is changing as a consequence of the lower level of fertility. In addition, the differentiation in living arrangements and changes in marriage behavior have also resulted in smaller households.

Lutz (1994) examined the fertility rates in 30 industrialized countries over the period 1950–90. In most European countries (except for eastern Europe) during the "baby boom" of the early 1960s, the average fertility rate varied between 2.2 and 3.0, except for Hungary (the lowest, at 1.8) and Iceland, Ireland, the Netherlands, and Portugal (all above 3.0). In the 1970s, a general decline in fertility began, reaching rates of 2.0 or less in the late 1980s.

The changing age structure of the populations in Europe has also led to decreasing household sizes. Both a declining proportion of young people and an increasing proportion of the elderly will result in smaller households. Young people are part of existing households, so that a reduction in their number in a population will therefore directly contribute to a decrease in the average household size. Today, many elderly people are postponing the decision to enter institutions and are living on their own to later ages.

The trend toward smaller households has been accompanied by changes in marriage behavior (i.e in the marital status unmarried, married, divorced, and widowed). An analysis of age-specific marriage rates has shown that both men and women now favor later marriage, and that the probability of marriage is lower (Lutz, 1994). At the same time, there has been a trend toward nonmarital unions in most European countries; younger age groups in particular show high rates of cohabitation. Furthermore, divorce rates have also increased; the broken family is no longer a rare phenomenon. The proportion of marriages ending in divorce ranges from 1 out of 10 in southern Europe, 3 out of 10 in central Europe, and about 4 out of 10 in Scandinavia and the UK.

4.5.2. Non-demographic factors

In other research the processes of household formation and dissolution have been examined using economic approaches, in which changes in households are considered to be due to macroeconomic circumstances or are related to economic parameters. Although most studies indicate a clear relationship between economic benefits and the formation of households, no unambiguous impact can be identified. Furthermore, the availability of housing frames the opportunities for and constraints on the household formation process. In the Netherlands the number of households and the number of available dwellings have been converging since 1960 (van Diepen, 1995); today, two or more households rarely share the same dwelling. In 1992, a dwelling in the Netherlands was occupied by 1.03 households on average. A shortage of available accommodation can slow down the processes of household formation and dissolution, whereas an ample supply can speed them up.

Haurin *et al.* (1990) attempted to assess the influence of economic variables such as rental costs, wealth, and the potential earnings of young people, on their decisions on whether to leave the parental home, to get married, or to live alone. Using the 1987 US Survey of Youth, they found a large economic impact. In low-rent areas the probability that a young person would be living outside the parental home was 18% higher than in high-rent areas, resulting in a 6% higher headship rate. Furthermore, they observed a 30% higher headship rate for young people from wealthy families than for those from poor families. Finally, in this study young people with high potential earnings were 17% more likely to leave the parental home than those with low potential earnings. Viewing the future, assuming a rent increase of 20% (1986), they estimated that half a million fewer households would be formed by people aged 20–30 years.

Skaburskis (1994) studied the impacts of changes in economic conditions in Canada on the process of household formation using the 1986 Canadian Census Public Use Micro Data File. He rejected the hypothesis that market conditions govern demographic trends; his findings showed that in the early 1980s lower income prospects did not lead to a decrease in the formation of new households in younger age cohorts. On the contrary, the headship rate of the 20–24 year cohort in 1981 was significantly higher than in 1986, implying that in 1986 fewer people in this age group were heads of households than in 1981.

All of the above studies, as well as that of Börsch-Supan (1986), focused on young people, since this age cohort forms the main category entering the housing market. But, because the courses through (family) life are so diverse, other age cohorts also need be taken into account. Marriages are no longer necessarily for life, and life paths are now far more diverse than in the past. Smith *et al.* (1984, cited in Skaburskis, 1994) observed similarities in changes in headship rates in Canada, the US, the UK, and France in the period 1960–1980, and distinguished between family and non-family headship rates. Whereas family headship rates remained almost constant during this period, non-family headship rates nearly doubled. Approximately 30% of this change could be ascribed to reduced rental costs.

4.6.   Official Household Projections by National Institutions

Understanding and explaining household developments is one thing, projecting future developments is quite another. What parameters and models can be used for household projections? Here, we present a picture of official household projections, based on the responses to a questionnaire survey of the statistical agencies of the EC member states and other industrialized countries, conducted in preparation for a ECE/Eurostat workshop (de Beer, 1994; de Jong, 1994; Hablicsek, 1994; Halus, 1994; Menthonnex, 1994; Salathiel, 1994; Prinz, 1994). The results of this inventory and our observations are given in the following.

Countries in Europe rely on different models – static or dynamic – for projecting household developments. Static models focus on changes in household structure at different points in time, and are used by Austria, Cyprus, Finland, Germany, Italy, Poland, Romania, Switzerland, and the UK. Dynamic models are based on the specification of household positions, and assumptions on the transitions between household positions. Therefore, dynamic models rely on extensive data collected at the individual level, and are consequently more complex. Such models are used in Norway and Russia. Mixed dynamic/static models are used by just two countries, the Netherlands and Hungary. Surprisingly, four countries (Belgium, Denmark, Ireland, and Sweden) replied that no official household projections were available. In Sweden the official statistics institute does not construct household projections, although during the late 1970s and early 1980s a dynamic household model was developed by Hårsman *et al.* (in Keilman *et al.*, 1988). However, at present Sweden is in the process of setting up a household projection model. Spain, Portugal, Greece, and France provided no information.

The main assumption underlying all official national household projections surveyed is that the trend toward smaller households will continue. The main reasons for this trend can be summarized as reduced fertility, resulting in fewer children per family, the aging population and, consequently, more elderly people, who are tending to live alone longer, increasing divorce rates, more nonmarital unions and living alone, and more single parents. Whatever type of model is employed, it has to be capable of including these trends, either implicitly or explicitly. Implicitly means that assumptions are made as to the directions of changes in static models; explicitly refers to the quantitative relation between transition probabilities and the resulting distribution of the population over types of households in dynamic and mixed static-dynamic models. All of the official national household projections surveyed include, implicitly or explicitly, trends on fertility, aging, migration, and on the formation and dissolution of households.

The projection models used throughout Europe are based on a variety of definitions of household types and positions. Notwithstanding these distinctions, all countries have experienced a trend toward smaller households, due to the increasing number of one-person households on the one hand, and fewer children in family households on the other. Yet no two countries use the same method for projecting the number of households in the future. The most recent research on household projection models concentrated on dynamic models, whereas official household projections in most European countries are still based on static models. This may be due to the limited availability of data, but also to the low priority that is given to household projections in many countries.

In constructing a projection model, emphasis should be put on the definitions of the types of households or household positions, which should adequately reflect the major current and future trends in the processes of household formation and dissolution. Whether such trends should be projected in a static or dynamic way is primarily a question of the availability of data. Further research is necessary to clarify whether dynamic models provide more accurate forecasts of the future number of households than static models. Rather than emphasizing the static or dynamic model building part, more weight should be given to the appropriate definition of the household types and positions to be defined for the projection model. Only if sufficient attention is paid to the formulation of the types of households or household positions, can a model build upon knowledge of the processes (and their changes) of household formation and dissolution, and thus provide more accurate projections of future trends.

4.7. Conclusions

Although they are small social groups, households are a complex phenomenon. Demographers have had a long tradition in describing and projecting overall population developments, but the grouping of people into households is a topic of more recent interest. In Europe, the increase in the number of households has significantly exceeded the population growth. In most countries the proportion of small households has increased at the expense of large households. In this chapter we have described the changes in households in the Netherlands in a broad geographical context. Within Europe, the Netherlands is not an ordinary case; there has been a shift from a relatively large proportion of large households, to a relatively large proportion of small households. The number of households has increased three times faster than the increase in population, and there has been a rapid reduction in the average household size. The changing age structure and increasing headship rates have also contributed to this increase. The finding that in all age groups more people are heads of households suggests a trend toward more individual lifestyles as far as living arrangements are concerned.

Many decisions concerning the consumption of goods and services are made at the household level, so that households should be regarded as important operational units. A better understanding of the grouping of people into households, and the changes in the processes of household formation that can be expected in the future, is therefore required in order to assess the future demand for services such as housing, energy, and water. Knowledge of the number and composition of households is a first step toward understanding the character and extent of household metabolism. Studies of the diverging lifestyles in people's organization of their lives, and their impacts on household metabolism, should be a next step in research. Then the various, often sweeping consequences of changes in household behavior – their implications and magnitude – may be examined within the perspectives of sustainability and environmental quality.

Summary

- Most European countries have experienced similar trends toward smaller households due to decreasing levels of fertility, changes in the age structure of the population, and the diversification in living arrangements. Consequently, the numbers of households have increased in many countries.
- Although all countries are experiencing similar trends, no two countries use the same method for projecting the number of households in the future.
- The changing number and size of households, and thus the formation of people into households, will have far-reaching consequences for the future demand for services such as housing, energy, and water.

Acknowledgments

I would like to thank IIASA for hosting and supporting my research during my stay in the spring of 1995. In particular, I am very grateful to Gabriele Doblhammer-Reiter for her enjoyable and faithful cooperation and for putting data at my disposal.

References

Becker, G. (1981) *A Treatise on the Family*, Harvard University Press, Cambridge, MA.

Börsch-Supan, A. (1986) Household formation, housing prices, and public policy impacts, *Journal of Public Economics*, **30**.

CBS (1989) *90 Years of Statistics*, Central Bureau of Statistics, SDU, The Hague.

CBS (1993, 1996) *Statistical Yearbooks*, 1995 and 1996, Central Bureau of Statistics, SDU, The Hague.

De Beer, J. (1994) *Projections of Households and Families: Overview of Current Practice*, Working Paper No. 30, ECE/Eurostat Joint Work Session on Demographic Projections, Luxembourg, 1–4 June 1994.

De Jong, A. (1994) *A Macro Simulation Model for Projecting Households by Size*, Working Paper No. 34, ECE/Eurostat Joint Work Session on Demographic Projections, Luxembourg, 1–4 June 1994.

Doblhammer-Reiter, G. (1993) *Household Projections to the Year 2050*. A UNCHS (Habitat) project, Research and Development Division, UNCHS, Nairobi.

Hablicsek, L. (1994) *Demographic Projections in Hungary with Special Regard to the Projections of Families and Households*, Working Paper No. 42, ECE/Eurostat Joint Work Session on Demographic Projections, Luxembourg, 1–4 June 1994.

Halus, R. (1994) *Methods and Assumptions Used in the Household and Family Projection Model in Romania*, Working Paper No. 44, ECE/Eurostat Joint Work Session on Demographic Projections, Luxembourg, 1–4 June 1994.

Haurin, D.R., P.H. Hendershott, and D. Kim (1990) *Real Rents and Household Formation: The Effects of the 1986 Tax Reform Act*, Working Paper No. 3309, National Bureau of Economic Research, MA.

Keilman, N. (1994) *Household Formation and Dissolution*, Working Paper, ECE/Eurostat Joint Work Session on Demographic Projections, Luxembourg, 1–4 June 1994.

Keilman, N., A. Kuijsten, and A. Vossen (1988) *Modelling Household Formation and Dissolution*, Clarendon Press, Oxford.

Latten, J.J. (1993) Household explosion in The Netherlands?, *Population Statistics Monthly 93/4*. Central Bureau of Statistics, The Hague.

Lesthaeghe, R. (1983) A century of demographic and cultural change in Western Europe: An exploration of underlying dimensions, *Population and Development Review*, **9**(3):411–435.

Lutz, W. (1994) Future reproductive behavior in industrialized countries, in: W. Lutz (Ed.), *The Future Population of the World: What Can We Assume Today?*, IIASA/Earthscan, London.

Menthonnex, J. (1994) *A Model of Household Projections for Switzerland*, Working Paper No. 46, ECE/Eurostat Joint Work Session on Demographic Projections, Luxembourg, 1–4 June 1994.

Prinz, C. (1991) *Marital Status and Population Projections*, Working Paper No. WP-91-12, IIASA, Laxemburg, Austria.

Prinz, C. (1994) *Problem Formulation, Model Selection and Data Quality: Some Issues in the Context of Living Arrangements Projections*, Working Paper No. 32, ECE/Eurostat Joint Work Session on Demographic Projections, Luxembourg, 1–4 June 1994.

Ploegmakers, M.J.H. and L.Th. Van Leeuwen (1994) *Dutch Households: Three Decades of Change, 94/2*, Ministry of Housing, Spatial Planning and Environmental Management, The Hague.

Salathiel, D. (1994) *Household Projections in England*, Working Paper No. 41, ECE/Eurostat Joint Work Session on Demographic Projections, Luxembourg, 1–4 June 1994.

Schmid, J. (1988) Principles emerging from sociology for definitions and typologies of household structures, in: N. Keilman *et al.* (Eds.), *Modelling Household Formation and Dissolution*, Clarendon Press, Oxford.

Skaburskis, A. (1994) Determinants of Canadian headship rates, *Urban Studies*, **318**:1377–1389.

UN (1980) *United Nations Principles and Recommendations for Population and Housing Censuses*, paras. 1223 and 1226.

UN (1981) *Estimates and projections of the number of households by country, 1975–2000*, UN Population Division.

UN (1987) *Demographic Yearbook*, ST/ESA/SER.R/17, Statistical Office, DIESA, United Nations, New York.

UN (1993) *The Sex and Age Distribution of the World's Populations: The 1992 Revision*, Dept of Economic and Social Development, United Nations, New York.

Van der Kaa, D. (1987) Europe's second demographic transition, *Population Bulletin*, **42**(1):1–57.

Van Diepen, A. (1995) *Population, Land Use, and Housing Trends in the Netherlands since 1950*, Working Paper WP-95-63, IIASA, Laxenburg, Austria.

Van Diepen, A. and E. Ennen (1996) The relevance of life style research in spatial planning, in: *Foundation of National Spatial Planning Discussion (ed): Beyond Policy*. Contributions to the National Spatial Planning Discussion, Part 2, pp. 597–606.

Van Diepen, A. and J. van Ginneken (1994) *Demographic Developments, Consumption Patterns and Environmental Load in the Netherlands* (Demografische ontwikkelingen, consumptiepatronen en milieubelasting in Nederland), Rep. No. 34, NIDI, The Hague.

Van Ginneken, J.K.S. and A. van Diepen (1994) Decrease of population growth: a condition for a sustainable future, in: Dutch Committee for Long-Term Environmental Policy (Eds.), *The Environment: Towards a Sustainable Future*, Kluwer Academic Publishers, Dordrecht, Chap. 13, pp. 351–369.

Van Imhoff, E. and N. Keilman (1991) *LIPRO 2.0: An Application of a Dynamic Demographic Projection Model to Household Structure in The Netherlands*, NIDI/CBGS Publications, The Hague.

Van Imhoff, E. (Ed.) (1995) *Household Demography and Household Modeling*, Plenum Press, New York.

Chapter 5

Spatial Aspects of Housing

A.M.L. van Diepen

Abstract

The daily surroundings of households are influenced by changes in the residents' demands and preferences concerning the dwelling. This chapter focuses on scale in the daily environment, and explores the changes in land use that have occurred in the Netherlands in the last four decades. Recent changes in the design and organization of dwellings, and the relationship between residential behavior and design are examined from a theoretical point of view. The changes in dwelling design are described, starting from nineteenth-century practice, with emphasis on the spatial changes that have occurred with regard to construction and design in general.

5.1. Introduction

The Netherlands is a small, densely populated country, so that the availability of space is an issue of constant concern. The growing population, and the demand for land for housing, industry, shops, and transportation routes, are placing increasing pressures on the available land. Although spatial claims can sometimes be mutually supportive, some kinds of land use may be mutually exclusive or in direct conflict. For these reasons, the spatial implications of human activities deserve special attention.

We start our analysis at the concrete level, focusing on the house and neighborhood as the spatial context of the household. Most household activities take place within or around the home, although this daily environment is not the same for all households. Over the last 200 years there have been considerable changes in the design and planning of the daily environment. Social developments have led to changes in design and construction, and new technical features have been incorporated, as well as new concepts, equipment, and devices that are regarded as desirable from economic, sociodemographic, ecological, or financial points of view. Therefore, housing has to be seen in its historical context, as the product of a particular architectural and planning period. The large variety of spatial design and building features we observe today reflects developments in planning and design in the past. This chapter highlights the main developments in housing in the Netherlands and their connection with household activities.

5.2. Mutual Relations Between Households and Dwellings

The goal of planning and design is to achieve the best possible mutual fit or adaptation between space and society. It deals with the tension between the existing and desired daily environment within certain constraints. Each individual can regard the spatial surroundings as enabling or constraining; each dwelling has to accommodate a wide range of activities that are performed within the home, such as cooking, eating, washing, and sleeping, as well as watching TV and doing homework. Residence behavior reflects the mutual relationship between people and their surroundings, considering the optimal tuning between the household and the house itself. In the habituation process of households to achieve a satisfying balance between the actual residential situation and their demands or desires, three types of reaction can be identified (Tazelaar, 1985).

First, households can adapt themselves and their preferences to the situation, such as by placing the washing machine near to the sink, locating the TV near to the signal input connector, to not buying a dishwasher if there is not enough space in the kitchen. In such reactions, households follow the "prescribed" residence behavior of the original layout as long as the necessary adjustments do not cause serious dissatisfaction. Second, to nullify any dissatisfaction, households can actively try to adjust (parts of) their daily environment to their own needs, such as by rebuilding or converting the house, or moving to another one. Such reactions include changing the initial, prescribed residence behavior by technical means, such as buying an extension lead and relocating the television, making one room out of two, or installing a new heating system. A third type of reaction involves a change in the household's sense of well-being. Feelings of stress and discontent can arise if the members of the household are unable to harmonize the situation with their own desires. Hence, they will try to reduce the annoyance caused by the discrepancy between the design of the dwelling on the one hand, and their specific wishes on the other; in other words, "living is the art of constant adjustment" (van Tijen, cited in Priemus, 1969).

This mutual adjustment between dwelling and household is not static but dynamic. Priemus (1969) distinguished between the cyclic and noncyclic changes that influence the initial habituation process. *Cyclic changes* take place at a regular intervals, and the initial circumstances will generally return. These changes are predictable and researchable, and thus their consequences are known. Dwellings must therefore be equipped to meet the recurrent changes that all households face, such as birthdays, the diurnal cycle, and changes of season. As we will see below, principles to take into account such changes were introduced in dwelling design during the first half of this century.

Noncyclic changes are more difficult to take into account, since their occurrence can not be predicted. In this case, a further distinction between internal and external noncyclic changes is useful. *Internal noncyclic changes* are specific to each household, and arise from the characteristics of the households themselves, e.g., size and composition, income, and preferences. Whether, when, and how these changes will occur in a particular household, however, is not known. Although these internal changes are specific to a particular household and their occurrence is unpredictable, they are seldom inconceivable. *External noncyclic changes* are beyond the control of the household, but influence the habituation process because they impact on internal noncyclic changes. Examples include population growth, technological innovations, increasing prosperity, natural disasters, and shifts in the housing market. These social changes are difficult to anticipate, and in practice, it is impossible to address their consequences in new dwelling designs.

5.3. Changes in Dwelling Design: Approaching Functional Quality

Ladde (1993) described the continuous strain between the household and dwelling design; no product is so sensitive to social changes as the house yet, simultaneously, no product is so tradition-bound. Innovations and new applications are always based on current building practice, and seldom lead to extreme about-turns in design. The fundamental purpose of a dwelling is to provide shelter for its residents, so the starting point of design has remained the same, yet there are evident differences between the houses built at the beginning of this century and those built in the 1990s.

By analyzing the current housing stock, we can get an indication of building types in the past. *Figure 5.1* shows the current housing stock according to the period of construction and type of dwelling. Single-family dwellings refer to those occupying whole buildings, with the main living areas situated on the ground floor; these include both detached and semi-detached houses. Multi-family dwellings refer to larger buildings consisting of several apartments. About 7% of the housing stock in 1995 was constructed before 1905; 65% of these old dwellings are single-family dwellings.

This section highlights some of the changes that have occurred in dwelling design during the twentieth century, mainly from the perspective of the functionality of dwellings for their residents. The functional quality of the housing stock refers to the utility and comfort of houses, and therefore does not refer to technical characteristics such as the durability and toughness of materials and construction,

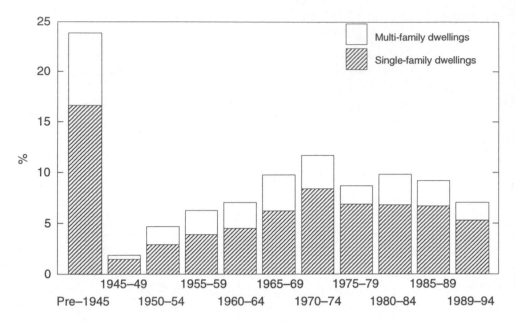

Figure 5.1. Housing stock in the Netherlands in 1995, according to period of construction and type of dwelling, as a percentage of all dwellings. Source: CBS (1995).

nor aesthetic characteristics such as beauty or amenity. First, however, we give a brief overview of nineteenth-century practice.

5.3.1. The nineteenth century

In the nineteenth century housing conditions were generally very poor. Most dwellings were not provided with services that today are regarded as standard requirements. Many facilities that are now part of basic home equipment were located outside the house. Households often shared facilities such as toilets and waste disposal facilities, water heating, laundry, and a pump for bathing. A typical public sector dwelling consisted of one or two rooms in which large families lived together, which meant that many household activities were performed in the same room. Space within the dwelling was therefore functionally undivided; the same area was used for sleeping, cooking, eating, and washing, and a mattress in an alcove could be used by different people at different times of the day. In urban areas houses received little fresh air and sunlight. Before 1900, terrace houses with only one floor were the most common building type; high-rise developments with three or four floors were found only in large cities.

5.3.2. 1900–1945

According to the Housing Act (1901) housing development plans had to comply with regulations concerning the location of buildings in relation to public roads and other buildings, the availability of water, access to sunlight and fresh air, and the minimum sizes of rooms.

During the first half of this century, more household activities were distinguished with regard to spatial needs inside the dwelling. The visible changes in building layouts reflect a process toward functionally differentiated dwellings (de Vreeze, 1993). Different areas were designated for particular purposes: an entrance hall, a living room for sitting and eating, a kitchen for cooking, bedrooms for sleeping, cellars and kitchens for storing food, and other storerooms for coal, etc. Gradually, the kitchen was designed as a separate area, equipped with a sink and draining board and cupboards. Areas for keeping food cool, the kitchen, scullery, and surplus space for provisions were situated on the north-facing side of the building. The distinct separation of bedrooms, the kitchen and other rooms is an example of accommodation to a cyclic change, in this case the diurnal cycle.

Lower-class dwellings soon came to resemble nineteenth-century middle-class dwellings, although the layouts were simpler. Some aspects of design that had been common in middle-class houses were incorporated into working-class houses during the early part of the century, such as separate bedrooms for parents and children. Like middle-class dwellings, the new lower-class dwellings also had two living rooms, although they were smaller. Only one of these rooms was used in winter, in order to reduce the use of fuel for heating. The kitchen was located in an extension at the rear of the house.

The quality of working-class housing improved significantly after the introduction of the 1901 Housing Act (de Vreeze, 1993). The development toward more functionally oriented spatial divisions can be seen in both single- and multi-family dwellings. The single-family dwelling was the dominant housing type in Amsterdam, Rotterdam, The Hague, Utrecht, and Groningen in this period. Almost 17% of the current housing stock was built between 1905 and 1945, more than 70% of which consists of single-family dwellings (see *Figure 5.1*).

Facilities that had previously been located outside the home gradually became part of the basic dwelling. The shared lavatory was replaced by a private indoor toilet, and outdoor washing facilities were replaced by indoor showers or washhouses. This "privatization" of amenities was made possible by the construction of network systems for energy and water. In 1904 the first electric light was turned on in Amsterdam and after World War I electricity was installed in all new dwellings. In the 1930s, most new dwellings were connected to electricity, gas, water, and sewerage systems, although the equipment to utilize these services was rarely provided (de Jonge, 1960). In this respect, the more expensive middle-class houses were better equipped, in that baths and central heating systems were often installed.

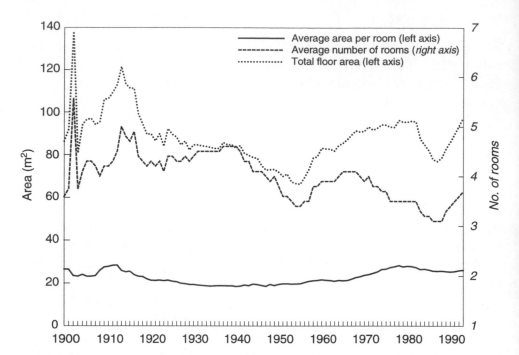

Figure 5.2. Average total floor area, area per room, and number of rooms per dwelling in the city of Groningen 1900–1993, generated from data on the housing stock in 1993; five-year moving averages.

The relocation of conveniences from outdoors to indoors, and the further division of space to provide functional diversity, inevitably meant that more space was needed inside. As an example, we now present data on the sizes of dwellings in the city of Groningen, obtained from an analysis of the current housing stock according to the year of construction (Groningen, 1994). *Figure 5.2* presents data (five-year moving averages) on the average total floor area, the average area per room, and the average number of rooms. These data should be regarded only as indicators of past conditions, since the original designs may have been changed over time. The averages in *Figure 5.2* show sharp declines after World War I. In Groningen, the average total floor area gradually but clearly decreased, from nearly 120 m^2 in 1910–1920, to 70 m^2 in 1950. The average number of rooms remained more or less the same, and even increased during the 1920s and 1930s, before a distinct decline began. Combining those two characteristics in time, the average area of rooms decreased. These findings confirm the indicated trend of increasing functional divisions, but give no evidence that the sizes of dwellings increased.

Figure 5.3 shows the average total floor area and number of rooms in single- and multi-family dwellings built in Groningen over the period 1900–1993. *Figure 5.3(a)* shows that in both categories the average total floor area has decreased,

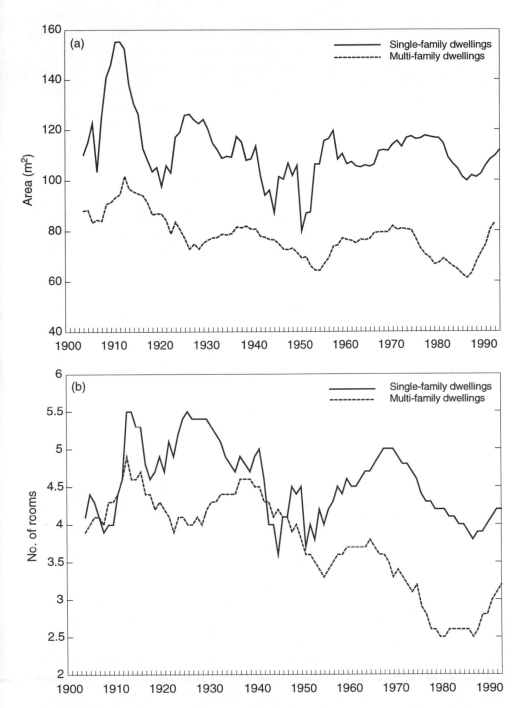

Figure 5.3. Average total floor area (a) and number of rooms (b) according to type of dwelling in the city of Groningen, 1900–1993, generated from data on the housing stock in 1993; five-year moving averages.

although the latter has shown fewer fluctuations. By 1950 the differences between single- and multi-family dwellings had diminished. *Figure 5.3(b)* shows that before and just after World War I the average numbers of rooms in single- and multi-family dwellings increased to 5.5 and 4.5, respectively. There was a general decline up to the early 1950s, followed by convergence and a crossing of the two lines.

In the first part of this century, as outdoor facilities were relocated indoors, more household activities were performed inside the house, thus producing a stronger inward orientation. The intimacy and privacy of home life became more important and had to be preserved. This shift in orientation is recognizable in neighborhood designs based on the "garden city" ideal, dating from the first decades of this century. First, the individuality of the house was stressed, with its own front door and chimney. Second, the identity of the neighborhood, with picturesque streets, gardens, inward-oriented arrangements, and south-facing dwellings underlined its seclusion from the outside world. These were the first signs that the interweaving of neighborhood and household activities was decreasing, since the functional relations and dependencies in terms of common facilities became weaker. The neighborhood was important as an extension of home life in a pleasant environment, but in a functional sense it no longer supported household activities.

5.3.3. Postwar construction and design

Postwar housing was characterized by the use of new materials, simple methods of construction, and rationalized layouts. The goal, above all else, was to reduce the enormous housing shortage at the end of the war. In the 1930s around 30,000 dwellings had been added to the housing stock each year, whereas during and immediately after the war, although there was some construction, the balance was negative.

Figure 5.4 shows the numbers of dwellings built each year since 1950. In 1973, 160,000 dwellings were added to the housing stock, more than three times as many as in 1950, but then building output dropped abruptly. In 1979–1982 there was a short but strong recovery, and since then output has been erratic. From *Figure 5.4* it can be seen that there were clear differences in output according to the source of finance. After the 1950s there was an enormous increase in output, peaking in the early 1970s, much of which was due to an increase in the construction of unsubsidized dwellings. The number of dwellings built partly with government finance also increased rapidly, especially in the 1960s and early 1970s. Dwellings built under the Housing Act accounted for a large proportion of postwar building, particularly in the form of high-rise developments built between 1945 and 1970. Some 29% of the present total housing stock dates from this period, 37% of which are multi-family dwellings (see also *Figure 5.1*).

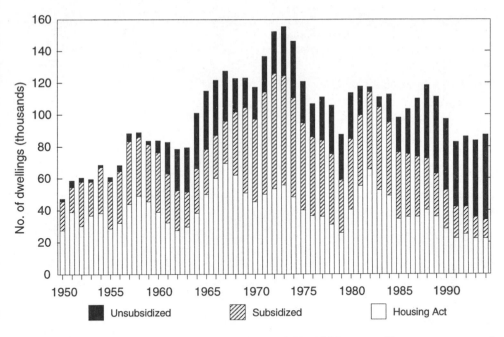

Figure 5.4. Number of dwellings built in 1950–1993, according to sources of finance. Sources: CBS (1989, 1994).

Dwelling Size

The size of a dwelling is related to the total floor area, the number of rooms, and the type of dwelling. In single-family dwellings the living room and kitchen were usually located on the ground floor and the bedrooms and bathroom upstairs. High-rise apartments were usually divided into two parts, separated by a supporting wall: the living room and kitchen in one part, bedrooms and bathroom in the other. Generally, a single-family dwelling contained one more room than an apartment (van Diepen, 1995). Single-family dwellings were about 5–10 m² larger than average, and apartments were a few square meters smaller than average. Until the late 1960s the increases in the sizes of both single- and multi-family dwellings followed generally similar trends.

Figure 5.5 shows the average total floor areas of new dwellings built in 1956–1982 (the only years for which data are available). The average area started to increase in 1961; multi-family dwellings peaked in 1967, and single-family houses 10 years later. After 1967, the average areas of the two types of dwelling began to diverge. A comparable trend is observable for the city of Groningen, although the level was higher (see *Figures 5.2* and *5.3(a)*). The decline in total floor area in 1980 turned into an increase in the late 1980s, to an average of 100 m² in the early 1990s.

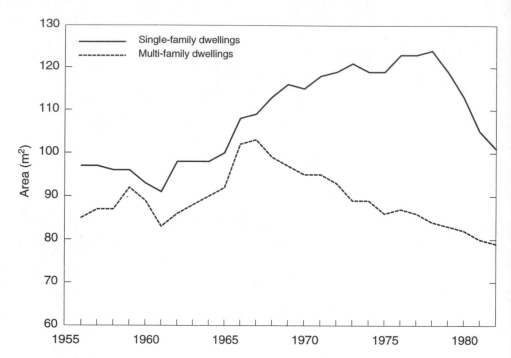

Figure 5.5. Average total floor area of single- and multi-family dwellings built in 1956–1982. Sources: CBS (1956–1984).

The reduction in average total floor area of multi-family dwellings after 1967 was achieved by eliminating all surplus space in corridors, halls, and the so-called wet compartments, i.e., toilet and bathroom (see *Figure 5.6*). Since both the surplus space and the total floor area in multi-family dwellings were reduced (*Figure 5.5*), an apartment built in 1967 had about 40% more surplus space than one built in 1982. Furthermore, single-family dwellings built in 1982 had about 10 m² more surplus space than multi-family dwellings. At the same time, living rooms become larger and more dominant. In 25% of the dwellings completed in 1994, living rooms were 20–30 m² in size, and almost 50% were more than 40 m².

All dwellings also had fewer rooms. In Groningen, the average number of rooms increased in the 1950s and 1960s, followed by a decline in the 1970s and 1980s (*Figures 5.2* and *5.3(b)*). After 1950, the sizes of single- and multi-family dwellings began to diverge, amounting to a difference of more than two rooms by the late 1970s. *Figure 5.7* shows the additions to housing stock in the Netherlands since 1956, according to the number of rooms. For decades, 30–40% of dwellings had been built with five or more rooms, but in the 1980s this figure fell to only 8%. In the period 1956–1994 more than 50% of new houses had only four rooms, and the proportion of three-room dwellings rose slowly from the late 1960s, reaching 25% of all new houses built in 1994. The share of one- and two-room apartments

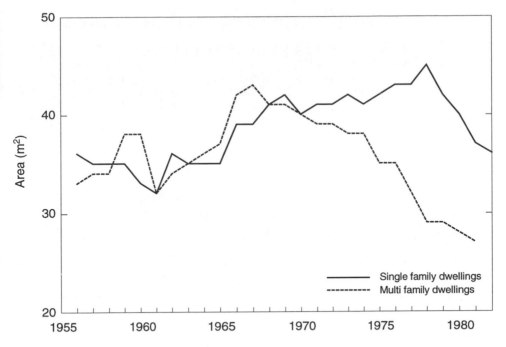

Figure 5.6. Average surplus space in single- and multi-family dwellings built in 1956–1982. Sources: CBS (1956–1984).

grew during the 1970s and early 1980s when many apartments for one-person households were built to meet the enormous demand. In 1984, nearly 20% of the dwellings completed each year consisted of three rooms or less, but this fell gradually to 5% in 1994.

We now examine to what extent these developments have transformed the characteristics of the housing stock. *Figure 5.8* shows the sizes of dwellings built in 1956 and 1993 according to the number of rooms (recalculated to exclude the kitchen in each case). The slowly declining share of large dwellings in new houses (from 38% in 1956 to 32% in 1993) is not yet reflected in the distribution of the housing stock. Also the share of houses with two rooms decreased only slightly, from 16% to 12%. The proportion of four-room houses increased from 28% to 38%, and is now the largest category.

In summary, both the diversity in the sizes of dwellings and average floor areas have increased over time. A comparison of the trends in dwelling size and demographic developments this century yields some interesting pictures. As the floor area (including the kitchen) has increased, the average number of rooms per dwelling has risen from 2.75 to 5.04, so that more space is now available for activities associated with running the household and housekeeping. There is now considerably more space per person, since the average household size has fallen to

A.M.L. van Diepen

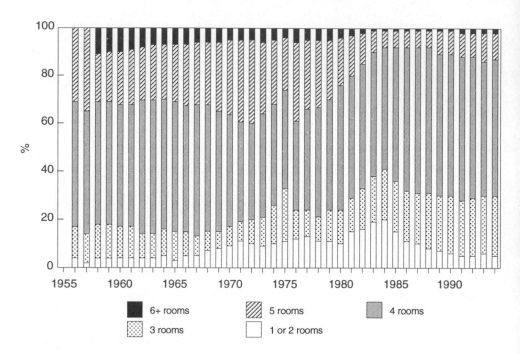

Figure 5.7. Additions to the housing stock according to the number of rooms, 1956–1994. Sources: CBS (1989, 1995).

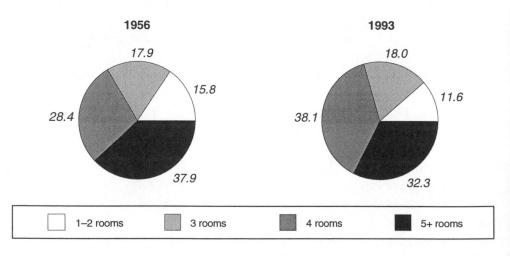

Figure 5.8. Sizes of dwellings according to the number of rooms, 1956 and 1993. Sources: CBS (1989, 1995).

2.4 (see Chapter 4), and the number of persons per room has decreased from 1.65 at the turn of the century, to 0.9 in 1947, and further to 0.54 in 1985. The desire for privacy has become an important factor that is now taken into account in dwelling design and construction.

Facilities

Technical improvements have greatly improved the utility of dwellings since the war. Central heating systems, ventilation, and better lighting have meant that the whole dwelling can be used more efficiently (de Vreeze, 1993). Before 1940 very few dwellings were equipped with central heating, but since the early 1970s such systems have been installed in all new dwellings and in many existing dwellings, supported by government policy (see Chapter 2). There are striking differences between high-rise and low-rise developments, however. In 1965, about 93% of all new multi-family dwellings were equipped with central heating systems, compared with only 18% of single-family dwellings. Sanitary facilities such as showers, baths, and second toilets were also installed, so that the average number of washstands and toilets per dwelling increased from 0.66 and 1.03, respectively, in 1955, to 1.61 and 1.43 in 1970. Garbage chutes and separate coal stores, which were often installed in the 1950s, are now no longer provided (CBS, 1956–1994).

The introduction of new domestic appliances has led to the rationalization of both dwelling design and household activities. Due to the growing demand, pushed by commercial interests, appliances such as refrigerators and washing machines soon became basic equipment (Baudet, 1986). The diffusion processes of these appliances were rather similar. Redesigned from a mechanical washtub in 1950, the new electric washing machine was more compact, and thus could fit inside most dwellings (Baudet, 1986), so that washing no longer had to be done outside. At the same time, the new compact refrigerator meant that cellars were no longer needed to store food, and self-service supermarkets began to encourage the storage of food at home. The first supermarket was opened in 1948, and the number increased gradually to 5 in 1950, 137 in 1955, and 1026 in 1958 (Association for Commerce, 1959). The rise of supermarkets has also meant that private purveyors no longer deliver goods to the door.

These conveniences and the availability of space for movable household appliances became integral parts of dwelling design, connected to the energy and water supply systems that had been constructed before the war. The inward orientation of household activities increased in the 1950s and 1960s, with an emphasis on material improvements by increasing the floor area and raising housing quality by installing facilities indoors.

5.4.   New Trends in Housing Design

The rationalization of the building process in the 1950s and 1960s resulted in a
tight and functional division of space inside the house, which had increasingly
restricted dwelling utility in general. In the 1960s, changes in residence behavior
and living preferences gave rise to a wider variety of housing types. High-rise
tower blocks and unvaried designs were no longer appreciated. The construction
practices of the late 1960s and early 1970s produced a further differentiation of the
housing supply to include detached and semi-detached houses, bungalows, terrace
or row houses, duplexes, and gallery apartments. In particular, as detached and
semi-detached houses became more popular, fewer high-rise developments were
built. Of all dwellings built between 1970 and 1990 (which represent 40% of
the current housing stock), 27% were multi-family dwellings, compared with 37%
between 1950 and 1970 (see *Figure 5.1*). Of the current total housing stock, 30%
are multi-family dwellings.

In the 1970s, the preferences of the various types of households began to be
taken more into account in dwelling design, resulting in specific housing types
for people living alone, the elderly, the disabled, and students. It became evident
that residence behavior should not be regulated by the layout, and housing designs
should be more flexible. Layouts incorporated more neutral divisions that were
less directed at specific uses, leading to more innovative "open-plan" divisions,
Z-shaped living rooms, and open kitchens. Central heating systems meant that
the entire dwelling could be heated, and the open layouts allowed residents to
communicate over longer distances between rooms. However, these changes also
contributed to greater internal nuisances within the home, such as noise, odor, and
loss of energy.

From an environmental point of view, the construction and utility of dwellings
received more attention. Starting with restricting noise, measures were taken
to improve housing quality by reducing annoyance within dwellings. Since the
Noise Annoyance Act (1972), architects have to take noise nuisance into account,
such as by locating noise-sensitive areas such as bedrooms on the quietest side of
the building, and by installing double glazing to reduce noise from the outside.
However, insulation has meant that more household activities cause more noise
annoyance within the home.

In response to the oil crises of the 1970s several attempts were made to reduce domestic energy demand, including the installation of double glazing, and
reductions in the volume of dwellings. The average volume, which determines
the energy demand for heating to a large extent, rose gradually during the 1960s
and 1970s (see *Figure 5.9*). The difference between subsidized and unsubsidized
dwellings is striking. The volume of unsubsidized dwellings increased steadily,
with only a brief interruption in the early 1980s, whereas the volume of all other
dwellings decreased after the first oil crisis.

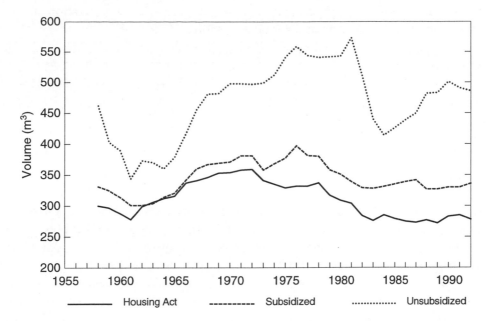

Figure 5.9. Average volume of dwellings according to the sources of finance, 1955–1992. Sources: CBS (1956–1994).

Planners and architects have introduced a number of new technical devices to reduce domestic energy consumption, including energy-saving appliances and solar collection panels, as well as improved physical planning measures relating to land divisions, reduced frontages, and dwelling orientation. During the 1980s some radical experiments were made to introduce energy-efficient systems of warm air and water ducts, and heat-absorbing walls, on the basis of which a number of ecological building practices have developed. Apart from saving energy, the emphasis is now on the use of so-called "sustainable building materials". The objectives of ecological building practices have now been extended to a larger scale; some self-contained neighborhoods have been built with their own small-scale water purification plants, waste separation and recycling facilities. Thus shared facilities outside dwellings have gained renewed interest, and households are being encouraged to attune their behavior in line with community objectives.

5.5. Residential Land Use

The wishes and demands of households concerning their environment have undergone several changes in response to a number of wider processes of social change. Here we describe the large-scale changes in residential land use since 1950 in relation to other human activities that require space.

Table 5.1. Population distribution according to degree of urbanization of the municipality, as percentages of the total population, 1950–1993.

Municipalities	1947	1960	1970	1980	1993
Rural	29	22	11	12	11
Urbanized rural	11	16	21	22	23
Predominantly commuting	5	7	13	14	15
Urban	54	55	55	52	51

Sources: CBS, 1989; 1995.

5.5.1.   Housing density

Since World War II planning policy in the Netherlands has focused on space saving, leading to a high housing density. In the 1950s, the goal of this policy was to protect agricultural land, and later to preserve open spaces as amenities for urban populations, and to reduce mobility (Ministry of Housing and Physical Planning, 1980). Few data on the density of residential areas are available, and several definitions are used, according to the type of land use considered, i.e., the total area, residential areas only, building areas only, etc. These different approaches to dwelling density prevent regional comparisons. Most of the available data on dwelling density relate to planning proposals, which suggest an increase in the number of dwellings per hectare in general, and very broad ranges of density according to when they were built and the type of neighborhood, i.e., low-rise, high-rise, or mixed (van Diepen, 1995). Except for mixed areas, there has been a slight increase in dwelling density since the early 1980s.

The increase in dwelling density in the postwar period, particularly in 1947–1993, was accompanied by rapid urbanization. *Table 5.1* shows the distribution of the population according the degree of urbanization of the municipality. In 1947, about 29% of the population lived in what could be called rural municipalities, and more than 50% in urban areas. During the 1950s and 1960s many rural munici-palities became urbanized and attracted many new residents, at the expense of the rural communities. In particular, the number of municipalities with large numbers of commuters showed a strong increase in the 1960s, reflecting the migration from the old city centers to smaller towns on the periphery. By 1993 the share of the population living in rural municipalities had fallen to 11%. The share of the pop-ulation living in urban municipalities has remained at roughly 50%. Over the last four decades the trend could be described as the urbanization of the rural areas.

5.5.2.   Changes in land use

The changes in dwelling design described above have led to a greater demand for residential space, and changes in the distribution of various types of land use. *Table 5.2* shows the quantitative changes in land use in the Netherlands since 1950, based

Table 5.2. Land use in The Netherlands, as percentages of the total land area, excluding water bodies, 1950–1989.

	1950	1960	1970	1980	1989
Built-up area	5.4	6.3	7.1	9.5	9.8
Infrastructure	2.9	2.6	2.0	3.8	4.1
Recreation	0.1	0.2	0.4	2.1	2.2
Agriculture	76.0	75.9	75.5	71.1	70.4
Forest	7.3	8.0	8.8	8.7	9.0
Uncultivated land	8.3	7.0	6.1	4.8	4.5
Total area ($\times 1{,}000$ ha)	3,297	3,363	3,378	3,393	3,387

Source: Van Diepen (1995).

on data from the CBS Soil Statistics (CBS, 1994), together with information based on earlier CBS data. In the past 40 years the system of land use classification has been changed considerably (van Diepen, 1995), so that some kinds of land use that were described in detail in 1950, had lost their specifications by the 1960s and 1970s. In particular, several (sub)categories of natural land use that indicated natural diversity have been omitted. The category "built-up area" has become more comprehensive, and now includes all kinds of urban functions, including industrial, commercial, and residential areas. In *Table 5.2* we have therefore reorganized the categories into comparable groups over time, and eventually gather them into the built-up area; such a procedure inevitably results in the loss of some information.

Between 1950 and 1989 the total land area of the Netherlands was increased by 2.7% due to land reclamation from the sea. From the total land area (excluding water bodies), the proportions of agricultural and uncultivated land fell, and those of built-up areas, infrastructure, recreation, and forest increased. The share of the built-up area rose from 5.4% in 1950 to 9.8% in 1989. However, although the total built-up area (including commercial areas) increased by 86%, the increase per capita was only 26.4%, from 178 to 225 m^2 per capita. In contrast, the total land area per capita in the Netherlands fell significantly, from 3236 m^2 per capita in 1950 to 2247 m^2 per capita in 1994.

5.6. Conclusions: Spatial Changes in Perspective

Throughout the last two centuries, the home has increasingly become a private domain. Houses have become larger and better equipped with all kinds of facilities, to contribute to a better level of daily care. The focus of the household activities has changed, from sharing outdoor facilities with neighbors, toward more privately oriented activities indoors. The functional relationship with the outside world has been reduced to one that provides access to water, gas, electricity, and sewerage systems. The degree of utility is controlled from within the dwelling, at the touch of a button: For more self-sufficient households the neighborhood has become less important, as life within the home has become more inward oriented.

In general, dwellings in the Netherlands have become larger, and their quality has improved, particularly since World War II. Single-family dwellings are usually larger than multi-family dwellings, and now dominate the housing stock. In the first half of this century, life within the home was to a large extent predetermined by the generally tight and functional division of the interior. In the late 1960s and early 1970s, dwelling design developed to provide a more neutral and flexible arrangement of space, as the idea of prescribed habituation behavior was abandoned. Dwelling designs now follow many lines of thought, leaving the process of habituation up to the residents themselves. Whereas in the last century dwelling design reflected income and social status, household characteristics and lifestyles are now increasingly being taken into account.

Various aspects of housing are now important in dwelling design, particularly the provision of facilities. The standards of basic facilities have risen as technical and economic means have become available and new norms for construction have been adopted. Since the oil crises of the 1970s, new challenges for dwelling design have been the inclusion of energy-saving devices, and ecological building construction. In ecological building practice there has been a revival in the use of shared facilities. More than 80% of the housing stock that will be needed in the year 2015, however, has already been built. In order to alleviate the effect of the coup de grace of the satisfaction of living in old dwellings by improving new ones, residential area renewal programs must meet the demands for functional quality, as well as those for better environmental standards.

The proportion of the dwelling stock that still has to be built for the future population will provide the best opportunities for changing to a more sustainable built environment. External noncyclic changes in society are still very difficult to incorporate into new designs, even though the ability to adjust to such changes will to a large extent determine the future utility of existing dwellings. Surplus space, spatial variability, and extended energy and water systems inside dwellings, as well as houses of various sizes are regarded as the most appropriate means to accommodate new developments in the habituation process, and to reduce the strain between existing and desirable housing conditions. The challenge for the future will be to design and plan dwellings and neighborhoods that will meet the demands for sustainability and environmental quality without ignoring the residents' demands for housing utility.

The Netherlands has faced a difficult task of planning for different kinds of land use in a limited amount of space. The expansion of built-up areas has left a clear mark on the total area available, particularly in terms of the loss of open space, in response to the increasing spatial demands of the population.

In this chapter we have approached the utilization of space on a very concrete level. Starting with the private domain of households, the space within the home has increased, so that the residents now perform a wider range of activities within the dwelling. Because of the decline in the average household size, the floor area per capita has increased, so that in the 1990s people have more private space than they did in the 1950s. Over the last 40 years the total built-up area has increased due to population growth and the higher per capita demand for space, and these trends are not expected to decrease in the near future. Planners and designers now need to carefully and deliberately balance these various desires and demands in order to maintain environmental quality.

Summary

- The functional relationship between households and their neighborhood has steadily diminished. Instead of shared outside facilities, households now have private facilities indoors, and access to water, gas, electricity, and sewerage systems that can be controlled from within the dwelling. Life within the home has become more inward oriented.
- Dwelling design has become less prescriptive regarding residence behavior. The interiors of dwellings built in recent decades are more neutral and flexible, providing space for different kinds of household activities.
- Within a short time various new facilities were installed in new dwellings, and increased the differences between new and existing dwellings.
- There has been a trend towards increasing space consumption per capita in the Netherlands, in terms of both the home and the built-up area in general.

References

Association for Commerce (1959) *Commercials and Consumers*, Report of the 21st Congress of the Association for Commerce, Groningen.

Baudet, H. (1986) *A Familiar World: 100 Years of Innovation in the Netherlands*, Bert Bakker, Amsterdam.

CBS (1956–1994) *Building Construction Monthly*, Central Bureau of Statistics, SDU, The Hague.

CBS (1989) *90 Years of Statistics*, Central Bureau of Statistics, SDU, The Hague.

CBS (1991, 1994–1996) *Soil Statistics*, Central Bureau of Statistics, SDU, The Hague.

CBS (1994, 1995) *Statistical Yearbook*, Central Bureau of Statistics, SDU, The Hague.

CBS (1995) *Housing Demand Survey 1993/1994: Housing Situation, Expenditures, and Removals*, National Statistics, Central Bureau of Statistics, SDU, The Hague.

De Jonge, D. (1960) *Modern Aspirations and Wishes for Living in the Netherlands*, VUGA Press, Arnhem.

De Vreeze, N. (1993) *Housing, Aspirations, and Ambitions: Qualitative Groundwork for Social Housing in the Netherlands*, National Housing Council.

Groningen (1994) *Dwellings on January 1, 1993 and 1994*, Information Center, Municipality of Groningen.

Ladde, E.E. (1993) *Tradition and Tophit: Dwelling Design 40 Years of Difference*, Farewell address, University Press, Delft.

Ministry of Housing and Spatial Planning (1980) *Dwelling Density*, Dept. of Urban Research, Zoetermeer.

Priemus, H. (1969) *Living, Creativity, and Adaptation: Research Toward Conditions for Optimal Opportunities for Adaptation in Housing*, Mouton, The Hague.

Tazelaar, F. (1985) *Quality of the Urban Environment: Reactions of Residents to Deficiencies*, University of Utrecht.

Van Diepen, A. (1995) *Population, Land Use, and Housing Trends in the Netherlands since 1950*, Working Paper WP-95-63, IIASA, Laxenburg, Austria.

Voogd, H. (1995) *Facets of Spatial Planning*, Samson Tjeenk Willink, Alphen aan den Rijn.

Chapter 6

From Household to Urban Metabolism: Ecological Renewal of Neighborhoods

A.G. Bus and H. Voogd

Abstract

The quality of the existing housing stock will determine the characteristics of household metabolism in the coming decades. Ecological renewal of the existing built environment will be necessary in order to reduce the rate of household metabolism, but this will be far from simple to implement due to the complex and heterogeneous structure of cities. This chapter therefore focuses on various ways of "regenerating" urban neighborhoods. First, we estimate the potential of ecological renewal by reviewing some urban renewal and conservation policies. We then present an outline of an ecological renewal approach for existing neighborhoods, followed by an overview of possible constraints on implementation.

6.1. Introduction

The negative impacts of household metabolism on the environment are not primarily caused by a few "luxury" households, but by the vast majority of "normal" households, each of which is responsible for "just a small" contribution. One important aspect of household metabolism is the dwelling itself. The average lifetime of a house is 50–100 years, so that the building, renovation and demolition of houses can be regarded as a kind of metabolism with a long time scale. This time scale, in combination with the growing populations and their increasing demands for housing and thus for space, justifies the attention given to the urban areas where these dwellings are concentrated. Other human activities in urban areas also contribute to processes of urban metabolism: the flows of materials and goods that support both urban activities and human consumption in turn give rise to resource depletion, the generation of waste, and the contamination of soils (see Tjallingii, 1995). The search for solutions to these problems has to be multidimensional; they can not be reduced to simple economic, social, psychological or physical planning issues. On the other hand, disciplines such as urban planning may contribute to a better understanding of how cities can become more "environmentally friendly". These contributions usually focus on rules and measures that may affect the spatial behavior of households and land use. This approach can be called "ecological urban planning".

Several towns and cities in Europe and the United States are already experimenting with ecological urban planning (e.g., Beatley and Brower, 1993). Well known examples include Boulder (Colorado), Portland (Oregon) and Seattle (Washington) in the USA, and in Berlin, Wiesbaden and Tübingen in Germany, which is no doubt the leading country in Europe in the field of ecological urban planning. In the Netherlands, examples can be found in smaller towns such as Alphen aan den Rijn (Ecolonia), Drachten (MorraPark), and Delft (Ecodus).

So far, the principles of ecological planning have been applied in the design of new neighborhoods, even though the vast majority of householders live and work in already urbanized areas. The Dutch Ministry of Housing, Physical Planning and the Environment (VROM) has estimated that by 2015, 7.6 million dwellings will be needed, so that 1.3 million new ones will have to be added to the housing stock (VROM, 1992a). In 1995 the 6.3 million existing dwellings (VROM, 1996) represented 80% of the housing stock that will be needed in 2015. This high percentage illustrates the importance of making greater efforts to identify ways to reduce both household metabolism in existing dwellings, as well as urban metabolism at the larger scale level of neighborhoods or even entire urban areas. To control or reduce urban metabolism through approaches such as ecological planning, clearly a broader scope is required than simply to build ecologically sound new neighborhoods. The principles of ecological planning must also be applied to the existing built environment, in order to introduce a more sustainable approach in processes that have traditionally been described as "urban renewal". In this chapter "ecological urban renewal" (or simply "ecological renewal") is defined as the implementation of changes in the existing city, in response to the need to resolve economic, social and physical problems, and to reduce or prevent further environmental degradation.

6.2.   The Historic Roots of the Built Environment

For centuries cities were established and grew as a result of economic activities, which in turn were determined by the geographical location of natural resources, sources of energy, and the availability of communication and transportation networks (e.g., Burtenshaw *et al.*, 1981). The pre-industrial city was small, consisting mainly of owner-occupied single-family dwellings. The Industrial Revolution changed this traditional pattern, as the concentration of industries attracted a flood of migrants from the countryside and accelerated the growth of the city. However, since these migrants were usually too poor to buy houses in the city, private construction companies were set up to build and rent out dwellings at reasonable rates. These companies acquired land on the outskirts of the city, and had a few simple goals: to achieve the highest possible housing density at the lowest possible cost, in order to get the most from their investments. In many industrialized countries, the appearance of these companies and the indifference of the authorities has resulted in immense, oppressive city districts with large numbers of tenement blocks.

When the authorities began to concern themselves with housing, they did not interfere much in the interplay of social forces. In many cities these high-rise blocks of rented apartments still predominate. In the centers and on the outskirts of cities, land ownership became increasingly attractive to building companies. Due to their vulnerability to discontinuities, they tried to secure the two main factors of production: capital and land. This has resulted in mergers between building firms and financiers, and the rise of development companies that acquire land for building projects. The power of the building firms over land and the power of the letting companies over dwellings undermine the effectiveness of government measures for regulating the housing market and the built environment. Deferring to the power of the building and letting companies, the urban authorities in many industrialized countries have moderated their objectives, and tower blocks have grown rapidly as a symbol of unrestrained commercialism.

In the nineteenth and early twentieth centuries, the prospects of employment initiated the flow of migrants to the city, but after World War II, the availability of housing and the growing car ownership exerted centrifugal forces on the city. Attracted by the relatively low prices, ample space, peace and tranquillity, and the freedom of a home of their own, many city dwellers are now returning to the countryside. In the case of the largest cities, such trends have worked to the detriment of inner city areas. There has been a long-term tendency, particularly in northern Europe and North America, for selective migration and the concentration of low-income residents in many urban neighborhoods (e.g., Herbert and Thomas, 1982). Due to changing public opinion, and better urban planning traditions, however, many small cities have managed to prevent the building of high-rise blocks within their boundaries. The need to protect open spaces and agricultural land from the ravages of urban sprawl took on a new urgency for assessing the indirect and environmental costs of development: the "real" costs. Many suburban areas promoted "no-growth" policies, usually in the form of zoning restrictions, although these have created artificial housing shortages and inflated land values.

In many countries such policies have resulted in urban landscapes with a number of common characteristics. On the outskirts of the city, particularly the suburbs, elite groups settle, while the older parts of town offer more accommodation to the lower-paid. Households become increasingly segregated, with income as the selecting factor. Many cities show ever widening rings of growth, with the old, usually inferior dwellings in the center, and the new, often more expensive houses on the outskirts. These social and structural characteristics must therefore be taken into account in the design of strategies for ecological renewal. It is much easier for authorities to deal with collective owners, such as housing corporations, than with many independent owners: households with multiple interests. Besides, private initiatives to improve dwellings and neighborhoods need money, and low-income households are characterized by the lack of this resource.

Around the world, the rate of urbanization has increased enormously. In 1810 London was the only city with a million inhabitants, whereas today there are 35 cities with populations of over 5 million, and 20 with over 10 million (Girardet, 1995). It is clear that the process of urbanization is changing the face of the Earth and the condition of humanity; cities cover less than 2% of the Earth's surface, but use 75% of its resources. Urban authorities will clearly have to learn to use their resources more prudently and more efficiently.

Since the oil crisis of 1973 the relationship between sustainable development and urban planning has attracted much attention (e.g., Chinitz, 1990; Breheny, 1992), particularly energy consumption and urban form (Owens, 1986). At the building scale, the insulation benefits of terraced or row houses or apartments relative to other forms of dwelling are now considered, as well as the benefits of optimizing layout and orientation in order to utilize solar energy. Emphasis is also given to the design of urban forms to minimize the need for travel (e.g., Keyes and Peterson, 1977; Rickaby, 1991). There is some empirical evidence showing that high urban densities, i.e., reduced travel distances and good public transportation systems, are correlated with lower fuel consumption (Newman and Kenworthy, 1989).

At present, most urban planners focus on urban extension, i.e., developing open land to allow the expansion of existing centers. This focus theoretically implies that ecological urban planning is restricted to just 1 or 2% of the total built environment. In practice the figure is likely to be much less, given that only a small number of new developments are based on sustainability principles. *Table 6.1* shows that in the Netherlands, despite the growing interest in ecological urban planning, only a very small fraction of recently built houses have been based on ecologically sound principles in five areas: energy, water, materials, waste reduction and the indoor environment. A "sustainable house" can be defined as one in which measures in at least two of these five areas have been implemented (VROM, 1996). Thus even in new houses the scale of implementation of sustainable building measures is still modest.

Table 6.1. Percentage of houses with sustainable measures compared to the total of houses built in the Netherlands, 1989–1994.

	Housing stock	New houses		Sustainable houses	
		No.	% of housing stock	No.	% of new houses
1989	5,699,400	111,233	1.95	79	<0.01
1990	5,802,400	97,384	1.67	46	<0.01
1991	5,892,200	82,888	1.41	847	1.02
1992	5,965,900	86,164	1.43	544	0.63
1993	6,044,000	83,689	1.38	2,154	2.56
1994	6,118,500	87,369	1.43	3,079	3.52

Sources: Adapted from VROM (1995, 1996).

6.3. Neighborhood Regeneration

It is obvious that for practical reasons ecological urban renewal should follow more traditional approaches to urban renewal. Urban renewal can be described as the need to replace in an existing city outworn or outmoded structures, facilities, and in time entire areas, in response to the need to resolve economic and social problems. In this sense, the process of urban renewal has been going on as long as cities have existed, although the reasons for renewal may have changed.

In many countries urban renewal began with policies of clearance and demolition, but in the 1950s the term acquired a more specialized meaning and is now associated with both the prevention and elimination of "urban blight" – the deterioration of, or deficiencies in, the quality of structures and their immediate environment. The term urban renewal is often replaced by the broader term "urban regeneration". Later, particularly after the 1973 oil crisis, the focus was on preservation and repair. The results of a recent comparative study of urban renewal policies in the Netherlands and other European countries, showed that the goals and motives of these policies differ considerably (Priemus and Metselaar, 1992). In some countries (Austria, Denmark, Sweden, Germany, the UK) such policies have been deliberately used as instruments to stimulate urban economies, particularly the building industry, whereas in others the emphasis has been on the resolution of social problems (Alterman and Cars, 1991), and improving parts of the housing stock. Although in the past urban renewal projects paid little attention to sustainability issues, the situation is changing rapidly. According to Priemus and Metselaar (1992) several countries mentioned "environmental protection" as one of the reasons for strengthening their urban renewal policies in the 1990s.

Three types of "treatment areas" for neighborhood regeneration can be distinguished, according to the degree of urban blight:

1. *Redevelopment areas* are neighborhoods in which urban blight has advanced to such a degree that by local standards nothing short of clearance is acceptable. These areas are characterized by structural deterioration, environmental pollution and poor quality services such as schools, and water and sewerage systems. The socioeconomic indicators of blight include high frequencies of juvenile delinquency and venereal disease, tax evasion, declining property values, and many vandalized abandoned buildings. General health and welfare indices also tend to be low.
2. *Rehabilitation areas*, where the signs of blight are less severe, can be restored to standard conditions. Rehabilitation measures include spot condemnation of buildings, stricter enforcement of building regulations in terms of repairs to or provision of sanitary facilities, public programs to improve or provide community facilities that are lacking, and voluntary campaigns for cleanup, painting, and improved building maintenance.
3. *Conservation areas* are those in "standard condition", to be protected from blight and maintained at least in their present state. Conservation means the preservation of predominantly built-up areas that are in "good" condition, by means of measures such as stricter enforcement of zoning regulations, minimum housing standards, and more vigilant maintenance of community facilities and private property. The idea of "recycling" could therefore be extended from aluminum cans and newsprint, to include the renovation of old buildings and adapting them to new uses. Many examples from around the world demonstrate the commercial potential of adaptive reuse, ranging from artists' lofts in Soho in London, to the renovation of Art Deco movie palaces and the conversion of railroad stations into cultural centers in the USA.

The process of revitalizing run-down urban areas has been widely discussed in the urban planning literature (e.g., Hall, 1988; Ashworth, 1994), usually with emphasis on social aspects. An important derivative source of concepts and ideas for regeneration has been "urban ecology" (e.g., Herbert and Thomas, 1982). Within this general theoretical framework, derived from analogy with the biological world, it is believed that the patterns and relationships evident there can be paralleled by land use and people within cities. Within the urban ecology framework, urban processes are explained in terms of symbiosis, competition, dominance, segregation, etc. The most crucial urban ecological processes are invasion and succession, which are viewed as elements of a cycle which proceed through a number of stages, with changes in land use and/or population type between the first and last stages.

Critics of urban ecology have noted its neglect of human and cultural factors, and have questioned the validity of using analogies, since they are often inadequate to explain urban sociogeographical patterns. Besides, urban ecology neglects the influence of politics and planning. In her influential book *The Death and Life of Great American Cities*, Jane Jacobs (1961) warned that land use segregation

Table 6.2. Housing stock in European countries: houses built in various periods as percentages of the housing stock.

	<1919	1919–1944	1945–1969	1970–1981	Total
Germany (BRD)	20	13	49	18	100
Spain	15	12	46	27	100
France	29	14	31	26	100
Italy	18	12	49	21	100
The Netherlands	13	15	35	37	100
United Kingdom	29	21	35	15	100

Source: Adapted from EC (1993).

and low-density dispersal were killing off the diversity that is the very basis of urban life. For Jacobs, the essential value of cities is the mixture of activities they support and encourage. She sees urban renewal as part of a broad strategy to reinvigorate cities. Previously, urban renewal involved replacing blighted areas with new developments, analogous to a farmer clearing a field and preparing it for a new crop. Jacobs, however, offered a different analogy: that of a living forest, a complex ecosystem in which old growth coexists with new, and are dependent on each other for sustenance.

The nominal urban ecology approach is restricted primarily to social land use processes. However, if expanded into an "urban metabolism" framework, it may become a valuable derivative source for ecological renewal.

6.4. The Potentials of Ecological Renewal

To gain a clearer insight into the potentials of ecological urban renewal, we now present some basic characteristics of the housing stock in the Netherlands. Compared with other European countries, the Dutch housing stock is relatively young (see *Table 6.2*).

Table 6.3 gives an overview of the quality of the housing stock, classified according to the estimated costs of repair. The table illustrates that during the period 1984–1992 most attention was paid to houses needing large-scale, costly repairs. The number of houses in relatively good condition (<10% cost category) increased from 59 to 80%.

About 55% of the Dutch housing stock consists of rented properties. This figure is higher than in most other European countries (average 30%), except for Germany (58%) and Sweden (60%). Most of these properties are owned by private housing corporations that are regulated by the government. *Table 6.4* shows the numbers of rented houses that were upgraded between 1987 and 1991, and illustrates the important contribution of the housing corporations to urban renewal.

Table 6.3. Quality of the Dutch housing stock measured in terms of the cost of repair as a percentage of the newly built value (1984 and 1992).

	<10%		10–20%		20–30%		>30%		Total	
	1984	1992	1984	1992	1984	1992	1984	1992	1984	1992
Pre-war dwellings	36	54	20	22	14	10	31	14	100	100
Post-war dwellings	70	89	17	8	7	2	7	1	100	100
Total	59	80	18	12	9	4	14	4	100	100

Source: Adapted from VROM (1994).

Table 6.4. Number of rented houses in the Netherlands upgraded by means of government subsidies.

		Houses upgraded by government subsidies		Rented houses upgraded by housing corporations	
Year	Total housing stock	No.	% of total stock	No.	% of houses upgraded
1987	5,289,300	78,600	1.5	57,800	73.5
1988	5,588,600	80,000	1.4	58,500	73.1
1989	5,699,400	68,100	1.2	45,600	67.0
1990	5,802,400	81,400	1.4	57,400	70.5
1991	5,892,200	79,500	1.4	56,700	71.3

Source: Adapted from VROM (1994).

The data in *Table 6.5* show clearly that the numbers of upgraded and new houses are gradually converging, providing some evidence for the point made earlier that more attention to ecological renewal is worthwhile. The last two columns in the table show that there have been improvements in both the physical state of houses (i.e., by demolition followed by building new ones), and in the standard of housing (such as more and larger rooms; see also Chapter 5) in response to changed opinions about preferred functions. Thus it is difficult to state the mean lifetime of a house. For example, houses along the canals in the center of Amsterdam are already more than 200 years old, but are still popular, whereas in many neighborhoods built after the war houses are already being or soon will be demolished. Thus both the quality of construction and the qualitative composition of houses are important.

Table 6.6 shows that the total government investments in urban renewal changed little between 1985 and 1993. The total budget in 1995 was Dfl 793 million (at real 1985 prices), a substantial reduction on 1993, but still considerable. Yet this was less than 10% of the total investment in building renovations. At real 1995 prices, the Dutch Economic Institute of Building Industry (EIB, 1997) estimated that in 1997 Dutch society will invest Dfl 7.2 billion in the renovation of houses, Dfl 16.2 billion in new houses, and Dfl 5.2 billion in maintenance. Thus in 1997 about Dfl 12.4 billion will be spent on the existing housing stock, about

Table 6.5. Number of new, renovated and upgraded, withdrawn and demolished houses in the Netherlands, 1987–1991.

	New houses	Houses upgraded by government subsidies	Houses withdrawn from housing stock[a]	Houses demolished
1987	110,091	78,600	12,455	5,439
1988	118,446	80,000	12,673	7,260
1989	111,233	68,100	12,953	9,145
1990	97,384	81,400	11,548	8,418
1991	82,888	79,500	12,754	8,765

[a]Houses withdrawn from the housing stock due to changed functions, merging, and demolition.
Source: Adapted from VROM (1992b, 1994).

Table 6.6. Government expenditures on urban renewal in the Netherlands (in Dfl, current prices).

	1985		1989		1993	
	Amount	%	Amount	%	Amount	%
Acquisition/demolition	690	50	546	30	509	26
Upgrading houses	130	9	262	15	346	19
Traffic measures	58	4	105	6	121	6
Organization costs	110	8	145	8	171	9
Housing environment	138	10	319	18	289	16
Heritage care	30	2	94	5	106	6
Industries	41	3	99	5	66	4
Pollution/nuisance	140	10	163	9	146	8
Social welfare	42	3	74	4	97	5
Total	1,379	100	1,807	100	1,851	100
Real prices of 1985[a]	1,379		1,622		1,480	

[a]Correction according to price index numbers from new to built dwellings (Central Planning Bureau, 1994).
Source: VROM (1988, 1996).

43% of all investments in the housing industry. The problem of the lack of funding could be resolved if just 1% of this amount – about Dfl 125 million – were to be reserved for the implementation of ecologically sound measures.

Table 6.6 also shows that in 1993 a larger proportion of the investments in urban renewal projects went into upgrading houses and improving the housing environment than in 1985. Unfortunately, the level of the investments provides no indication of how the housing environment was improved, nor the extent to which these improvements helped to reduce environmental degradation. Nevertheless, it is a challenge to visualize the relations between the housing environment, its impact on urban metabolism, and the contribution of this metabolism to environmental degradation.

Table 6.7. Production of primary and secondary resources used in the building industry in the Netherlands in 1989.

	Production	Imports	Exports	Used	Utilization
Primary resources					
Sand for landfill	59,500			59,500	Dwellings,
Industrial sand	25,600	6,300	9,000	22,900	infrastructure,
Clay	5,750	250		6,000	and other
Limestone	2,160	160		2,320	functional
Gravel[a]	10,900	12,800	21,450	21,450	buildings
Total	103,910	20,210	11,250	112,170	
Secondary resources					
Building and demolition rubble[b]	5,000			5,000	Road building
Asphalt rubble	1,000			1,000	Road building
Cleaned soil[c]	500			500	Landfilling

[a]Gravel includes river and mountain gravel.
[b]Including 500,000 tonnes sieved sand.
[c]V&W (1994).
Source: Adapted from BMT (1990).

One example of an ecologically sound renewal measure is to reduce the input and output flows of various building materials in neighborhood renewal projects (see *Figure 6.1*; V&W, 1994). Some efforts have been made to encourage the use of sustainable building materials. As shown in *Figure 6.1*, the reuse of building materials is an essential ingredient in reducing the rate of urban metabolism. Here a distinction is made between "primary" building resources and the reuse of these products as "secondary" materials. Obviously, sustainable neighborhood renewal implies that the use of secondary materials is encouraged.

Table 6.7 lists the secondary resources used by the building industry in the Netherlands for three main categories of building: dwellings, infrastructure, and other functional buildings such as offices (V&W, 1994). Excluding the sand used for landfilling and as a secondary resource, in 1989 the building industry used a total of 52.7 million tonnes (Mt) of materials (industrial sand, gravel, clay, limestone). To build an average house, about 175 tonnes of materials are needed (FODI, 1989). Thus in 1989 about 19.5 Mt of building materials were used for constructing new houses, or 37% of all the materials used by the industry in that year. At the same time, the demolition of old houses generated about 1.6 Mt of building rubble.

Unfortunately, not everything that could be reused is reused. In 1989, for example, about 11.5 Mt of building and demolition rubble were generated, of which 9 Mt (about 85%) could have been reused if it had been reprocessed into rubble stone or sieved sand. However, only about 4.5 Mt of rubble stone and 0.5 Mt of sieve sand were produced, or 43% of the total 11.5 Mt (BMT, 1990). Assuming

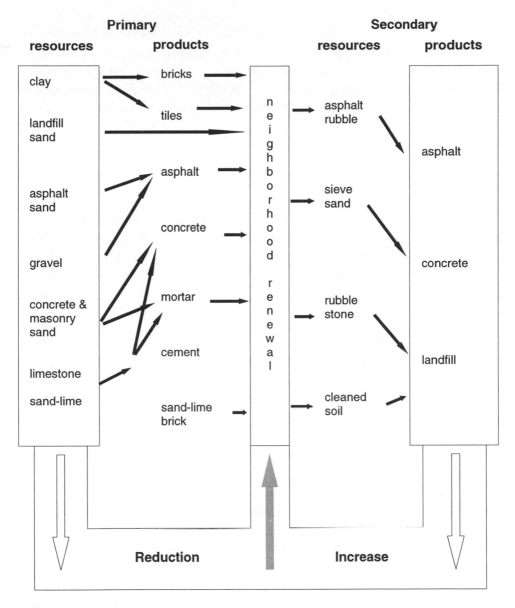

Figure 6.1. The relation between neighborhood renewal and input and output flows of building materials.

an annual growth rate of building production of 1.5%, and that the proportion of building and demolition rubble remains the same, by the year 2000 the production of building and demolition rubble could increase to 13.3 Mt. Clearly, there is much room for improvement.

As well as reducing the use of new building materials, the qualitative composition of housing could also be upgraded. Improving the quality of neighborhoods
may be the best way to reduce urban metabolism in the long term, but it is necessary
to bear in mind that the inhabitants and other users of a neighborhood often have
different opinions as to what constitutes quality in a residential area (see van Poll,
1997), and such opinions are likely to change over time. These aspects make it very
difficult to design high-quality neighborhoods that can be used for a long period.

6.5.   Towards an Ecological Renewal Approach

The preceding sections have provided some empirical evidence that ecological
planning principles should not be limited to urban expansion schemes.   Urban
rehabilitation, in its various forms, offers many opportunities to apply principles
of sustainable development. In this section, we present some preliminary ideas on
spatially oriented solutions to reduce the environmental impacts of activities at the
neighborhood level, in order to protect ecological systems from further destruction.

The designers of neighborhoods in the past paid little attention to the environmental issues that are regarded as important today. According to Alterman and Cars
(1991) urban renewal processes have so far been guided mainly by socioeconomic
considerations. For this reason it may be assumed that the environmental quality
of existing neighborhoods can be improved by neighborhood renewal. The authorities involved in neighborhood renewal projects face the challenge of improving
the existing environmental quality and to prevent further environmental degradation, while at the same time finding solutions to more immediate socioeconomic
problems.

From an urban planning point of view, the primary aim of neighborhood
renewal is to improve the quality of existing neighborhoods and to keep them
functional for at least 25 years without the need for costly structural changes. The
quality of a neighborhood is determined by factors that influence the quality of
both the housing stock (i.e., technical factors, maintenance, and the arrangement of
houses), and the residential area itself (i.e., the presence, quality and accessibility of
facilities, the identity of the neighborhood, security, environmental quality, ecological quality ("green" areas), and street cleanliness). These factors are also important
in determining its sustainability. It is likely that neighborhoods characterized as
"high-quality living areas" will fulfil their functions for a longer period of time,
and so may reduce their rate of metabolism. The paramount question is therefore
how to implement environmental measures in neighborhood renewal projects.

Environmental quality can be assessed at the local level (livability) and the
global level (sustainability), and they are closely related. Environmental quality
at the local level has a direct impact on the quality of life in cities, villages, and
areas designated for nature and recreation. It is therefore important to prevent

or reduce environmental annoyance caused by activities in a neighborhood or its surroundings. Factors that influence the local environmental quality of a neighborhood include: safety; contamination of soils; water and air pollution; and nuisance or annoyance due to noise, odor or dust.

The relationship between neighborhood and global environmental quality is more indirect. At the neighborhood level, transport, domestic heating systems, etc., contribute to environmental degradation at the global level. In the long run, this degradation may also have negative impacts on local environmental quality, and thus the quality of the neighborhood. For example, the thinning of the ozone layer may mean that sunbathing is a hazardous activity, so that owning a garden may become less attractive. As another (perhaps not global but still very large scale) example, severe air pollution levels can cause respiratory problems, so that people are advised not to engage in outdoor sports on sunny and windless days. Environmental degradation at the global scale could clearly be prevented or reduced by implementing ecological measures in neighborhood renewal projects.

Many factors influence global environmental quality, including the loss of biodiversity, ozone depletion, acidification, production of greenhouse gases, waste disposal, squandering of resources, destruction of ecosystems, desertification, eutrophication of lakes, and the dispersal of pollutants. To translate these abstract global issues into concrete measures at the neighborhood level, the first step is to introduce measures that will help to reduce the flows of materials and goods (water, fossil fuels, and materials, as well as the production of waste); to limit the use of space for urban expansion; and to preserve or improve ecological systems (see Tjallingii, 1995).

Before suitable measures can be chosen, however, it is first necessary to analyze the existing situation with respect to these themes and to anticipate local, regional or even international developments that could have consequences for the neighborhood. To identify which measures could reduce environmental degradation, it is important to understand the relations between human activities and how they contribute to such degradation. Evidently, urban environmental planners need to anticipate demographic changes (see Chapter 4), technical improvements (see Chapter 2), economic developments (see Chapter 8), political commitment (see Chapter 9), and environmental and physical planning relations.

Knowledge of all these relations is essential for improving the environmental quality of neighborhoods by means of ecological renewal projects that are appropriate to local conditions. But even if the uncertainties about external developments are reduced, it is still difficult to choose between different measures. Some measures could improve aspects that are important for global environmental quality, while at the same time could have a bad influence on aspects which are important for local environmental quality. For example, the construction of a railway line may be seen as desirable from the point of view of sustainability, but at the local level it may reduce the environmental quality of a neighborhood. In other words, the pros and cons have to be carefully weighed in order to find the right solutions for a neighborhood.

Urban environmental degradation is closely related to the physical design or urban form. This is also the case at the scale of a neighborhood. Physical design improvements include upgrading the existing housing stock, such as small-scale renovation, demolition and rebuilding, as well as improvements to the existing spatial structure, e.g., roads or recreation areas. Another approach closely related to the physical design of a neighborhood is environmental management. With a given physical design different approaches may have different environmental impacts.

Figure 6.2 shows the main relations that influence ecological neighborhood renewal. In the past, neighborhood renewal was seen as the answer to many socioeconomic and physical problems. To ensure that existing problems will be solved not only in the short term, planners have to anticipate demographic, economic, technical and cultural trends and developments 10 or 20 years from now. In addition to addressing traditional socioeconomic and physical problems, the ecological approach also sees the deterioration of environmental quality, both local and global, as a problem. Planners now also need to take into account the rights of future generations (see White, 1994), which means that they have to take a longer-term view than they have been used to. To be able to redesign neighborhoods that reduce environmental degradation, knowledge of the effects and the efficiency of spatial principles on environmental aspects/issues is necessary.

In meeting the challenge of achieving ecological neighborhood renewal from the physical planning point of view, both the substantive and implementation components of environmental protection need to be elaborated. The substantive component consists of spatial-functional planning principles aimed at reducing environmental degradation. Although there are many such principles, they have rarely been elaborated and tested at the neighborhood scale. It is therefore important to realize that before the new ecological principles can be implemented, the parties involved will want to know, in as much detail as possible, the costs (investment and maintenance), and the other pros and cons of these measures. It is likely that physical or environmental management measures that reduce environmental degradation will be more easily accepted by the parties involved if those measures contribute to the solution of existing problems or to other important goals as well.

6.6.   Possible Constraints on Ecological Renewal

Given the large potential for reducing environmental degradation through ecological neighborhood renewal, and knowing that in practice very little is actually being done, it is essential to explore all possible constraints. This section focuses on the factors responsible for the poor record of implementation so far, and presents some suggestions for reducing or even eliminating them.

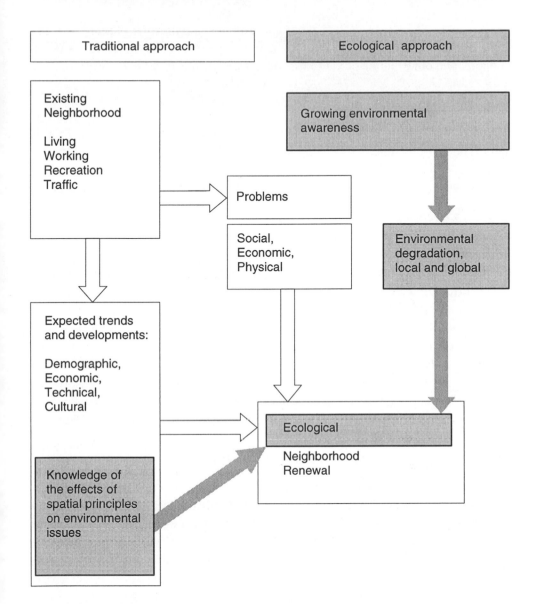

Figure 6.2. Ecological neighborhood renewal. The shaded boxes and arrows illustrate that the ecological approach is an extension of the traditional approach.

Financial Constraints

With the introduction of urban renewal legislation in 1985, Dutch municipalities were provided with the instruments necessary to take action in areas in need of renewal or rehabilitation. However, the present government budget restrictions have meant that projects to deal with environmental problems are having to compete for funding with those designated for resolving socioeconomic and physical problems.

To choose the right solutions it is important to understand the interrelations between these problems, and to assess the pros and cons of the different solutions (from financial and other points of view) for each of the parties involved.

Exchanging Information

Before a municipality can choose the most appropriate measures, information is needed on many technical, socioeconomic and environmental issues. This demands the professional knowledge of various agencies, and their full cooperation. Organizations that are poorly informed and inefficient will probably select less appropriate solutions.

Sectoral Approach

Urban renewal has evolved from a housing issue to a much wider approach, yet there is still little knowledge about the relations between different system approaches. For example, if a local authority wants to improve the environmental quality of a neighborhood by improving the housing stock and living area, they will have also to take into account the incomes of the residents in relation to their living expenses. Otherwise it is possible that neighborhood renewal will result in higher rents that the residents can not afford. Research is therefore needed to ensure that an integrated approach is taken. It is also important that planners understand the networks in a neighborhood, and the common and conflicting aims of the residents.

Lack of Knowledge about Environmental Cost-effectiveness

At present, little is known about the impacts and effectiveness of ecological principles that have been applied, so it may be difficult to persuade institutions and individuals to adopt them. Knowing the costs of the different ecological renewal principles, but not of their effects nor likely effectiveness, will not be conducive for their implementation. Research is therefore needed to identify the costs, returns and other consequences.

Uncertainty About Future Developments

Another issue of concern is the uncertainty about future developments that may be important for a neighborhood. Although much experience, knowledge and data are available for using or developing different scenarios at the national scale, it is often difficult to translate these national scenarios to the local level. This is especially the case if local scenarios are being used to explore which ecological renewal principles would yield the greatest benefits. Before scenarios can be used in this sense, it is necessary to understand the qualitative and quantitative aspects of the various human–environment relations at the neighborhood level.

"Fuzzy" Character of Concepts

To enable a fruitful exchange of opinions about the concepts of "living area quality" and "sustainability" between individuals and institutions, it is essential to elaborate these concepts in the framework of neighborhood renewal. Ecological renewal implies the definition of a range of conditions that are measurable and can be compared with a set of "standards", which in turn are based on generally recognized criteria for health, safety, waste management, building materials, and other issues of public and ecological concern. The standards employed will determine the range of conditions for different types of treatment areas to be identified, and are important at the international, national as well as local levels. Standards for building materials, occupancy, and sanitary facilities are usually specified in building, housing, fire and sanitation codes, whereas those relating to the design of lots, blocks, streets, population densities, and the type and intensity of developments are included in district regulations and zoning ordinances. Where existing standards are inadequate or lacking, trial standards for survey purposes need to be upgraded or set in reference to general standards, or to standards already in force in communities of similar size and character that are most consistent with local objectives.

Differing Values

The residents and other users of a neighborhood often have different opinions about the quality of their living area, and the responsibility of the neighborhood towards sustainability. It is therefore essential to investigate the various opinions and to involve all parties in the process of ecological neighborhood renewal (see Teisman, 1992). It is essential to obtain local support before implementing any renewal plan; consensus-building is essential in order to find solutions that will benefit all participants (Woltjer, 1995).

Legislation

Urban renewal processes are always surrounded by legislation. The problems that will be addressed by renewal activities are complex and dynamic, and are often difficult to address within the inflexible regulations of the law. This is especially the case when neighborhood renewal plans are also dealing with soil contamination. The challenge is therefore to make optimal use of the possibilities offered by existing legislation. This demands extensive legal knowledge, in particular the consequences at the local level. If only poor solutions can be found within existing legislation, then changing the legislation could be a solution. But in new legislation the protection of the individual against negative environmental impacts should still be of great importance.

6.7. Recycling the City: Conclusions

Issues such as social justice, housing, transport and health have always dominated the urban agenda. Because of the unprecedented rate of urbanization and
its associated negative environmental impacts, the issue of urban environmental
sustainability is gaining increasing attention. In assessing the impacts of cities
on the environment, it is useful to understand their metabolism, their inputs of
resources and their outputs of waste. The needs of cities can be met with greatly
varying throughputs of resources. In the industrialized countries, urban metabolism
is characterized by resources flowing through the system with little concern about
their origin, nor about the destination of the associated waste. These characteristics
of urban production, consumption and disposal are quite detached from the overall
ecological viability of the urban system, and tend to disrupt natural cycles. They
are profoundly different from natural metabolic processes.

Urban authorities who want to take responsibility for the environmental impacts
of their cities at different levels will have to adopt policies that aim at circular
metabolic systems. In the past local environmental pollution that causes poor
living conditions was sometimes a reason for urban renewal. It is to be expected
that inhabitants of Western countries will increasingly take action against activities
that threaten the living area quality, including local environmental pollution, of their
neighborhood. It is less likely that they will take action against activities that cause
environmental degradation at a larger scale. Local authorities should therefore focus
on ways to reduce environmental degradation at this larger scale, with the aim of
creating neighborhoods and cities that are people-friendly, environmentally friendly
and culturally rich. To be successful in this endeavor, the focus should be not only
on restricting urban expansion and development, but also on encouraging prudent
investments to upgrade the ecological quality of the existing built environment.
Urban planners have amassed considerable knowledge about the functioning of
the urban system, but this knowledge base needs to be widened to include ways
of increasing energy and resource efficiency. Urban planners cannot claim to be
knowledge-led unless they also acquire the know-how to make urban metabolism
more ecologically sound.

Summary

- Ecological neighborhood renewal is defined as the implementation of renova-
  tive changes in the physical neighborhood, in response to pressures to resolve
  economic, social and physical problems, that will reduce or prevent environmental degradation. However, every neighborhood has its own implementation
  constraints and possibilities – technical, financial, as well as social.

- About 80% of the housing stock that will be needed in the year 2015 already exists. Therefore more attention should be paid to the implementation of environmentally benign measures in the process of urban renewal.

- In urban ecological planning, attention has so far been limited to urban expansion, especially to sustainable buildings. Sustainable houses are defined as those in which substantial measures in at least two of the themes energy, water, material, garbage and the internal environment have been implemented. However, from this definition, and the fact that only 4% of the houses built in 1994 could be described as "sustainable", it is clear that the scale of adoption of sustainable principles in urban expansion schemes is still very modest.

- In theory, spatial planning can contribute to a structural reduction in environmental pollution. However, one has to deal with existing spatial structures that were designed at times when environmental issues were not considered important. Although some of these structures could be changed to make them more environmentally friendly, such changes can of course not be made for an entire city at once. However, it would be realistic to pursue the implementation of measures to reduce environmental pollution in ongoing urban renewal projects, notably at the neighborhood level.

- Further research is necessary to identify the factors that restrict the implementation of ecological measures in neighborhood renewal plans, and ways to tackle them. The problem of the lack of funding could be solved if just 1% of the total annual investments in the Dutch housing stock, currently about Dfl 12.5 billion, were to be reserved for the implementation of ecologically sound measures.

References

Alterman, R. and G. Cars (1991) *Neighbourhood Regeneration: An International Evaluation*, Mansell, London.

Ashworth, G.J. (1994) *Heritage Planning*, Geo Press, Groningen.

Beatley, T. and D.J. Brower (1993) Sustainability comes to Main Street, *Planning*, **59**(5): 16–19.

BMT (1990) *Has the Market To Do It?: Market Exploration for Bulk Minerals in the Building Industry in the 1990s*, Management and Marketing Advisers in the Building Sector (in Dutch).

Breheny, M.J. (Ed.) (1992) *Sustainable Development and Urban Form*, Pion, London.

Burtenshaw, D., M. Bateman and G.J. Ashworth (1981) *The City in Western Europe*, Wiley, Chichester.

Central Planning Bureau (1994) *59 years Statistics in Time Series*, SDU, The Hague (in Dutch).

Chinitz, B. (1990) Growth management: good for the town, bad for the nation?, *Journal of the American Planning Association*, **56**:3–21.

EC (1993) *Statistics on Housing in the European Community*, European Commission, Directorate General V: Employment, Industrial Relations and Social Affairs.

EIB (1997) *The Expectations for Building Production and Employment*, Economic Institute of the Building Industry, Amsterdam (in Dutch).

FODI (1989) Dutch Federation of Aggregates Industries, Clay, Gravel, Sand, etc., Letter to the Cabinet informer, drs R.F.M. Lubbers, Nijmegen (in Dutch).

Girardet, H. (1995) *The Urban Age: Sustainable Cities in an Urbanizing World*, Jonathan Cohen and Associates, New York.

Hall, P. (1988) *Cities of Tomorrow: An Intellectual History of Urban Planning and Design in the Twentieth Century*, Blackwell, Oxford.

Herbert, D.T. and C.J. Thomas (1982) *Urban Geography*, Wiley, Chichester.

Jacobs, J. (1961) *The Death and Life of Great American Cities*, Random House, New York.

Keyes, D.L. and G. Peterson (1977) *Urban Development and Energy Consumption*, WP-5049, Urban Land Institute, Washington, DC.

Newman, P.W.G. and J.R. Kenworthy (1989) Gasoline consumption and cities: A comparison of US cities with a global survey, *Journal of the American Planning Association*, **55**:24–37.

Owens, S. (1986) *Energy Planning and Urban Form*, Pion, London.

Priemus, H. and G. Metselaar (1992) *Urban Renewal Policy in a European Perspective: An International Comparative Analysis*, Delft University Press, Delft.

Rickaby, P.A. (1991) Energy and urban development in an archetypal English town, *Environment and Planning B*, **18**:153–176.

Teisman, G. (1992) *Complex Decision-Making: A Pluricentric Approach to Decision-Making about Spatial Investments*, VUGA, The Hague (in Dutch).

Tjallingii, S.P. (1995) *Ecopolis: Strategies for Ecologically Sound Urban Development*, Backhuys, Leiden.

Van Poll, R. (1997) *The Perceived Quality of the Urban Residential Environment: A Multi-attribute Evaluation*, PhD thesis, University of Groningen.

VROM (1988) *Housing in Numbers 1987*, Ministry of Housing, Planning and the Environment, The Hague (in Dutch).

VROM (1992a) *Trend Report Housing 1992*, No. 43, Ministry of Housing, Planning and the Environment, The Hague (in Dutch).

VROM (1992b) *Environmental Policy in the Netherlands*, Ministry of Housing, Planning and the Environment, The Hague (in Dutch).

VROM (1994) *Housing in Numbers, 1993*, Ministry of Housing, Planning and the Environment, The Hague (in Dutch).

VROM (1995) *Housing in Numbers, 1994*, Ministry of Housing, Planning and the Environment, The Hague (in Dutch).

VROM (1996) *Housing in Numbers 1995*, Ministry of Housing, Planning and the Environment, The Hague (in Dutch).

V&W (1994) *Structure Plan Surface Minerals*, Part 1, Ministry of Traffic and Public Works, The Hague (in Dutch).

White, R.R. (1994) *Urban Environmental Management: Environmental Change and Urban Design*, Wiley, Chichester.

Woltjer, J. (1995) Consensus-building in infrastructure planning, *Planologische Diskussiebijdragen*, part II, pp. 447–456 (in Dutch).

Chapter 7

Household Consumption, Quality of Life, and Environmental Impacts: A Psychological Perspective and Empirical Study

B. Gatersleben and Ch. Vlek

Abstract

Household consumption in the Netherlands has increased substantially since 1950. Many household activities have been mechanized, and more and more goods for personal development and entertainment have been produced and consumed. In this chapter we examine the factors underlying this increase in consumption, focusing on the Needs, Opportunities, and Abilities of consumers, following the NOA model. From a historical analysis of changes in Dutch household consumption, it appears that the opportunities to consume constitute an important factor. Because of increased opportunities, people increasingly satisfy their needs through consumer behavior. We have conducted a diagnostic and evaluative field study to examine the importance of the abilities and the needs components, and to evaluate household consumption patterns in terms of their environmental impacts. It is shown that the ability and the opportunity to consume are the most important factors underlying Dutch consumer behavior. When people possess a particular good it soon becomes a necessity to their household, which means that they are not willing to give it up. Household goods obviously contribute to the respondents' quality of life, by satisfying several needs. To the extent that goods are more important to them, respondents are less willing to change their behavior. The Dutch are well aware of the environmental impacts of their own behavior, although this has little effect on their willingness to change.

7.1. Introduction

Household metabolism may be described as the conversion of energy, water, materials, goods and services into various household functions and waste products. As shown in Chapter 2, both the indirect and direct uses of energy and water in the Netherlands have increased strongly over the last 40 years. In the social-psychological research described in this chapter we have studied the behavioral determinants (rather than the environmental effects) of household metabolism.

We try to understand the various social and psychological mechanisms underlying household consumption patterns over time (Diagnosis). We study the perceptions and attitudes of individuals concerning their environmental effects (Evaluation) and we investigate possible ways and means to arrive at "sustainable" consumption patterns (Change). We focus on the diagnosis and evaluation of household consumption patterns. We first give an overview of changes in household consumption since 1950, and then present a conceptual model comprising the Needs, Opportunities and Abilities (NOA) to consume, in order to arrive at a diagnosis of specific factors underlying consumer behavior. This is done both at the macro-level of society as a whole, and at the micro-level of the individual household. We present a short historical analysis of the various driving factors, followed by a methodological description of a field study in which household consumption patterns are studied in relation to the NOA concepts, as well as with regard to their environmental impacts. Most of this chapter is devoted to major results of our first empirical investigation.

For a representative coverage of household consumption we focus on five major household needs: living accommodation, personal hygiene, food storage/preparation, leisure activities within the home, and transportation, as shown in *Table 7.1*. More specifically, we consider the ownership (related to indirect energy consumption) and the use (direct energy consumption) of consumer goods for home heating, laundry, bathing, food storage/preparation, audiovisual entertainment, as well as the use of the computer at home, and the use of private cars.

7.2. Developments in Consumption Styles

As was shown in other chapters in this book, several major changes have taken place in Dutch household consumption since 1950 (see Gatersleben and Vlek, 1997 for a description following *Table 7.1*). In a study of the environmental impacts of changing consumption styles in six European countries and the USA, Uusitalo (1982) identified three major changes in Western consumption styles: modernization, enrichment, and the centrality of the automobile. Uusitalo showed that these three developments have increased the environmental impacts of household consumption in terms of the amount and composition of household waste, the amount and composition of energy used, the levels of environmental pollution and the rate

Table 7.1. Five categories of household needs.

	Accommodation	Personal hygiene	Food storage/preparation	Leisure time	Transportation
Ownership	Dwelling	Washing machine	Cooker	Video recorder	Car
	Heating equipment	Tumble dryer	Dishwasher	TV	Bicycle
		Spin dryer	Freezer	CD player	Motorbike
	Waterbed	Shower	Microwave oven	Stereo equipment	Moped
	Electric blanket	Bath	Food processor	Personal computer	
			Electric kettle	Fax machine	
Use of	Heating equipment	Washing machine	Cooking equipment	TV, video	Car, bicycle, etc.
		Shower and bath		Stereo, computer	Public transport

of resource depletion. The modernization of consumption, defined by Uusitalo as "the increased use of mass-produced goods and services", has two characteristics. The first is increased consumption of ready-made products or decreased home production of goods. The second characteristic, market efficiency, is described as an increased consumption of time-saving products. Uusitalo defined the enrichment of consumption as "the increased variety and many-sidedness of the consumption basket resulting from the higher amount of discretionary spending and leisure".

The modernization of Dutch household consumption patterns is reflected in the increased consumption of goods that make housekeeping tasks (heating, laundry, bathing, and cooking) easier, more comfortable and less time-consuming. For instance, 50 years ago, heating the home involved laborious activities such as emptying the ashes and carrying coal, whereas now only the thermostat of the central heating system needs to be turned up. Whereas in 1950 most people washed clothes by hand, today almost 100% of Dutch households possess a washing machine. There have also been major changes in the equipment used for cooking. The oil stove and the wood furnace have virtually disappeared; between 1947 and 1987 the number of households using a gas cooker increased by a factor of 5.7. Another example is the microwave oven; in 1985 such an appliance did not even exist, whereas in 1992 20% of Dutch households possessed one.

The enrichment of Dutch consumption styles may be found in the increased use of goods related to entertainment and personal development, particularly over the last 20 years. New goods are constantly being produced and bought (e.g., video recorders, CD players), and old ones discarded (e.g., the substitution of black and white for color TVs; see Chapter 2). In 1987 only 13% of Dutch consumers possessed a computer, compared with about 40% in 1997. Another important development related to the enrichment of consumption is the time and money spent on holidays. Between 1966 and 1980 the number of Dutch holidaymakers increased from 41% to 88%, and the number of times they went on holiday increased from an average of 1.24 to 1.58 per year. It was shown in Chapter 2 that private car ownership has increased substantially over the last 40 years, and the distances driven per capita per year have increased even more.

Due to these developments in household consumption styles, residential energy use and water use increased significantly since 1950, as well as the amounts of waste generated. More extensive overviews of the substantive changes in household consumption are given elsewhere in this volume. For an overview of recent historical developments in household consumption patterns, for the period 1950–1990, following *Table 7.1*, see Gatersleben and Vlek (1997).

7.3. Diagnosing Household Consumption: The NOA Model

To arrive at a synthesis of the main factors underlying consumer behavior we use the "Needs–Opportunities–Abilities" (NOA) model of consumer behavior (Vlek *et al.*,

1997). This model was inspired by the Motivation–Opportunities–Abilities (MOA) model of consumer behavior (Robben and Poiesz, 1992; Ölander and Thøgerson, 1994). To be able to better predict intentional consumer behavior, the latter authors extended the Fishbein–Ajzen theory of reasoned action (Fishbein and Ajzen, 1975) to include opportunity and ability components. In the MOA model, opportunities and abilities are seen as stimulating and limiting factors, respectively, which influence the relation between existing consumer motivation and behavior. However, we believe that opportunities can also evoke motivations; having the opportunity to buy might make people want to buy. Furthermore, abilities and opportunities give people the behavioral control to perform a given consumption act. In our view, consumer behavior is the result of consumer needs, opportunities, and abilities (see Vlek *et al.*, 1997; Jager *et al.*, 1997). Needs and opportunities together constitute the motivation to buy something, while opportunities and abilities together constitute the behavioral control needed to be able to buy.

Figure 7.1 presents the NOA model of consumer behavior. As can be seen, the motivation to consume results from certain consumer needs and opportunities to fulfill these needs. We presume that people have certain needs that they can satisfy only when they have the ability and the opportunity to do so. This is in line with the means–end chain theory of consumer behavior (Reynolds and Guttman, 1988; van Raaij, 1994), according to which people do not want goods for their own sake, but for what they can do for them. People therefore buy certain goods in order to satisfy needs, which might be satisfied in another (e.g., less energy-consuming) way as well. When people have a material opportunity to fulfill a need they may be motivated to use this opportunity and buy the good. For instance, when someone needs to express his or her identity or status to other people, and the opportunity arises to buy a special type of car, he or she may use this opportunity to satisfy the need. Being motivated to buy something, however, is not enough. The relevant opportunities (for instance, places where goods can be bought), and abilities (e.g., enough money) are also required. If either of the latter are not available, the person may become frustrated. Opportunities and abilities determine the degree of behavioral control people have. In order for a certain kind of consumer behavior to emerge, people need to have both the motivation and the behavioral control to do so.

Following *Figure 7.1*, the NOA model is embedded in a societal context by the addition of five general macro-level factors, which inevitably influence the individual behavior concepts. The societal context is divided into five kinds of driving forces: technology, economy, demography, institutions, and culture; the TEDIC complex (see Opschoor, 1989; Stern, 1992; Vlek, 1995).

Each of these aspects of the model is briefly described in the following. Wherever possible, we give a short historical description of each factor to indicate how it has influenced changes in Dutch household consumption. We then give a short

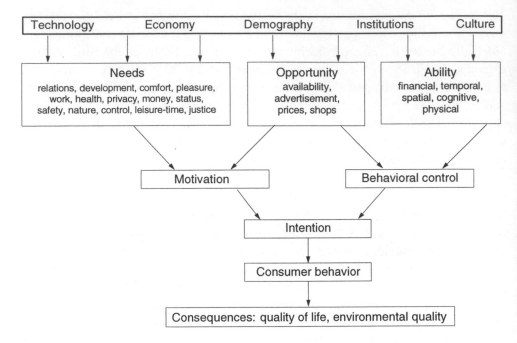

Figure 7.1. The Needs–Opportunity–Ability model of consumer behavior.

account of developments in the five macro-level forces. For a more extensive
overview, see Gatersleben and Vlek (1997).

7.3.1. Needs

Individuals pursue a number of objectives in order to maintain or improve their
"quality of life" or "well-being". Many theorists have tried to formulate lists
of these objectives, under different names such as basic needs (Maslow, 1954,
Max-Neef, 1992, Allardt, 1994), instincts (McDougall, 1932), values (Rokeach,
1979), quality of life indicators, and indicators of well-being at both the individual
level (Andrews and Whitney, 1976; Campbell *et al.*, 1976), and at a societal level
(OECD, 1976; Henderson, 1994).

Hareide (1994), for instance, described the variables that make life worth
living: social relations, health, nature and environment, meaningful work, and
material possessions. Allardt (1994) studied the central conditions necessary for
human development and existence, which he formulated as "having" (material
conditions), "loving" (social relations) and "being" (personal growth). McDougall
(1932) listed 18 propensities or instincts, such as "to seek food", "to shelter the
young", or "to wander to new scenes". Maslow (1954) formulated a "hierarchical
theory of needs" in which needs (like McDougall's instincts) were divided into five
hierarchical levels (physiological, safety, a feeling of belonging, self-esteem and

self-actualization). Rokeach (1979) created the Rokeach value survey in which he formulated 18 terminal values (such as "a comfortable life", "a world of beauty", and "social recognition") and 18 instrumental values (personality characteristics, such as responsible, independent and loving) to achieve the end values. This theory has been related to means–end theory in describing and defining consumer behavior and consumer lifestyles (de Bruin *et al.*, 1993; Breemhaar *et al.*, 1995). By doing so, lifestyles are described as means–end chains. The relative importance of end values directs choices in the consumption process, because of which individuals differ and their behaviors can be grouped into consumer lifestyles.

Whereas the Rokeach values are seen as end goals in life, social indicators research, following the tradition of Diener (1993, 1995a,b,c), Veenhoven (1989, 1994), Inglehart (1990) and Easterlin (1974, 1995) add one more step. The final goal in this tradition is well-being, happiness, or quality of life. Social indicators are used to measure the level of well-being or happiness of individuals (Andrews and Whitney, 1976; Campbell *et al.*, 1976) and individuals within societies (OECD, 1976; Henderson, 1994). We can distinguish personal indicators such as health, safety, education, labor, and leisure time; environmental indicators such as the physical and social environment, and culture; and economic indicators such as the availability of goods and services and mobility. So far, emphasis has been given to economic indicators of well-being. The GNP, for instance, is still the most important indicator of the level of (economic) well-being of a nation. A number of studies have shown that people in rich countries are indeed, on average, happier than people in poorer countries (Veenhoven, 1989, 1994; Diener, 1993, 1995a,b,c; Inglehart, 1990; Easterlin, 1974, 1995). Furthermore, within countries, these studies have found a small, but consistent correlation between income and happiness. Several authors, however, have tried to focus on social rather than economic indicators (e.g., Henderson, 1994).

On the basis of various studies on social indicators, as well as the need and value theories discussed above, we have drawn up a list of 15 indicators of well-being or quality of life (see *Table 7.2*). We believe that this list provides a reasonably representative range of aspects that are important to individuals in Western consumer societies.

7.3.2.   Opportunities

Opportunities can be seen as a set of external facilitating conditions, such as the objective availability of goods, materials and services, their accessibility, the relevant information that is available, and prices. As noted above, many goods and services are now available that did not exist 50 years ago. Furthermore, the increased availability of some goods and services makes it possible or impossible to consume others; for example, the substitution of LPs by CDs has meant that it is

Table 7.2. The 15 major quality of life aspects; see also the motivation component in *Figure 7.1*

Social relations	Having good relations with friends, colleagues, neighbors and family; having the opportunity to improve these relations and to make new ones.
Development/education	Having the opportunity to get a good education and to develop one's general knowledge.
Comfort	Having a comfortable and easy daily life.
Pleasure/arousal	Experiencing nice, enjoyable and exciting things in daily life.
Beauty	Being able to have and enjoy beautiful things in and around the house.
Work/labor	Having or being able to find a pleasant and good job, and being able to perform that job pleasantly and as well as possible.
Health	Being in good health; having access to adequate health care.
Privacy	Having the opportunity to be yourself, to do your own thing, and to have a place of your own.
Money	Having enough money to buy and do the things that are necessary and pleasing.
Status	Being appreciated by others because of your skills, achievements and possessions.
Safety	Personal safety in and around the house, and being protected from crime and accidents on the streets and in the house.
Nature/environment	Clean air, water and soil; healthy plants and animals.
Freedom/control	Freedom and control over the course of one's own life, to be able to decide for yourself, what you do, and when and how.
Leisure time	Having enough leisure time.
Social justice	Having equal opportunities and rights to own and do things.

now almost impossible to by recorded music on LPs. Because of decreasing prices (relative to income) and the opportunity to buy on credit, consumption has grown as well. The range and number of outlets where these goods and services can be bought (e.g., mail order or via TV home shopping) have also increased.

7.3.3. Abilities

The abilities of consumers are described as the set of internal capacities of an individual or household to procure goods and services. These abilities include the financial, temporal, spatial, cognitive, and physical means and skills. Financial abilities refer to the incomes of consumers. The Dutch today are able to spend almost twice as much money in real terms as they did in 1950, and the availability of credit, loans, and instalment plans means that they are able to buy things that they cannot immediately afford. Temporal abilities refer to the time available for consumption; for instance, people now have more time to take holidays. Spatial ability refers to the amount of space within the home to store goods, as well as to the distance of the household to relevant shops and services. More people now live in larger dwellings, with fewer people per household, and the car provides easy access to work and shops. Physical capacity refers to health, fitness and strength, and to the possession of licenses and permits.

7.3.4. Macro-level factors

Developments in technology, economy, demography, institutions and culture (see *Figure 7.1*) have influenced changes in consumer behavior by changing abilities, opportunities, and consumer needs. Technological and economic developments, for instance, have increased opportunities because more services and materials are available now than 50 years ago, while due to mass production, people's actual abilities and opportunities have increased because of falling prices. Not only are more goods available, but there are also more people to consume them. Demographic developments can therefore be seen as having a multiplier effect on consumption.

Technological and economic developments have so far yielded several impressive benefits, such as the reduction of poverty and better standards of living. Society keeps striving for further economic and technological growth, as can be seen in the way in which society is organized into social structures and institutions. Consumption and consumption growth have also penetrated into cultural norms and values, in that for many people, their sense of well-being depends to a large extent on their earnings and possessions, and perception of others is influenced by their material possessions. The importance of nature tends to have been reduced to the extent that it is able to serve human needs (see Gatersleben and Vlek, 1997).

7.4. Household Consumption Patterns: A Field Study

From the above description of changes in Dutch household consumption it would appear that the availability of opportunities to consume constitute an important factor underlying consumer behavior. Because of increased opportunities, people increasingly satisfy their needs through consumer behavior. In the diagnostic and evaluative field study described in the following, we assess the importance of the abilities and the needs components. We also examine and evaluate household consumption patterns in terms of their environmental impacts. First, we list the specific research questions, the design of the study and the research methods used, and then present and discuss the main results.

7.4.1.   Research questions on consumer behavior

The research questions address two major topics: diagnosing the underlying mechanisms of household consumer behavior, and evaluating this behavior in terms of environmental impacts.

Concerning the diagnosis we studied whether different household consumption patterns are related to different household consumer abilities (e.g., income, level of education, and where they live), and consumer needs (as expressed in quality of life aspects). First, we asked a representative sample of Dutch households about which goods they possess and use. The specific research questions were as follows:

1.   (a) What are the penetration rates of different household goods, concerning accommodation, personal hygiene, food storage/preparation, leisure activities, and transportation?
     (b) How frequently and intensively are the various goods used?

Second, we studied whether the respondents' consumption patterns differed according to the household composition and their abilities.

2. To what extent can differences between consumption patterns be explained by differences in household composition (and age) and respondents' consumer abilities (income, level of education, and where they live)?

To get an idea of the changes in household consumption, the respondents were also asked what goods they possessed in the past, and what they expected to possess in the future.

3.   (a) What goods did Dutch consumers possess in the past?
     (b) What goods do Dutch consumers think they will possess in the future?

We asked the respondents about the importance they attached to various household goods: whether they perceived them as a necessity or a luxury. According to adaptation level theory, people become used to the things they possess, and do not want to lose them, while at the same time they are looking out for new things. This would mean that once people possess a good, they are more likely to regard it as a necessity; the goods they do not yet possess may only be desirable to them.

4.   (a) To what extent are various household goods regarded as a necessity or an unnecessary luxury for the household?

(b) To what extent does the evaluation of a good as a necessity depend on the actual possession of the good?

According to means–end chain theory people do not want goods for their own sake but for what they can do for them. Household goods contribute to the satisfaction of certain needs or quality of life requirements. The possession of a household good may then be explained by the extent to which it contributes to the satisfaction of certain important quality of life aspects of the individual.

5. (a) What aspects are important to people's quality of life?
    (b) To what extent do certain household goods contribute to satisfying these aspects?
    (c) To what extent can the possession of a household good be explained by the extent to which it contributes to the quality of life of the individual?

Apart from studying what household goods Dutch consumers possess and how they use them, we also examined how they evaluate the environmental impacts of their own behavior.

6. (a) What do people perceive to be the environmental effects of their own households?
    (b) To what extent can differences in these evaluations be explained by people's actual possession and use of household goods?

We also studied whether the respondents think it is necessary and possible to change their household's behavior, and to what extent they would be willing to change. We asked to what extent the willingness to change depends on the perceived impact of the household on the environment, their attitudes concerning the necessity and possibility to change, and the importance of several goods to their quality of life (question 5b).

7. To what extent do people think it is necessary and possible to change household consumer behavior in view of its environmental impacts?
8. (a) To what extent would people be willing to change their household consumer behavior?
    (b) To what extent does people's willingness to change depend on differences in their perceptions of the environmental impacts of their own household, of the necessity and possibility to change, and of the importance of relevant household goods to their quality of life?

Figure 7.2 shows the main concepts of the field study and the interrelations studied; the numbers refer to the eight research questions listed above.

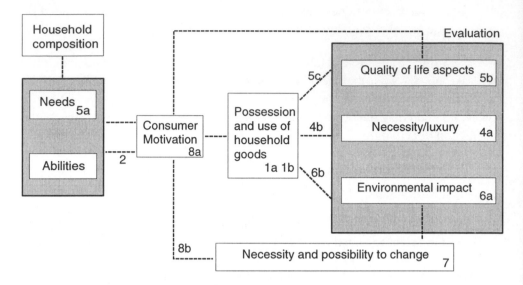

Figure 7.2. The major research concepts and their relations: the research questions.

7.4.2. Method

A total of 1746 randomly selected Dutch households participated in the field study, of which 496 were interviewed personally and 1250 later completed a written questionnaire. In the rest of this chapter we present the methods and results of the interview study. The questionnaire survey was mostly a large-scale replication of this interview study; the methods and results will be reported elsewhere.

Procedure

The 496 home interviews were conducted in November and December 1995 in three areas of the Netherlands (north, southeast, west). The interviewees were selected on the basis of postal codes. Within these regions an *a priori* selection was made of respondents in four age groups (a variable related to household composition), three income groups, and two types of residential area (rural and urban). In each of the three areas 9–13 interviewers were trained to conduct 15–20 structured interviews each. All of the interviewers had previous general interview practice or training, and most of them had interview experience. Specific training was provided to ensure that they would interpret and handle the interview questions and possible problems adequately and consistently. Each interviewer was then given a list of the names, addresses and telephone numbers of candidate respondents. These invitees had been sent a letter informing them about the study and that they would be phoned in a few days to ask them to participate. Each interviewer called several respondents and asked them a number of questions in advance to make sure that

Table 7.3. Personal interview questions.

A.	Possession of 39 household goods
B.	Necessity of 39 goods
C.	Ranking of 15 quality of life aspects
D.	Possession and use of dwelling
E.	Possession and use of car
F.	Possession and use of washing machine, bathing facilities
G.	Possession and use of home heating equipment
H.	Possession and use of cooking equipment
I.	Possession and use of audio/video equipment
J.	Possession and use of computer equipment
K.	Multi-attribute evaluation of 5 goods in relation to 15 quality of life aspects
L.	Perception of environmental impacts of household behavior
M.	Necessity and possibility to change consumer behavior
N.	Willingness to change consumer behavior
O.	Past and future possession of household goods
P.	Demographic questions (sex, age, income, level of education, etc.)
Q.	Questionnaire evaluation

an even number of men and women, of different income groups and different age groups would be interviewed. If a respondent met the requirements and was willing to participate, an appointment was made and the interviewer visited the respondent at his or her home. Each interview lasted about 90 minutes.

The Interviews

The questionnaire used for the interviews consisted of 18 parts (A–Q; see *Table 7.3*). In part A, the respondents were asked to indicate which items on a list of 39 household goods they possessed. The list included goods from each of the five consumption categories shown in *Table 7.1*. A number of goods had been deliberately selected because less than 40% of Dutch households in 1993 possessed them (VEEN, 1994). The response pattern therefore gives an indication of the material luxury and novelty of the household. In part B, the respondents were asked which of these same 39 goods they regarded as either necessary or an unnecessary luxury. In part C, the respondents were asked to rank the list of 15 quality of life aspects (see *Table 7.2*) in order of importance to their household's quality of life. Parts D–J contained questions about their homes, and about the possession and use of five household facilities. Two parts (D and G) focused on accommodation; part E on transportation; part F on personal hygiene; part H on food storage/preparation; and parts I and J on leisure activities. In part K, the respondents were asked to evaluate five of their possessions (major consumer goods) in terms of their contribution to the 15 quality of life aspects in *Table 7.2*. For each aspect, the respondents were asked to what extent their car, washing machine, home heating equipment, cooking equipment and audiovisual equipment contributed to their quality of life. Part L contained questions about respondents' perceptions of the environmental impacts of their own household. The questions in part M asked about the necessity and the possibility to change household consumption patterns in a "sustainable" direction (i.e., moderation). In part N respondents were asked about the things they already did, had done, or would be willing to do to reduce the environmental impacts of their household. Part O consisted of the same list of household goods as used in part A. Respondents aged 45 years or younger were asked what items they thought they would possess in 20 years' time; those aged over 45 years were asked what they possessed 20 years ago. The questionnaire ended with demographic questions about the household and the respondent, and some questions to evaluate the questionnaire itself.

The Respondents

A total of 496 Dutch households were interviewed; 195 from the north of Holland (in and around Groningen), 131 from the west (Leiden, Amsterdam, The Hague, and Rotterdam), and 170 from the south/southeast (Nijmegen, Eindhoven). About 30% of the households who were sent a letter (about 1500) actually participated. The non-responses were mainly due to incorrect phone numbers on the address lists, no answers after repeated phone calls, and households who did not meet the study requirements (in terms of household composition, age or income). Of the households that could be reached and who met the requirements, 30% refused to cooperate, usually because of lack of time. The mean age of the respondents was 47 years. About 27% of the respondents said they worked full time and 25% part-time; others were retired, or otherwise unemployed (or occupied as housewife/man or studying).

Table 7.4 shows several characteristics of the respondents who participated in the interview study and the actual composition of the Dutch population in 1996 (taken from CBS, 1996). As can be seen, respondents aged 40–64 years were over-represented, and the age group 0–19 was under-represented, for obvious reasons. Women were also over-represented, which again is not surprising, since they were most likely to be able to participate in a 90 minute interview. The average level of education was above the general population average.

7.4.3. Results

We now present the response patterns for each part of the questionnaire. The differences between respondent groups according to household composition and age are described, and those according to their abilities (income, level of education, and where they live). We first present the results on the possession and use of

Table 7.4. Characteristics of the sample respondents compared with a national sample (%).

		Study sample interviews ($n = 496$)	National sample (CBS)	
Age	0–19	0.0	24.0	
	20–39	37.4	32.0	
	40–64	46.3	30.0	
	65–79	13.3	10.0	
	80+	3.0	3.0	
Sex	Male	38.0	49.5	
	Female	62.0	50.5	
Household size	1 person	25.2	31.3	
	2 persons	39.7	33.2	
	3 more persons	35.1	35.6	
Level of education[a]	Low	17.9	47.2	
	Intermediate	31.7	42.2	
	High	50.4	25.1	
Monthly income[b]		4.1	2731	
Residential location[c]	Rural	54.5	Rural	18.7
			Low	20.7
			Medium	20.8
	Urban	45.5	High	20.7
			Very high	19.1

[a]Level of education: low = primary and secondary school, low vocational education, mid = lower general, intermediate vocational or technical, high = higher general, pre-university, high vocational, university.
[b]Monthly income: 7-point scale: 1 = less than Dfl 1000 per month; 7 = more than Dfl 6000 per month; thus 4.1 is about Dfl 3000 per month (in mid-1997, Dfl 100 = US$51 = £31).
[c]Here and in subsequent tables, "residential location" refers to the degree of urbanization of the area in which the respondent's household is situated; defined as the number of addresses per km^2.

household goods and their contribution to the quality of life (parts A–K), and then the results of the questions on environmental impacts (parts L–N).

Possession of Household Goods: Part A

What are the penetration rates of different household goods concerning accommodation, personal hygiene, food storage/preparation, leisure time activities, and transportation? It is beyond the scope of this chapter to describe the results on all the 39 household goods separately. To reduce the amount of data, we investigated whether the 39 variables could be clustered into a smaller number of consumption patterns, but no interpretable clusters could be distinguished. We therefore focused

Table 7.5. Possession (penetration) rates of household goods in the five main consumption categories.

(a)

	Overall mean	Household type ($F = 12.5$, $df = 24$, $p < 0.00$)			Age of respondents ($F = 3.4$, $df = 36$, $p < 0.00$)			
		Single $n = 171$	Couple $n = 104$	Family $n = 166$	<33 $n = 102$	34–45 $n = 119$	46–59 $n = 119$	60+ $n = 101$
Size of dwelling (no. of rooms)	4.2	3.5	4.7	5.2**	3.9	4.7	4.8	4.4**
Central heating system	51	38	50	63	46	61	56	37
Heating appliance	26	37	28	16	35	16	19	44
Washing machine	97	88	99	102**	95	100	98	96
Tumble dryer	46	20	43	71**	37	62	53	31
Microwave	52	37	47	71**	54	65	54	40
Dishwasher	28	11	27	41	24	36	35	13
TV	148	110	138	189**	141	167	164	117
Video recorder	72	46	69	95**	75	93	73	46*
Computer	65	41	56	93**	75	85	77	19**
Car	93	54	96	116*	92	99	103	75
Bicycle	267	121	224	427**	236	373	285	166**

(b)

	Income $(F = 5.1, df = 24, p < 0.00)$			Education $(F = 1.2, df = 24, p =ns)$			Residential location $(F = 4.3, df = 12, p < 0.00)$	
	Low $n = 171$	Mid $n = 104$	High $n = 166$	Low $n = 75$	Mid $n = 143$	High $n = 223$	Rural $n = 235$	Urban $n = 206$
Size of dwelling (no. of rooms)	3.8	4.5	5.1**	4.1	4.6	4.5	5.0	4.0**
Central heating system	38	51	64*	36	55	55	58	43
Heating appliance	43	28	9**	33	26	24	23	30
Washing machine	92	99	101*	96	99	97	99	96
Tumble dryer	34	45	62	41	53	46	57	36*
Microwave	35	57	70**	42	57	54	63	44**
Dishwasher	11	27	46**	21	24	33	35	20
TV	123	162	169*	144	159	144	164	134*
Video recorder	53	84	85*	62	76	73	79	66
Computer	35	65	97**	29	56	82*	65	64
Car	59	98	125**	82	94	95	111	77**
Bicycle	222	250	335	253	294	260	312	225*

Note: The numbers of respondents do not add to 496 due to missing values.
* < 0.05; ** < 0.01.

on the most representative goods in the categories listed in *Table 7.1*. For the first category, accommodation, we considered the number of rooms in the home as representing the spatial aspect of the household (see Section 7.3.3), and the possession of a central heating system and heating appliances as relevant home heating equipment. For the second category, personal hygiene, we looked at the possession of a washing machine and tumble dryer. For the third category, food storage/preparation, we considered the possession of a microwave oven and dish-washer. Concerning leisure time activities, we considered the possession of a TV, video recorder and personal computer. For the last category, transportation, we used the possession of a car and a bicycle.

Table 7.5 shows the mean penetration rates of each of these goods among the respondent groups. The first column of *Table 7.5(a)* shows the overall means for the possession of household goods, and the other columns show the results for the different household types and age groups. *Table 7.5(b)* shows the results according to income, education, and where they live. Note that the penetration rates (number of goods per 100 households) can be more than 100 for items such as the TV and the bicycle, although this does not mean that every household has a TV or a bicycle. The differences between respondent groups were analyzed with one multivariate analysis of covariance per respondent variable. With these analyses, differences between respondents in one of the respondent variables were studied, and at the same time correlations with other respondent variables were controlled. The upper rows of *Tables 7.5(a)* and *(b)* show the multivariate tests of significance. If this test is significant ($p < 0.05$, which depends on the F and df values; the larger the F-value, the stronger the effect), this means that the respondent groups (e.g., income groups) differ on the total set of dependent variables (possession of items). The second row of each column gives the number of respondents for which the analysis was done. Note that the numbers of respondents do not add to 496 due to missing values in the dependent or independent variables.

As can be seen in *Table 7.5*, the largest differences in the possession rates of household goods occur between income groups and household types. Higher-income groups and families possess more of almost everything. Better-educated respondents more often possess a personal computer. Middle-aged respondents live in the largest houses, young ones in the smallest. The oldest respondents least often possess a video recorder, a computer and bicycles. Respondents living in urban areas less often possess a clothes dryer or a microwave oven.

Necessity or Luxury of Household Goods: Part B

In part B of the interviews, the respondents were asked to study the list of goods used in part A once gain, and to indicate which goods they regarded as necessary or a luxury for their own households. *Table 7.6* shows the percentage of respondents who indicated that a particular household good was a necessity for them. The first column of *Table 7.6(a)* shows the scores for all respondents. Only heating appliances and dishwashers are "necessary" to less than 50% of households. The goods that most respondents regard as necessary are the washing machine and the TV. *Table 7.6* also shows the results for the different respondent groups; we examined whether these percentages differ significantly by conducting a number of chi-squared tests. *Table 7.6(a)* shows that a higher percentage of households with children said the central heating system, the microwave oven, the dishwasher, the computer, the car and the bicycle were necessary than households without children. Respondents aged 34–45 years more often regard the central heating system, the microwave oven and the video recorder as necessary. *Table 7.6(b)* shows that most goods, except for heating appliances, are more necessary to high-income groups than to low-income groups. There are few differences between respondents according to the level of education. The computer is more often evaluated as a necessity by better educated than by less well educated respondents. The last two columns of *Table 7.6(b)* show that the central heating system, tumble dryer, microwave oven, TV, video recorder, and the car are necessary to more people living in rural areas than those living in urban areas.

Comparing *Tables 7.6* and *7.5*, it appears that respondents who indicated that a good is necessary to their household, also possessed the good more often. To study the extent to which the evaluation of the goods as a necessity or a luxury depends on the actual possession of the good, a number of correlations were computed. *Table 7.7* again shows the overall possession rates of the same goods listed in *Table 7.5*, together with the percentage of respondents who own at least one of them (these numbers can therefore never exceed 100%), and the percentage of respondents who said the good is necessary to them. The third column then provides the phi-correlation coefficient between these two variables. The phi-coefficient (a fourfold point correlation) is a measure of the association between two variables having two categories each (possess/not possess for part A, necessary/luxury for part B). All correlations are significant at the 1% level. From these correlations it appears that if the respondents possessed a good, they more often regarded it as a necessity to them, whereas those who did not possess one more often regarded it as an unnecessary luxury. The highest correlations in *Table 7.7* were found for the tumble dryer, the computer and the car. The lowest correlations were found for the washing machine and the central heating system. The low correlation for the washing machine is probably due to a ceiling effect, because almost all households possess one.

Use of Household Goods: Parts D–J

In parts D–J of the interview, the respondents were asked a number of questions about their use of household goods. Again, it is beyond the scope of this chapter to describe the responses to all questions, so we focus on one or two items from each consumption category in *Table 7.1*. These items mostly concern the intensity of use

Table 7.6. Respondents' evaluation of household goods as a necessity (%).

(a)

	Overall mean	Household type			Age of respondents			
		Single $n = 124$	Couple $n = 191$	Family $n = 174$	< 33 $n = 117$	34–45 $n = 131$	46–59 $n = 130$	60+ $n = 110$
Central heating system	92	84	93	98**	91	98	94	86**
Heating appliance	48	53	48	45	51	44	49	49
Washing machine	99	97	100	99	99	100	98	98
Tumble dryer	62	48	58	76**	60	69	65	53
Microwave	62	52	58	74**	63	70	65	48**
Dishwasher	35	22	31	48**	34	43	34	26
TV	96	94	97	96	93	95	98	99
Video recorder	73	64	71	82**	74	80	76	60**
Computer	59	46	55	73***	71	77	64	18**
Car	84	70	85	92**	80	87	89	77
Bicycle	96	93	97	98*	97	99	99	90**

(b)

	Income			Education				Residential location	
	Low	Mid	High	Low	Mid	High		Rural	Urban
	n = 186	n = 114	n = 169	n = 87	n = 155	n = 247		n = 255	n = 224
Central heating system	87	91	98**	88	95	92		89	96*
Heating appliance	55	47	41*	52	48	47		48	48
Washing machine	99	93	99	100	98	99		99	99
Tumble dryer	57	60	69*	60	65	61		55	69**
Microwave	52	68	69**	62	65	60		57	68**
Dishwasher	23	27	51**	32	30	39		30	39
TV	96	97	96	98	98	94		94	98*
Video recorder	67	76	78	67	79	72		69	77*
Computer	42	54	82**	24	52	76**		59	60
Car	74	85	92**	81	86	83		76	93**
	95	97	98	97	96	96		95	97

Note: The numbers of respondents do not add to 496 due to missing values.
* < 0.05; ** < 0.01.

Table 7.7. Ownership of household goods and facilities (i.e., households that possess at least one), their perceived necessity, and the correlation between these variables.

Household good	Possession rate (%)	Necessity score	Phi correlation
Central heating system	51	92	0.25
Heating appliance	17	48	0.40
Washing machine	96	99	0.27
Tumble dryer	46	62	0.58
Microwave oven	52	62	0.47
Dishwasher	28	35	0.47
TV set	98	96	0.40
Video recorder	67	73	0.46
Computer	54	59	0.62
Car	77	84	0.57
Bicycle	95	96	0.44

of the household goods mentioned in *Table 7.5*. From the category accommodation we considered the temperature to which people heat their homes. Concerning personal hygiene, we focused on how often respondents wash their laundry per week and how often they take a bath or shower per week. The number of times per week respondents use a microwave oven and a dishwasher were considered for the category food storage/preparation. Concerning leisure activities, we considered the number of hours respondents watch TV, use a video recorder and home computer, and the number of holidays taken in the year before the study. Concerning transportation, we looked at the distances driven per year with the car that was used most by the household, as well as the distances driven to and from work. The differences between respondent groups were analyzed with a number of multivariate analyses of variance; the results are shown in *Table 7.8*.

It appears that the use of various household goods differs mostly between different income groups and household types. *Table 7.8(a)* shows that larger households use a microwave oven more often, watch more TV and more videos, and use their computer more often. Members of larger households bathe or shower less often than those in smaller households; the youngest respondents bathe the most, the oldest the least. The latter also wash laundry less often and use the car less. *Table 7.8(b)* shows that high-income groups more often use a microwave oven, a dishwasher and a personal computer. Surprisingly, higher-income groups watch less TV per day, even though they possess more TV sets (see *Table 7.5(b)*). The use of the car differs greatly between income groups. High-income groups not only possess more cars, they also seem to use them more, especially for commuting. The same goes for differences between respondents living in urban and rural areas; those living in rural areas drive greater distances, probably because they live further away from facilities and from their work. *Table 7.8(b)* also shows a number of differences according to the level of education. Better-educated respondents bathe more often, watch less TV, and use a computer more often than those with a lower level of education.

The differences between respondent groups in the use of household goods probably depend to a large extent on the possession of those goods. To study this, we computed a Pearson correlation coefficient between the possession and use of each good, as shown in the second column of *Table 7.8(a)*. The use of the microwave oven, dishwasher, and computer depends to a large extent on the possession of these goods, especially the dishwasher. The use of a video recorder and car depends to some extent on the possession of these goods. The home heating temperature and the number of times respondents wash laundry do not depend on the possession of a central heating system or washing machine, respectively. The number of hours respondents watch TV and the distances they drive to and from work depend to only a small extent on the possession of a TV and a car, respectively.

Past and Future Possession of Household Goods: Part O

In part O of the interview, respondents aged over 45 years were asked which of the 39 goods listed in part A they possessed 20 years ago, and those aged less than 45 years were asked which goods they thought they would possess in 20 years' time. *Table 7.9* shows the responses, and the percentages of respondents in each age group who said they possessed the good at the time of the interview. Again, not all 39 goods are reported in *Table 7.9*.

When the first two columns of *Table 7.9* are compared, it can be seen that for most goods (except for heating appliances, the washing machine, TV, and bicycle) the possession rates increased between 1975 and 1995, probably because these goods have become more easily available. When the last two columns of the *Table 7.9* are compared, it can be seen that the possession of most goods can be expected to keep on growing. For a number of goods, however, the number of respondents who said they expected to possess the good in 2015 was no higher than the number of people who possessed it in 1995. This holds both for goods that almost everyone owns today (washing machine, TV), as well as for some that are not so widely owned, such as the tumble dryer, video recorder, and computer; these items therefore appear to have reached saturation. The possession of heating appliances decreases steadily over time, from 1975 to 1995 and up to 2015.

For most goods the described trends are evident both within and (for the present) between the two groups. When the present possession rates of the two groups are compared, it can be seen that younger respondents possess most goods more often. It was shown in *Table 7.5(a)* that respondents in the 33–45 age group possess goods more often than either the younger or older respondents. Respondents aged over 60 years possess the fewest of those goods.

Table 7.8. Intensity of use of household goods and facilities.

(a)

	Overall mean	Correlation[a]	Household type ($F = 4.4$, df $= 22$, $p < 0.00$)			Age of respondents ($F = 3.7$, df $= 33$, $p < 0.00$)			
			Single n = 95	Couple n = 178	Family n = 157	< 33 n = 99	34–45 n = 113	46–59 n = 118	60+ n = 100
Home heating temp. (°C)	19.6	0.04	19.5	19.7	19.6	19.7	19.6	19.5	19.7
Washing machine (pp pw)	1.6	0.03	1.6	1.4	1.7	1.7	1.7	1.6	1.1**
Bathing (pp pw)	5.3	–	5.7	5.2	5.2*	6.1	5.7	5.7	3.7**
Microwave (pw)	4.0	0.62**	2.7	3.0	6.5**	4.3	5.9	4.2	2.3
Dishwasher (pw)[b]	1.6	0.93**	1.3	1.9	1.8	1.3	1.4	2.8	1.4
TV (hours/day)	4.0	0.19*	3.4	3.8	4.7**	3.8	3.9	4.1	4.1
Video (hours/day)	2.6	0.36**	1.3	2.0	4.3**	3.1	3.6	2.6	1.4
Computer (hours/day)	4.5	0.58**	2.9	3.1	7.7**	4.6	6.4	6.3	0.9*
Car (km/year)	13.5	0.44**	7.6	14.3	17.8	15.5	15.6	16.6	8.1**
Work (km)	6.3	0.14*	3.0	6.0	9.8	10.1	7.8	7.7	0.9
Holidays (no./year)	1.8	–	1.6	1.9	1.9	1.8	1.8	2.1	1.4

(b)

	Income (F = 3.6, df = 22, p < 0.00)			Education (F = 2.9, df = 22, p < 0.00)			Residential location (F = 2.1, df = 11, p < 0.05)	
	Low n = 159	Mid n = 105	High n = 166	Low n = 70	Mid n = 142	High n = 218	Rural n = 220	Urban n = 210
Home heating temp. (°C)	19.7	19.6	19.6	19.9	19.7	19.6	19.6	19.6
Washing machine (pp pw)	1.5	1.7	1.6	1.7	2.0	1.5*	1.6	1.6
Bathing (pp pw)	4.8	5.4	5.7	4.1	4.9	6.0*	5.0	5.7
Microwave (pw)	2.3	3.7	6.4**	2.3	4.3	4.8	5.1	5.7
Dishwasher (pw)[b]	0.9	2.4	2.1*	1.2	2.1	1.7	2.1	1.4
TV (hours/day)	4.4	4.2	3.5**	5.3	4.6	3.2**	4.1	3.9
Video (hours/day)	2.1	3.4	2.8	2.7	3.3	2.3	3.1	2.3
Computer (hours/day)	2.3	3.6	7.7**	1.3	3.7	6.4*	4.8	4.6
Car (km/year)	7.9	12.9	20.7**	8.7	13.5	16.2	17.1	11.2**
Work (km/year)	0.9	6.2	10.6**	3.6	6.5	7.9	8.4	5.1*
Holidays (no./year)	1.5	1.7	2.1	1.7	1.5	2.1	1.7	1.9

Note: The numbers of respondents do not add to 496 due to missing values.
[a] Correlation between these use variables and the possession of a central heating system, washing machine, microwave oven, dishwasher, TV set, video recorder, computer, and car, respectively (see *Table 7.5*).
[b] Frequency of use on a four-point scale; 0=never, 1=less than once per week, 2=one to three times per week, 3=four to seven times per week, 4=more than once per day.
* < 0.05; ** < 0.01.

Table 7.9. Past and future possession of household goods: the percentage of older respondents who owned each item 20 years ago, and younger respondents who expect to own each item in 20 years' time.

	Older than 45 ($n = 231$)		Younger than 46 ($n = 261$)	
	Past (1975)	Present (1995)	Present (1995)	Future (2015)
Central heating system	6.1	44.6	53.3	84.3
Heating appliance	34.2	19.5	15.3	4.6
Washing machine	90.5	91.8	96.6	96.6
Tumble dryer	13.4	41.1	50.6	55.9
Dishwasher	14.7	23.8	31.4	36.0
Microwave oven	–	45.0	59.4	95.4
TV set	43.7[a] 55.2[b]	99.1[a]	96.6	95.4
Video recorder	5.6	57.6	75.1	77.0
Computer	1.7	38.5	71.6	68.2
Car	18.1	77.5	77.0	83.1
Bicycle	93.1	94.4	98.1	97.3

[a]Color TV.
[b]Black and white TV.

Ranking Aspects of Quality of Life: Part C

In part C of the interview, the respondents were asked to rank a list of 15 quality of life aspects in order of importance to the overall quality of life of their households; see *Table 7.2*. The first column of *Table 7.10(a)* shows the overall mean ranking of these aspects. It appears that health is valued most, followed by social relations, and nature and the environment. Having beautiful things in and around the house is the least important aspect overall. The other columns in *Table 7.10* show the differences between various respondent groups in the mean rankings of the 15 aspects. To study whether these differences are significant, we conducted a non-parametric Kruskall–Wallis analysis of variance. As can be seen in *Table 7.10(a)*, respondents living in larger households (with children) value health, safety, work, and personal development more than those who live alone; freedom, privacy and beauty are less important to them. The youngest respondents value nature, privacy, safety, and comfort the least. The two middle age groups value social relations less than the younger and older respondents. The oldest respondents value privacy, safety, comfort and beauty more than the other age groups, especially the youngest. The oldest respondents value work, development, and leisure time less than the other age groups, especially the youngest. *Table 7.10(b)* shows that low-income groups value health, work and development less than the other income groups. The higher the respondents' level of education, the more important are freedom, work and development, and the less important are safety and comfort. Respondents who received either a low or a high level of education value health less than those with an intermediate education. Respondents living in rural areas value health, nature, and safety more than those living in cities. Freedom is less important to them than it is for city dwellers.

To study whether respondents rely on any underlying dimensions when evaluating what aspects are important to their quality of life, we conducted a principal components by alternating least squares analysis (Princals); the results are shown in *Table 7.11*. The upper row of the table gives the eigenvalue of each dimension and the interpretation of the dimension. The numbers in the columns show the component loadings of each quality of life aspect on the three dimensions. The three dimensions of the Princals solution explain only 41% of the total variance in the rankings of the 15 quality of life aspects. The first dimension explains 17% (the eigenvalue), the second dimension explains 13%, and the third dimension explains 11%. To be "significant", the eigenvalue should be more than $1/15 = 0.07$. Five dimensions could be found according to this criterion, although the fourth and fifth dimensions could not be given a useful interpretation. As can be seen in *Table 7.11*, the aspects development and work have high negative loadings on the first dimension, the aspects comfort and beauty load positively on this dimension. This first dimension is interpreted as conservative versus progressive. The second dimension distinguishes responsibility (good health, safety) and hedonistic aspects (experiencing pleasure, leisure time). The third dimension is characterized by having social relations and experiencing social recognition versus having privacy and freedom and control over the course of one's life; this dimension is described as social versus individual orientation.

We investigated how the various respondent groups differ on these dimensions by conducting several multivariate analyses of variance; the results are shown in *Tables 7.12*. It appears that most of the respondents who value conservative aspects more than progressive aspects are aged over 45, not highly educated, and live in rural areas. Respondents who can be found on the responsible side of the second dimension are mostly families with children, aged 46–59, and live in rural areas. On the hedonic side of the dimension we find that respondents are mostly single, aged less than 33, and live in urban areas. Respondents who value individual aspects more than social aspects are mostly 60 years or older, whereas those who value social more than individual aspects are mostly younger than 33. These conclusions are in line with the patterns of group differences that can be observed in *Table 7.10*.

Consumer Goods and Quality of Life

In part K of the interview, the respondents were asked to indicate, on a three-point scale, to what extent five different household goods contributed to each of the 15 quality of life aspects (1, not at all; 2, a little; 3, a lot). One household good

Table 7.10. Mean rankings of the 15 quality of life aspects.

(a)

	Overall mean	Household type			Age of respondents			
		Single $n = 124$	Couple $n = 196$	Family $n = 173$	< 33 $n = 117$	34–45 $n = 131$	46–59 $n = 133$	60+ $n = 111$
Health	1.9	2.6	1.7	1.7**	2.1	2.0	1.6	2.1
Relations	4.9	4.4	4.7	5.4	4.5	5.0	5.4	4.5*
Nature	6.2	6.5	6.0	6.1	7.1	5.8	5.7	6.2*
Freedom	7.1	6.2	7.3	7.4**	7.1	7.0	7.0	7.2
Privacy	7.3	6.4	7.5	7.8***	8.4	7.3	7.0	6.5**
Safety	7.5	8.3	7.4	6.8***	8.7	7.8	7.6	5.6***
Work	7.8	8.6	8.3	6.5**	6.7	6.6	7.3	11.2**
Social justice	7.9	8.1	7.7	8.2	8.2	7.7	8.0	8.0
Development	8.0	8.4	8.5	7.2**	6.8	7.5	7.7	10.5**
Income	9.3	9.5	9.0	9.4	9.6	9.6	9.2	8.6
Leisure time	9.5	9.6	9.6	9.3	8.9	9.1	9.7	10.6**
Recognition	9.9	9.8	10.0	9.7	9.2	10.1	10.3	9.8
Pleasure	10.5	10.0	10.3	11.0	8.8	10.7	11.2	11.1**
Comfort	11.0	10.1	10.7	11.2	12.0	11.6	11.0	8.9***
Beauty	11.5	10.7	11.3	12.3**	12.2	12.6	11.5	9.4***

(b)

	Income			Education			Residential location	
	Low $n = 185$	Mid $n = 114$	High $n = 172$	Low $n = 88$	Mid $n = 157$	High $n = 248$	Rural $n = 257$	Urban $n = 226$
Health	2.3	1.6	1.8**	2.0	1.6	2.1**	1.7	2.1**
Relations	4.6	4.9	5.0	5.1	5.1	4.6	5.1	4.7
Nature	6.3	6.5	5.9	6.1	6.1	6.3	5.8	6.2**
Freedom	6.9	7.2	7.0	8.6	7.1	6.6**	7.7	6.5**
Privacy	7.0	7.7	7.5	7.4	7.2	7.4	7.3	7.4
Safety	7.1	7.1	8.1	5.6	6.5	8.7**	6.7	8.0**
Work	9.1	6.8	7.1**	9.3	8.2	6.9**	8.0	7.7
Social justice	7.8	8.1	8.0	7.8	8.2	7.8	8.2	7.8
Development	8.9	7.9	7.3**	9.9	8.6	7.0**	8.1	8.0
Income	9.0	9.3	9.7	8.4	9.0	9.7	8.9	9.6
Leisure time	9.5	9.5	9.5	9.5	9.9	9.3	9.8	9.3
Recognition	10.0	9.6	9.9	10.0	10.0	9.7	9.9	9.9
Pleasure	10.1	10.8	10.8	10.2	10.2	10.7	10.8	10.2
Comfort	10.6	11.3	11.1	9.9	10.5	11.6**	10.7	11.1
Beauty	11.0	11.9	11.8	10.7	11.7	11.7	11.4	11.6

Note: The numbers of respondents do not add to 496 due to missing values.
* <0.05; ** <0.01.

Table 7.11. Three dimensions underlying the valuations of quality of life aspects.

	Dimension 1: Conservative versus progressive Eigenvalue = 0.17	Dimension 2: Responsible versus hedonistic Eigenvalue = 0.13	Dimension 3: Social versus individual orientation Eigenvalue = 0.11
Health	0.12	**0.57**	0.26
Relations	−0.06	−0.30	**0.49**
Nature	0.15	0.49	−0.17
Freedom	−0.20	−0.29	**−0.63**
Privacy	0.08	−0.12	**−0.64**
Safety	0.44	**0.56**	−0.10
Work	**−0.70**	0.09	0.30
Social justice	−0.38	0.36	−0.12
Development	**−0.76**	0.20	−0.03
Income	0.42	−0.08	0.31
Leisure time	−0.15	**−0.56**	−0.23
Recognition	−0.02	−0.24	**0.48**
Pleasure	−0.06	**−0.57**	0.18
Comfort	**0.71**	−0.11	0.05
Beauty	**0.59**	−0.19	−0.07

was chosen from each of the five major categories: the car, washing machine, home heating system, cooking equipment, and the TV (see *Table 7.1*). On average, the respondents indicated that the car contributes mainly to maintaining social relationships (mean 2.5), experiencing pleasure (2.5), doing their job (2.1), having privacy (2.1), having freedom and control over their lives (2.6), and saving time for leisure (2.3). The washing machine mainly contributes to comfort (2.7), control (2.1), and time saving (2.3). Heating equipment mainly contributes to comfort (2.8), and health (2.3). Cooking equipment contributes to comfort (2.7) and health (2.3). The TV and video recorder mainly contribute to development (2.0) and comfort (2.2).

In part C, the respondents were asked to indicate how important each of the 15 aspects were to their overall quality of life (see above). If we multiply the rated contribution of each good to an aspect by the (ranked) relative importance of that aspect for overall quality of life, we can create a "multi-attribute" quality score that indicates the aggregated contribution of each good to the overall quality of life of the individual. The overall results of this computation are given in the first column of *Table 7.13(a)*. It appears that the car contributes most to the quality of life of the average household, followed by the central heating system, the washing machine, and cooking equipment. The TV is the least important good to people's overall quality of life. *Table 7.13* shows the mean importance of the five goods for the different respondent groups. These differences were analyzed with a multivariate analysis of variance. As can be seen in the upper rows of both tables, the multivariate

Table 7.12. Differences between respondents on the three quality of life dimensions.

(a)

Quality of life dimension	Household type ($F = 3.4$, d$f = 6$, $p < 0.01$)			Age of respondents ($F = 14.5$, d$f = 9$, $p < 0.00$)			
	Single $n = 115$	Couple $n = 187$	Family $n = 161$	< 33 $n = 109$	34–45 $n = 122$	46–59 $n = 125$	60+ $n = 107$
Conservative–progressive	0.04	0.14	−0.16	−0.45	−0.30	−0.06	0.91**
Responsible–hedonistic	−0.35	0.04	0.21**	−0.36	0.08	0.20	0.04**
Social–individual	−0.23	0.04	0.10	0.24	−0.03	−0.03	−0.21**

(b)

	Income ($F = 1.6$, d$f = 6$, $p =$ ns)			Education ($F = 4.4$, d$f = 6$, $p < 0.00$)			Residential location ($F = 4.4$, d$f = 3$, $p < 0.01$)	
	Low $n = 183$	Mid $n = 111$	High $n = 169$	Low $n = 77$	Mid $n = 148$	High $n = 238$	Rural $n = 248$	Urban $n = 215$
Conservative–progressive	0.22	−0.08	−0.16	0.66	−0.18	−0.31**	0.17	−0.13**
Responsible–hedonistic	−0.12	0.11	0.06	0.00	0.17	0.11	0.18	−0.15*
Social–individual	−0.14	0.13	0.06	0.03	−0.01	0.01	0.03	−0.04

Note: The numbers of respondents do not add to 496 due to missing values.
* < 0.05; ** < 0.01.

Table 7.13. Importance of five household goods to the 15 quality of life aspects of different respondents.

(a)

	Overall mean	Household type ($F = 2.0$, $df = 10$, $p < 0.05$)			Age of respondents ($F = 2.6$, $df = 15$, $p < 0.00$)			
		Single $n = 54$	Couple $n = 139$	Family $n = 138$	< 33 $n = 68$	34–45 $n = 98$	46–59 $n = 103$	$60+$ $n = 62$
Car	220	217	223	219	231	220	214	218
Washing machine	191	186	188	192	187	195	185	191
Heating equipment	196	199	198	192	188	195	192	210
Cooking equipment	189	203	198	194	201	198	192	202
TV	172	175	174	164	172	166	166	183

(b)

	Income ($F = 2.2$, $df = 10$, $p < 0.05$)			Education ($F = 0.7$, $df = 16$, $p =$ns)			Residential location ($F = 3.0$, $df = 5$, $p < 0.01$)	
	Low $n = 97$	Mid $n = 93$	High $n = 141$	Low $n = 52$	Mid $n = 110$	High $n = 169$	Rural $n = 150$	Urban $n = 181$
Car	217	222	221	220	217	222	225**	214
Washing machine	195	192	183	202	185	188	188	191
Heating equipment	201	201	188	206	194	193	196	195
Cooking equipment	207	197	191	206	196	196	195	200
TV	181	173	161**	183	168	168	169	172

Note: The numbers of respondents do not add to 496 due to missing values.
** < 0.01.

effects are modest but significant for all respondent variables, except for the level of education. This means that respondent groups differ in their evaluations of all five goods together. *Table 7.13(a)* reveals that the effect for different household types seems to depend largely on differences in the importance attached the TV. The TV is more important to people who do not have children, although this effect is rather small and is not significant. The age groups seem to differ mostly in the importance they attach to the car (highest among the youngest respondents) and the TV (highest among the oldest respondents), but again these differences are not significant. *Table 7.13(b)* shows that the washing machine, heating equipment, and the TV are less important to higher-income than to low-income groups. However, only the effect for the TV is significant. Furthermore, the car is significantly more important to respondents living in rural areas.

Environmental Impacts of Household Consumer Behavior

In this section we discuss the responses to a number of questions concerning environmentally relevant behavior. In part L of the interview, the respondents were asked about their perceptions of the environmental impacts of their own households, part M whether they thought it necessary and possible to change household consumption patterns, and part N to what extent they would be willing to adopt various environmentally sound behaviors.

Environmental Impacts of Household Consumption: Part L

In part L respondents were asked to evaluate the environmental impacts of their household behavior compared with other Dutch households, on a five-point scale ranging from very little (1) to very much (5). Below we describe the responses to the questions on transportation, bathing, laundry, home heating, cooking, audiovisual equipment, the computer, the size of dwelling, and holidays. The first column in *Table 7.14(a)* shows the overall scores; the respondents evaluated all of their behaviors as moderately damaging to the environment, except for the use of the computer. The differences between the evaluations of the respondent groups were analyzed with a multivariate analysis of covariance. It appears that larger households evaluate their bathing, laundry, cooking, and possession and use of their computer as more harmful to the environment than do smaller households. The oldest respondents evaluate all behaviors, except for their dwelling, as less harmful to the environment than do younger respondents. High-income groups evaluate their transportation behavior and the size of their dwellings as more environmentally damaging than do the low-income group. Respondents with a low level of education evaluate their use of a computer as being less harmful than do those with a high level of education. Respondents living in urban areas evaluate

Table 7.14. Respondents' evaluation of the environmental impacts of the behavior of their own household.

(a)

	Overall mean	Household type ($F = 3.4$, d$f = 16$, $p < 0.01$)			Age of respondents ($F = 3.6$, d$f = 24$, $p < 0.00$)			
		Single n = 108	Couple n = 181	Family n = 161	< 33 n = 105	34–45 n = 120	46–59 n = 124	60+ n = 101
Transportation	2.5	2.1	2.5	2.7	2.5	2.6	2.7	2.0**
Bathing	2.6	2.4	2.6	2.7*	2.9	2.7	2.7	2.1**
Laundry	2.6	2.3	2.5	2.9**	2.7	2.9	2.6	2.2**
Home heating	2.6	2.5	2.6	2.6	2.8	2.6	2.6	2.4**
Cooking	2.4	2.2	2.4	2.5**	2.7	2.4	2.4	2.0**
Audio/video use	2.4	2.3	2.4	2.6	2.6	2.5	2.4	2.1**
Computer use	1.7	1.5	1.6	2.2**	2.1	2.0	1.9	1.2**
Size of dwelling	2.5	2.4	2.5	2.7	2.4	2.6	2.7	2.4

(b)

	Income ($F = 4.2$, d$f = 16$, $p < 0.00$)			Education ($F = 2.0$, d$f = 16$, $p =$ns)			Residential location ($F = 2.6$, d$f = 8$, $p =$ns)	
	Low n = 175	Mid n = 110	High n = 165	Low n = 74	Mid n = 142	High n = 234	Rural n = 241	Urban n = 209
Transportation	2.1	2.5	2.9**	2.4	2.4	2.6	2.7	2.3*
Bathing	2.5	2.6	2.6	2.5	2.5	2.7	2.6	2.6
Laundry	2.6	2.5	2.7	2.6	2.6	2.6	2.6	2.6
Home heating	2.6	2.6	2.5	2.7	2.5	2.6	2.5	2.6
Cooking	2.4	2.3	2.5	2.4	2.3	2.5	2.4	2.4
Audio/video use	2.4	2.4	2.4	2.5	2.4	2.4	2.4	2.4
Computer use	1.5	1.6	2.2	1.3	1.6	2.1**	1.8	1.8
Size of dwelling	2.4	2.5	2.8**	2.6	2.5	2.6	2.7	2.4

Note: The numbers of respondents do not add to 496 due to missing values.
* < 0.05; ** < 0.01.

their transportation behavior as more environmentally harmful than do those living in rural areas.

Although the differences between respondent groups are small, when compared with *Tables 7.5* and *7.7*, it seems that respondents who actually possess and more often use a good perceive their relevant behavior as more environmentally harmful. To study this relationship, we conducted a number of regression analyses in an attempt to explain the differences in the environmental evaluation of the behavior on the basis of the respondents' actual possession and use of goods. Only small percentages of the variance in the evaluations could be explained. Furthermore, only the use (not the possession) of the goods contributes significantly to the explanation. In general, the more often respondents use a certain household good, the greater they judge the environmental impacts of their behavior to be: 10% of the variance in the evaluation of transportation behavior appears to be explained by the distances the respondents drive each year; 8% of the evaluation of bathing behavior is explained by the number of times respondents take a bath or shower per week. Seven percent of the differences in the environmental evaluation of laundry washing is explained by the number of times per week respondents use a washing machine; and 4% of the environmental impact of heating the home is explained by the actual heating temperature. The evaluation of the environmental impact of cooking behavior cannot be explained by the use of the microwave oven and dishwasher; and 15% of the perception of environmental impacts of audiovisual equipment is explained by the number of hours respondents watch TV. The number of hours respondents use their computer explains 29% of the evaluation of this behavior. The size of the respondent's dwelling explains 9% of the variance in the evaluation of the household's use of space. Some of these limited explanations suffer from ceiling effects in the possession and use variables.

Necessity and Possibility to Change: Part M

In part M of the interview, the respondents were asked to what extent they thought that a number of changes are necessary in household behavior in general, and whether it would be possible for them to change. *Table 7.15* shows the mean scores obtained for each of these questions. It can be seen that respondents thought it most necessary to recycle goods, repair goods, reduce the use of the car, and reduce gas and electricity use. For most of these behaviors, the respondents indicated that it would be possible for them to change, although the possibility to reduce the use of the car was evaluated much lower than the necessity to do so. Overall, the respondents did not think it very necessary to take holidays closer to home, nor to reduce their living space by moving to a smaller house. There were no significant differences between respondent groups concerning these questions. This seems to imply that there is hardly any relationship between the respondents' own possession

Table 7.15. Perceived necessity and possibility to change household consumer behavior.

	Necessity[a]	Possibility[b]
Repair goods	4.1	3.6
Move to smaller house	2.4	2.6
Reduce car use	4.1	3.1
Reduce use of water for laundry and bathing	3.7	3.6
Reduce purchases of luxuries	3.6	3.5
Reduce electricity use	4.0	3.8
Recycle household goods	4.3	4.1
Reduce use of energy for home heating	4.1	4.0
Take holidays closer to home	3.0	3.1

[a]Five-point scale from not at all necessary (1) to essential (5).
[b]Five-point scale from not at all possible (1) to very well possible (5).

Table 7.16. Respondents who already do, are willing to, or are unwilling to behave in environmentally sound ways.

	Already do	Willing	Not willing
Move to smaller house	14	22	63
Insulate house	56	29	15
Reduce car use	44	19	37
Drive smaller car	35	29	37
Use washing machine more efficiently	84	11	5
Bathe less often	48	20	33
Turn down thermostat	64	12	24
AV equipment not on standby	59	28	13
Take holidays closer to home	35	17	48

and use of various household goods and the extent to which they think it is necessary and possible to change their behavior in general.

Willingness to Change: Part N

In part N of the interview, the respondents were asked about their willingness to change their own household behavior in a more sustainable direction. For each of nine "environmentally sound" behaviors, *Table 7.16* shows the percentages of respondents who stated that they already have changed their behavior, those who have not done so yet but would be willing to, and those who would unwilling to change their behavior.

Most respondents stated that they already had a well insulated house, that they already used the washing machine efficiently (e.g., they did not run it half-full), that they had already reduced their water consumption by bathing less often, that they had already tried to save energy by turning down the thermostat, and that they had already tried to save electricity by not leaving audiovisual equipment on standby. Most of the respondents who said that they did not do these things indicated that they would be willing to, except for bathing less often and turning down the thermostat. Most respondents were not willing to move to a smaller house or to take holidays closer to home. Similar numbers of respondents indicated that they already drive a small car; do not drive a small car but would be willing to; and do not drive a small car and would not be willing to. Fewer respondents said that they would be willing to use the car less than either those who said they already did, or those who said that they did not would not be willing to.

Explaining Differences in Willingness to Change

We also studied to what extent the respondents' willingness to change their behavior depends on their perception of the environmental impact of the household, and of the necessity and possibility to change. *Table 7.17* shows the mean scores on these three variables for the three groups of respondents according to their willingness to change. The differences were analyzed with a multivariate analysis of covariance. As can be seen in *Table 7.17*, respondents who indicated that they are not willing to reduce their living space and water use for bathing also said that it is less necessary and possible to do so, than respondents who already behave in an environmentally sound way or would be willing to. To a lesser extent, the same holds for other behaviors, except for driving a smaller car and for not leaving audiovisual equipment on standby. For these latter behaviors there was no difference between the three groups of respondents. Furthermore, respondents who indicated that their behavior is more environmentally harmful were neither more nor less willing to change their behavior. Thus, even if respondents are more aware of the environmental impacts of their behavior, this does not necessarily mean that they are more willing to change.

Second, we studied whether the extent to which respondents are willing to change differs according to household composition, age, income, level of education, and where they live. We conducted a number of chi-squared tests, but found few differences. Older respondents are slightly more willing to live in a smaller house than younger respondents. The latter were more willing to turn down the thermostat and to insulate their homes. Respondents living with a family are less willing to use the car less or to drive a smaller car, but they were more willing to bathe or shower less often. There are no significant differences between income groups, education groups, or rural versus urban respondents.

Finally, we studied whether the extent to which consumer goods contribute to the quality of life of individuals (*Table 7.13*) influences their willingness to change, by conducting a number of analyses of variance. The importance of the washing machine, cooking equipment, and heating systems to the respondents' quality of life has no effect on their willingness to change their behavior concerning the

Table 7.17. Respondents' evaluation of the environmental impacts of their own consumer behavior, and the necessity and possibility to change among respondents who already do, are willing, or are not willing to behave in environmentally sound ways (mean scores).

		Already do	Willing	Not willing
		$n = 69$	$n = 110$	$n = 309$
Move to smaller house	Impact	2.1	2.8	2.6**
($F = 9.8$, d$f = 6$, $p < 0.00$)	Necessary	2.8	2.7	2.2**
	Possible	2.9	2.9	2.5**
		$n = 261$	$n = 136$	$n = 69$
Insulate house	Impact	2.5	2.8	2.4**
($F = 4.2$, d$f = 6$, $p < 0.00$)	Necessary	4.2	4.1	3.9**
	Possible	4.1	3.9	3.9
		$n = 202$	$n = 85$	$n = 171$
Reduce use of car	Impact	2.2	2.8	2.9**
($F = 18.4$, d$f = 6$, $p < 0.00$)	Necessary	4.3	4.0	3.7**
	Possible	3.3	3.3	2.9**
		$n = 140$	$n = 114$	$n = 149$
Drive smaller car	Impact	2.7	2.6	2.8
($F = 0.6$, d$f = 6$, $p =$ns)	Necessary	4.0	4.0	4.0
	Possible	3.0	3.1	3.2
		$n = 401$	$n = 53$	$n = 21$
Use washing machine	Impact	2.6	2.7	2.8
more efficiently	Necessary	3.8	3.6	2.9**
($F = 4.7$, d$f = 6$, $p < 0.00$)	Possible	3.7	3.6	3.2*
		$n = 234$	$n = 96$	$n = 158$
Bathe less often	Impact	2.4	2.9	2.7**
($F = 14.1$, d$f = 6$, $p < 0.00$)	Necessary	3.9	3.9	3.4**
	Possible	3.8	3.7	3.5**
		$n = 312$	$n = 59$	$n = 116$
Turn down thermostat	Impact	2.5	2.8	2.7*
($F = 3.8$, d$f = 6$, $p < 0.01$)	Necessary	4.2	4.0	4.0**
	Possible	4.0	4.0	3.9
		$n = 274$	$n = 128$	$n = 61$
AV equipment not on standby	Impact	2.4	2.6	2.4
($F = 2.0$, d$f = 6$, $p =$ns)	Necessary	3.5	3.4	3.4
	Possible	3.7	3.6	3.2*
		$n = 162$	$n = 79$	$n = 222$
Take holidays closer to home	Necessary	3.4	3.2	2.5**
($F = 13.7$, d$f = 4$, $p < 0.00$)	Possible	3.3	3.2	2.9**

Note: For each behavior in the first column, analyses were performed on different numbers of respondents.

possession and use of these goods. The importance of the car, however, was related to people's willingness to change. The car appears to be significantly less important to respondents who said they already use the car less (mean importance 210; see *Table 7.13*), than to those who said they were willing to use it less (220) but had not done so yet. To respondents who were not willing to use the car less, the car was significantly more important (232).

7.5.   Conclusions

Household consumption in the Netherlands has increased substantially since 1950. Many household activities have been mechanized, and more and more goods for personal development and entertainment have been produced and consumed. In this chapter we have studied the factors underlying this increase in consumption, by focusing on the Needs, Opportunities and Abilities of consumers, following the NOA model. From an historical analysis of changes in household consumption it appears that the availability of opportunities to consume constitutes an important factor. Because of increased opportunities, people increasingly satisfy their needs through consumer behavior. In this diagnostic and evaluative field study, we have examined the importance of the abilities and the needs components. We also evaluated household consumption patterns in terms of their environmental impacts. In our first research questions, we studied what consumer goods Dutch households possess, how often they use them (research questions 1a and 1b), and whether this possession and use differs between respondents according to the household composition, age, and their abilities (income, level of education, and where they live; research question 2). It was shown that income and household composition were the most important variables influencing consumer behavior. High-income groups and families of three or more possess and use more than lower-income groups, and couples or single respondents. The level of education seems to have almost no effect on household consumption. Second, we studied what goods respondents possessed in the past and what they expect to own in the future (research questions 3a and 3b). Younger consumers expect to own more of most goods in the future than they do at present, and they already possess more goods than older respondents. Young consumers who do not possess such goods will probably buy them as soon as their income enables them to do so. When respondents possess a good, they also perceive it as a necessity for their households (research questions 4a and 4b).

To study why people want to have and use consumer goods, we examined to what extent they think that the possession of household goods contributes to various aspects of their quality of life. First, we examined what aspects are important to people's quality of life (question 5a). Health appears to be the most important, followed by social relations. The least important aspects are comfort and having beautiful things in and around the house. Important differences between these aspects can be described along three dimensions: "conservative" (comfort and beauty) versus "progressive" (development and work) values, "responsible" (health and safety) versus "hedonistic" (pleasure and leisure time) values, and "social" (social relations and social recognition) versus "individual" (freedom and control and privacy) values. Conservative-oriented respondents are mostly poorly educated, live in rural areas, and are aged over 60. Progressive-oriented respondents are mostly well educated, live in urban areas, and aged less than 33. People who value "responsible" above "hedonistic" aspects generally live in families, in rural areas, and are aged 46–59. Respondents with a more social than individual orientation are generally aged 33 or younger.

Next, we examined to what extent a number household goods contribute to respondents' quality of life (research question 5b). The washing machine, cooker, and home heating equipment are considered to contribute most to comfort and health. The car contributes most to maintaining social relations, experiencing pleasure, doing a job, having privacy, having freedom and control, and saving time for leisure. The TV mostly contributes to personal development and comfort. Respondents who possess more of these goods do not value these aspects any more than those who possess fewer of them (research question 5c). High-income groups and families possess most of these goods, and value health, development, and work more than more modest consumers. There also seems to be a relation between the importance of several aspects and the use of household goods. The TV and washing machine are used more often by respondents with low incomes and a low level of education. These respondents value comfort more than those with high incomes and a high level of education.

A multi-attribute score was computed to study the importance of the five household goods to respondents' overall quality of life. The car appeared to contribute most, and the TV least. The extent to which each of the five goods contributes to the overall quality of life is related to the actual possession and use of the goods. The possession of a car, for example, is more important to groups who actually possess more cars and use them more often (respondents living in rural areas). The TV is more important to people who watch television more often (respondents with low incomes).

Dutch consumers seem to be well aware of the environmental impacts of their household behavior (research question 6a), but this awareness is related to the use, rather than to the possession of household goods (question 6b). This means that respondents are probably not aware of the indirect energy consumption of their household, as embodied in the goods they own. On average, respondents agree that it is necessary and possible to change most household consumer behaviors, except for living in a smaller house and taking holidays closer to home. This does not seem to be related to their own consumer behavior. No differences were found between respondent groups concerning these variables. For reducing car use, a discrepancy was found between the judged necessity and the possibility to change.

Respondents agreed that it is necessary to reduce the use of the car, although they judged it only slightly possible to do so.

Finally, we studied to what extent the respondents would be willing to change their own household consumer behavior (question 8a). Most respondents said that they would be willing to change most behaviors if they do not already behave in an environmentally sound way, except for moving to in a smaller house and taking holidays closer to home. Furthermore, we studied whether the respondents' willingness to change depended on their evaluation of the environmental impacts of their own behavior (question 8b). Respondents who were aware that their behavior had a greater impact on the environment than that of other households did not appear to be more willing to change their behavior. Moreover, respondents who were least willing to use the car less, seem to drive most and to evaluate their transportation behavior as environmentally harmful. Furthermore, the car is most important to the quality of life of these respondents.

It can be concluded that Dutch consumers will keep on buying consumer goods as long as they have the (increasing) opportunity and ability to do so. It was shown that several household goods, especially the car, contribute to the perceived quality of life of the respondents. It seems that as soon as people are able to buy these goods, they will do so. Moreover, the more important some goods are to their quality of life, the more often they use them. The more often people use several household goods, the higher they evaluate the environmental impact of their household to be, although this does not influence their willingness to change. Most respondents think household consumer behavior should become more environmentally sound, although this does not seem to motivate them to change their own behavior.

Summary

- Dutch consumers will keep on buying consumer goods as long as they have the (increasing) opportunity and ability to do so.
- When people possess a good it becomes a necessity to their household, which means they are not willing to give it up.
- Household goods contribute to people's perceived quality of life by satisfying several consumer needs, especially the car. The more important the goods are, the more often they are used, and the less willing people are to change their behavior.
- Dutch consumers seem to be well aware of the environmental impacts of their household behavior. However, this awareness seems to be related only to the use, and not to the possession of household goods.
- In general the Dutch believe that household consumer behavior should become more environmentally sound. This, however, does not seem to lead to motivate them to change their own household behavior.

References

Allardt, E. (1994) Having, loving, being: an alternative to the Swedish model of welfare research, in: M. Nussbaum and A. Sen (Eds.), *The Quality of Life*, Clarendon Press, Oxford.

Andrews, F. and S. Whitney (1976) *Social Indicators of Well-being: Americans' Perception of Life Quality*, Plenum, New York.

Breemhaar, B., W. van Gool, P. Ester and C. Midden (1995) *Leefstijl en huishoudelijke energieconsumptie: Analyse van patronen van huishoudelijke energieconsumptie en mogelijkheden voor besparing: een benadering volgens de middel-doelketen theorie* (Lifestyles and household energy consumption, Analysis of household energy consumption patterns and energy-saving options: an approach following means–end chain theory), Institute for Social Scientific Research and Advice (IVA), Tilburg.

Campbell, C. (1991) Consumption: The new wave of research in the humanities and social sciences, in: F. Rudmin (Ed.), To have possessions: A handbook on ownership and property, Special issue of the *Journal of Social Behavior and Personality*, 6:57–74 .

Campbell, A., P. Convers and W. Rogers (1976) *The Quality of American Life: Perceptions, Evaluations and Satisfactions*, Russel Sage Foundation, New York.

CBS (1996) *Statistisch jaarboek*, SDU, The Hague.

De Bruin, P., R. Custers and A. Scholten (1993) *Voorwaarden voor consumptie verandering: een oriëntatie op normen en waarden* (Conditions for changes in consumer behavior: an orientation on norms and values), Swoka Rep. 148, Swoka, The Hague.

Diener, E. and C. Diener (1995) The wealth of nations revisited: income and quality of life, *Social Indicators Research*, 36:275–286.

Diener, E, M. Diener and C. Diener (1995) Factors predicting the subjective well-being of nations, *Journal of Personality and Social Psychology*, 69(5):851–864.

Diener, E., E. Sandvik, L. Seidlitz and M. Diener (1993) The relationship between income and subjective well-being: relative or absolute? *Social Indicators Research*, 28:195–223.

Diener, E., E. Suh, H. Smith and L. (1995) National differences in reported subjective well-being: why do they occur? *Social Indicators Research*, 34:7–32.

Easterlin, R. (1974) Does economic growth improve the human lot? Some empirical evidence, in: R. Silverstone and R. Hirhs (Eds.), *Consuming Technologies: Media and Information in Domestic Spaces*, Routledge, New York, pp. 48–66.

Easterlin, R. (1995) Will raising the incomes of all increase the happiness of all? *Journal of Economic Behavior and Organization*, 27: 35–47.

Fishbein, M. and I. Ajzen (1975) *Belief, Attitude, Intention and Behavior: An Introduction to Theory and Research*, Addison-Wesley, Reading, MA.

Gatersleben, B. and Ch. Vlek (1997) Understanding household metabolism in view of environmental quality and sustainable development, in: G. Antonides, W. van Raaij and S. Maital (Eds.), *Advances in Economic Psychology*, Wiley, Chichester .

Hareide, D. (1994) Has the quality of life improved in western Europe? in: M. Nussbaum and A. Sen (Eds.), *The Quality of Life*, Clarendon Press, Oxford.

Henderson, H. (1994) Paths to sustainable development, *Futures*, 26(2):125–137.

Inglehart, R. (1990) *Culture Shift in Advanced Industrial Society*, Princeton University Press, Princeton, NJ.

Jager, W., M. van Asselt, J. Rotmans, Ch. Vlek and P. Costerman Boodt (1997) *Consumer Behaviour: A Modelling Perspective in the Context of Integrated Assessment of Global Change*, Rep. No. 461502017, RIVM, Bilthoven.

Maslow, A. (1954) *Motivation and Personality*, New York.

Max-Neef, M. (1992) Development and human needs, in: P. Ekins and M. Max-Neef (Eds.) *Real-life Economics: Understanding Wealth Creation*, Routledge, London.

McDougall, W. (1932) *The Energies of Men*, Methuen, London.

OECD (1976) *Measuring Social Well-being, A Progress Report on the Development of Social Indicators*, Organization for Economic Cooperation and Development, Paris.

Ölander, F. and J. Thøgerson (1994) *Understanding of Consumer Behavior as a Prerequisite for Environmental Protection*, Keynote Address, 23rd Int. Congress on Applied Psychology, Madrid, July 17–22, 1994 .

Opschoor, J. (1989) *Na ons geen zondvloed; voorwaarden voor duurzaam milieugebruik* (After us no deluge: conditions for sustainable use of the environment), Kok/Agora, Kampen, ch. 5.

Reynolds, T. and J. Gutman (1988) Laddering theory, method, analysis, and interpretation, *Journal of Advertising Research*, **28**: 11–31.

Robben, H. and Th. Poiesz (1992) The operationalization of motivation, capacity, and opportunity to process an advertising message, in: W. van Raaij and G. Bamossy (Eds.) *Advances in Consumer Research*, Association for Consumer Research, Amsterdam, pp. 160–168.

Rokeach, M. (1979) *Understanding Human Values, Individual and Societal*, Free Press, New York.

Stern, O. (1992) Psychological dimensions of global environmental change, *Annual Review of Psychology*, **43**:269–302.

Uusitalo, L. (1982) Environmental impact of changes in consumption styles, *Journal of Macromarketing*, Fall, 16–30.

Van Raaij, W. (1994) Consumentengedrag en milieu, in: C.J.H. Midden and G.C. Bartels (Eds.), *Consument en milieu, Beoordeling van milieurisico's en sturing van gedrag* (Consumers and the environment, evaluation of environmental risks and managing behavior), Bohn Stafleu Van Loghum.

VEEN (1995) *Basisonderzoek elektriciteitsverbruik kleinverbruikers (BEK)* (Basic research on electricity use by private consumers), Vereniging van Exploitanten van Elektriciteitsbedrijven in Nederland, EnergieNed, Arnhem.

Veenhoven, R. (1989) National wealth and individual happiness, in: K. Grunert and F. Olander (Eds.), *Understanding Economic Behavior*, Kluwer, Dordrecht.

Veenhoven, R. (1994) Is happiness a trait? Tests of the theory that a better society does not make people any happier, *Social Indicators Research*, **32**:101–160.

Vlek, Ch. (1995) *Technical versus Socio-behavioral Solutions to Environmental Problems: Psychology's Unexploited Potential*, Invited address, Environmental Psychology Division, American Psychological Association, New York, August 1995.

Vlek, Ch., W. Jager and L. Steg (1997) Modellen en strategieën voor gedragsverandering ter beheersing van collectieve risico's (Models and strategies for behavioral change to manage collective risks), *Nederlands Tijdschrift voor de Psychologie*.

Chapter 8

Economic Aspects of Household Metabolism

V.G.M. Linderhof and P. Kooreman

Abstract

This chapter analyzes the postwar changes in the nominal and real prices of natural gas, electricity, and water. In order to take into account improvements in the efficiency of domestic appliances, we estimate the price per unit of service provided by these appliances. We discuss major developments in the amounts of waste generated by households, and the costs of waste removal. Finally, we summarize recent developments in private car ownership and fuel use.

8.1. Introduction

One does not need to invoke the microeconomic theory of consumer behavior to ascertain that prices have a large impact on consumption. As each guilder or pound can be spent only once, a very high price per unit of a good forces consumers to consider carefully their decision to purchasing that good. On the other hand, a very low price per unit may induce consumers to act almost as if the good is for free. These observations are just as valid for household metabolic flows, such as natural gas, electricity and water, as they are for other goods and services.

In this diagnostic research carried out within the framework of the economic aspects of household metabolism, we focus on the prices paid by households in the Netherlands for natural gas, electricity, and water over the period 1950–1990. To obtain a clear picture of real prices, three adjustments need to be made. The first, and most trivial, is correction for inflation. Inflation is measured from the changes in the prices of a fixed "basket" of goods over the years. *Figure 8.4* shows, for example, that average nominal electricity prices increased only slightly between

1950 and 1994, whereas the general price level increased substantially. As a result, the real electricity price in 1950 was more than double that in 1985. Second, the costs of services such as gas, electricity and water are influenced by changes not only in the price level, but also by changes in tariff structures. In the Netherlands there have been several such changes over the last four decades; for natural gas supplied to small consumers, for example, the tariff structure was changed from a regressive to a progressive one. These aspects are analyzed in Section 8.2.

Third, when investigating the consumption of natural gas, electricity, or water, the price per service unit of domestic appliances is the most appropriate concept to explain the household consumption of services. We have analyzed this aspect of the price for using refrigerators, freezers, washing machines and dishwashers. These appliances have become more energy efficient in recent years, so that the electricity price per service unit decreases even if the real electricity price per kWh remains constant. Moreover, to take into account the possible changes in the *quality* of these appliances (in terms of their energy efficiency and other attributes), we estimate hedonic price equations that relate electricity and water consumption to their characteristics and a trend. This allows us to elicit a quality-corrected price per service unit (Section 8.3).

Within the HOMES project, two other areas of interest are domestic waste and the ownership and use of cars per household, both of which are major areas of government policy. This are summarized in Sections 8.4 and 8.5, respectively, over the period 1950–1990. Some concluding remarks follow in Section 8.6.

8.2.   Household Consumption, Prices and Tariff Structures of Energy and Water

8.2.1.   Natural gas

A major aspect of household metabolism is the consumption of natural gas by private households and the corresponding prices. We have used data on natural gas consumption and prices over the period 1950–1990 compiled by the Netherlands Central Bureau of Statistics (CBS, 1995a). Annual data on prices and consumption of natural gas are available only from 1961, when natural gas was substituted for oil and coal. The precursors of natural gas and household consumption were discussed in detail in Chapter 2; here, we only provide only a brief summary.

In Chapter 2 natural gas consumption is expressed in gigajoules (GJ),[1] but for our purposes it is more suitable to analyze the changes in natural gas consumption in cubic meters (m^3), although the observed trends are similar. *Figure 8.1* shows household consumption and expenditures on natural gas; after 1961 consumption increased steadily, except for a brief fall after the 1973 oil crisis. The peak (so far) was reached in 1979, when the second oil crisis caused a general downward trend.

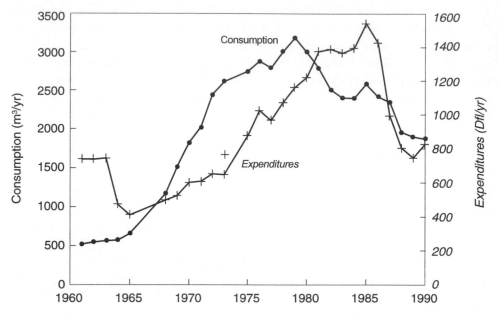

Figure 8.1. Natural gas consumption and expenditures by households, 1961–1990. Source: CBS (1995a).

Figure 8.1 also shows that in 1961 households spent an average of Dfl 740 (in real prices) on natural gas, but in 1964 expenditures declined sharply due to a major price reduction. Expenditures gradually fell until 1973, and then increased to an average of Dfl 1540 in 1985, and then fell to Dfl 823 in 1990, again due to a substantial reduction in prices. *Figure 8.2* shows the nominal and real prices of natural gas from 1961 to 1990. Real prices declined steadily until the oil crises of the 1970s, and then increased sharply until 1985. Only recently have prices been increasing again.

In 1990, the real price of natural gas was about 44 cents per cubic meter (ct/m^3), less than one-third of the 1961 price of 142 ct/m^3, and about the same as in 1980. Booij *et al.* (1992) estimated that the (short-term) price elasticity for household natural gas consumption lies in the range -0.4 to -0.1. Thus, a 10% increase in the gas price corresponds to a decline in consumption of 1–4%.

Tariff Structure for Natural Gas

Here we have used data on the natural gas tariff structure over a 30-year period from *EnergieNed*, published by the energy supply companies in the Netherlands. Between 1967 and 1980 a *regressive block tariff* was charged, in which the first 300 m^3 of natural gas were the most expensive. In 1967–1975 natural gas consumption

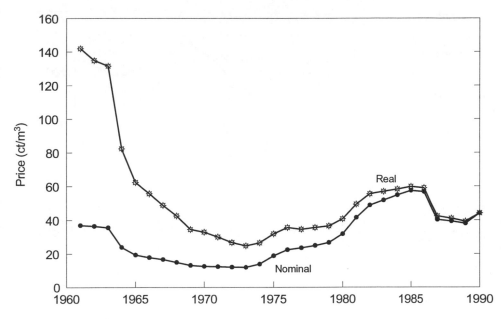

Figure 8.2. Natural gas prices for households, 1961–1990; base year is 1990. Source: CBS (1995a).

was divided into four blocks, and after 1975 the two smallest and two largest blocks of consumption were combined and a regressive two-block tariff structure was maintained until 1980. In 1975, the first 600 m^3 of natural gas cost 27 ct/m^3, and additional units 16.7 ct/m^3. In 1980, the tariff structure was changed from a regressive block tariff to a *proportional tariff*, so that all households paid a fixed charge and a price per unit of natural gas consumed.

Independent of the tariff structure, a number of tax changes have also affected the price of natural gas. In 1978 the rate of value added tax (VAT) on natural gas was raised from the low level (then about 4%) to the high level of 17.5%. In 1967 an environmental consumption tax was introduced at 0.03 ct/m^3, but in 1990 this was increased to 2.08 ct/m^3. In 1991 the gas supply companies introduced an Environmental Action Plan tax ("Milieu Aktie Plan", or MAP tax) of 0.5–2% of the natural gas price, to finance their environmental activities.

In 1996 the so-called "ecotax" was introduced as a means of reducing household natural gas consumption. This new tax transformed the proportional tariff structure into a progressive tariff structure, since it is charged on gas consumption over 800 m^3 per year. This is being introduced in stages; for 1996 the ecotax was set at 3.8 ct/m^3, and will be raised to 11.2 ct/m^3 in 1998. The expected increase in household energy expenditures will be offset by lower income taxes.

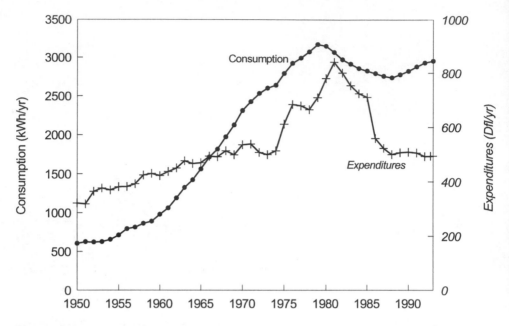

Figure 8.3. Electricity consumption and expenditures by households, 1950–1993. Source: *EnergieNed* (several volumes).

8.3. Electricity

For household electricity consumption, we have used data published in *EnergieNed* (several volumes) between 1950 and 1993 (see *Figure 8.3*). Electricity consumption increased steadily for almost 30 years, except for a slight fall immediately after the 1973 oil crisis. In 1979–1988 consumption declined, but since then has been rising again (for details of household electricity consumption, see Chapter 2).

Expenditures on electricity grew steadily until 1973. In the years following the two oil crises, expenditures continued to grow, but fell steeply in 1987 due to a large price reduction. *Figure 8.4* shows the nominal and real prices of electricity between 1950 and 1993. Real prices fell steadily until 1973, and then increased for some years. After the 1979 energy crisis the real price started to fall, and is still decreasing, whereas the nominal price of electricity has remained constant in the last few years.

Electricity Tariff Structures

There have been no major changes in the tariff structure of electricity since the introduction of the two-band tariff in 1950. Since 1984, some households have been able to choose whether to be charged the two-band tariff (peak-hour rate on weekdays, and half that rate during the night and at weekends), or a proportional

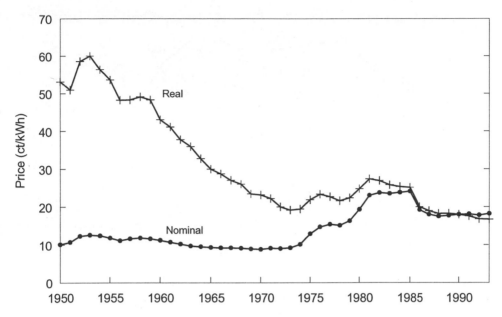

Figure 8.4. Electricity prices for households, 1950-1993; base year is 1990. Source: *EnergieNed* (several volumes).

tariff (approximately the "peak-hour" rate); the latter is often charged when an electric boiler is present. According to van Oortmarssen (1991), 30% of Dutch households were charged this tariff in 1987. The penetration of this double tariff varied from 5 to 95% among the regions of the electricity distribution companies. Booij *et al.* (1992) showed that the price elasticity for electricity in the case of the peak-hour tariff hardly deviated from that in the single tariff case; both elasticities were about −0.15. The peak-hour tariff structure was introduced to improve load management by smoothing out the fluctuations in the demand for electricity throughout the day, allowing for more efficient production.

Budget Shares of Natural Gas and Electricity

Separate information on budget shares (the shares of net income spent on particular commodities) of natural gas and electricity has been available only since 1978. Prior to 1978, data on the joint budget shares of heating and lighting were published (it fell from 5% in 1964 to 4% in 1974), so that the contributions of natural gas and electricity separately are not known. *Figure 8.5* shows that the combined budget share of natural gas and electricity over the period 1978–1990 (calculated from CBS annual budget surveys) fluctuated considerably, reaching a peak of 6% in 1985, and a low of 3% in 1989. These results correspond with the findings of Booij *et al.* (1992).

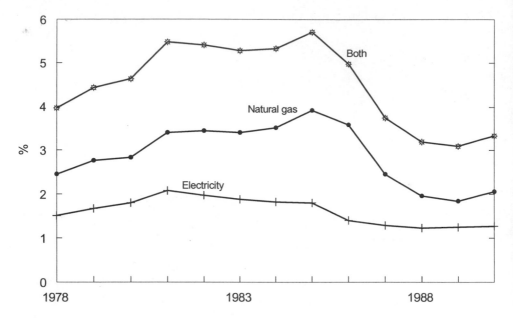

Figure 8.5. Budget shares of energy in household expenditures, 1978–1990. Source: Booij *et al.* (1992).

Figure 8.5 shows that the share of natural gas has always been larger than that of electricity. The largest share for natural gas was reached in 1985, when households spent twice as much on natural gas as on electricity. The largest share for electricity was reached in 1981. In 1990 households spent about 3% of their net income on natural gas and electricity.

8.3.1. Water

For a long time water has been available at relatively low cost. In the absence of "water crises" analogous to the oil crises of the 1970s, there has been little political and scientific interest in economic aspects of water provision and charges. Only in recent years have water services and water prices become recurring items on the political agenda,[2] as a result of the steady growth in water demand and increasing supply problems (associated with adverse environmental effects and rising costs). Over the period 1965–1990 domestic water consumption increased steadily by 1.1% per capita per year (see Chapter 2), and further increases in total water demand are expected until the year 2010, as a result of both demographic factors and behavioral changes.

Table 8.1 shows the domestic water price index in the Netherlands between 1970 and 1995 for a household using 200 m³ per year, together with the nominal and real prices charged by the supply companies. There were substantial regional

Table 8.1. Water prices in the Netherlands, 1970–1995 (Dfl per 200 m^3; base year is 1990).

Year	Price index	WLF (Friesland) nom.	real	WOG (East Gelderland) nom.	real	PWN (North Holland) nom.	real	DZH (The Hague) nom.	real
1970	38	134	353	133	350	192	505	118	311
1975	59	227	385	182	308	348	590	220	373
1980	78	277	355	197	253	390	500	354	454
1985	96	363	378	238	248	379	395	398	415
1990	100	389	389	243	243	407	407	412	412
1995	114	510	447	411	361	562	493	627	550

Sources: *VEWIN* (several volumes).

Table 8.2. Metering rate and water prices across water companies, 1986–1991.

Year		1986	1987	1988	1989	1990	1991
Number of companies		58	61	61	61	50	39
Residential water use	mean[a]	124.0	124.0	128.0	131.0	130.0	128.0
(liters per capita per day)	min	90.0	90.0	93.0	96.0	95.0	91.0
	max	196.0	183.0	168.0	177.0	181.0	184.0
Metered	mean[a]	84.7	88.1	89.2	88.7	91.0	93.0
households (%)	min	4.0	4.0	4.0	3.9	3.9	4.6
	max	100.0	100.0	100.0	100.0	100.0	100.0
Population in district of	mean	228.0	230.1	239.7	241.0	298.0	369.6
company (in thousands)	min	9.9	10.0	10.0	10.0	10.4	10.5
	max	1,196.0	1,212.0	1,212.0	1,225.0	1,237.0	1,242.0
Marginal water price	mean	1.157	1.162	1.135	1.156	1.167	1.218
(for metered households)	min	0.616	0.626	0.660	0.680	0.680	0.740
(Dfl/m^3)	max	2.450	2.450	2.450	2.410	2.350	2.350

[a]Weighted according to the population in the district.

differences in the real prices. For two companies (WOG and PWN) real prices are the same now as they were 25 years ago, while those of the other two companies increased substantially, especially the company supplying The Hague. The differences in price reflect the different water sources (ground or surface water).

Tariff Structures for Water

Traditionally, water company tariff structures have been based on cost-effectiveness, i.e., the companies set their rates such that the revenues will cover their costs. The use of water meters is usually advocated on the grounds of equity and efficiency. The equity argument is that it is reasonable that households that use more should pay more, and those that conserve water should be rewarded. Whether

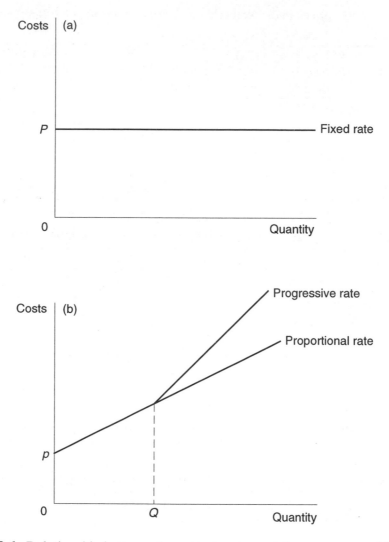

Figure 8.6. Relationship between the cost of water and the amounts used in (a) an unmetered, and (b) a metered household.

the installation of water meters is efficient at an aggregate level will depend on the cost of installation, and on the price sensitivity of water use. Only if the latter is sufficiently large will the costs of metering be justified by the savings in water supply. Recently, some companies have introduced progressive rates explicitly to encourage water conservation. One water supply company, for example, charges Dfl 1.22/m^3 for the first 120 m^3 per year, and Dfl 1.47/m^3 thereafter (*Table 8.2*).

Water meters have been installed in about 90% of households in the Netherlands, except for some large cities, such as Amsterdam, Rotterdam and Groningen (although Groningen started to introduce metering in 1996). For households without meters, the rate is fixed according to the number of rooms, the number of faucets, baths, showers or garden, or the size of the water supply pipe.

Figure 8.6 shows the theoretical relationships between the cost of water and the amounts used by unmetered and metered households under various tariff schemes. In (b) the effects of a proportional tariff (the real price per unit) and a progressive rate are shown; above a certain level of consumption the price per unit is higher. Whether a progressive rate is an effective means of reducing water consumption is again a matter of price sensitivity. Kooreman (1993) estimated the (short-run) price elasticity of domestic water use in the Netherlands to be -0.10 (a 10% price increase induces a 1% reduction in consumption), close to estimates reported by Herrington (1987) for Finland and Sweden. This implies that the effect of a progressive rate will be small. It would be much more effective to make all water-related charges completely dependent on use, since this would imply a multiplication of the nominal marginal price by a factor of 3 to 4 (see Kooreman, 1993).

8.4. Possession Rates and the Energy and Water Use of Appliances

The increased demand for energy and water for domestic use coincided with the introduction of various appliances. *Figure 8.7* shows the possession rates of some domestic appliances over time (CBS, 1995a; van Ours, 1986). In this case the possession rate is defined as the number of households owning an appliance, divided by the total number of households. However, van Maanen (1994; see also Chapter 2) introduced the penetration rate, defined as the number of appliances owned by households divided by the total number of households. Thus, if a household has two refrigerators, both are included.

In 1990, 98% and 95% of households owned a refrigerator and a washing machine, respectively, about 50% had a separate freezer, and only 11% a dishwasher. *Figure 8.7* shows that the possession rates of these four appliances have been stable over the last decade. These appliances account for a substantial part of domestic electricity consumption, which is about 3132 kWh per household per year (van Maanen, 1994, pp. 29–32). Of this, refrigerators and freezers account for 17.7% and laundry equipment 16.1%, more than one-third of the total. *Table 8.3* shows the average shares of domestic appliances in the total electricity consumption.

Domestic appliances use either electricity or both electricity and water. Below, we summarize the changes in the electricity and water use of these appliances, adjusted to take into account quality improvements. For this purpose we have used data on household appliances published in the Dutch Consumer Guide (*Consumentengids*) for 1964–1992 (for details, see Appendix A).

To analyze the electricity use and water use of appliances, we applied the hedonic price equation technique, which relates electricity use of refrigerators to their characteristics, and we added a time trend as well. With this method we can disentangle the effects of changing characteristics (e.g., the increasing average

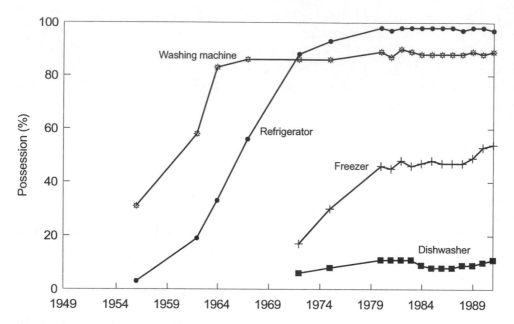

Figure 8.7. Possession of household appliances in the Netherlands, 1956–1990. Sources: Van Ours (1986); CBS (1995a).

Table 8.3. Electricity use of some appliances and the shares of household electricity consumption, 1993.

Household appliance	Electricity use (kWh/yr)	Share of electricity consumption (%)
Refrigerator	368.0	11.7
Freezer	186.6	6.0
Washing machine	232.7	7.4
Dish washer	220.0	7.0
Tumble dryer	52.9	1.7
Total	1,060.3	33.8

Source: *EnergieNed* (1994).

volume of refrigerators) on electricity use from the effects of pure increases in energy efficiency. Appendix B summarizes the hedonic regression technique and the estimation results.

8.4.1. Refrigerators

In 1966 only one type of refrigerator was available, a cabinet-sized model, whereas today many models have separate freezer compartments, placed either above (top freezer) or below (bottom freezer) the refrigerator compartment. In the latter case

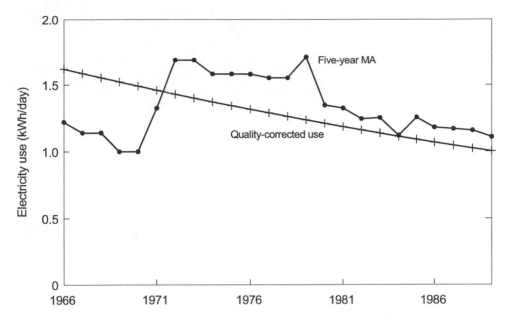

Figure 8.8. Electricity use of refrigerators, 1964–1990.

the two compartments have separate compressors. The volume of refrigerators has increased over time.

Figure 8.8 shows that electricity use[3] of refrigerators decreased steadily until the early 1970s when wardrobe-size models were introduced. In 1989 the electricity use of refrigerators was the same as in 1966, despite the increase in volume. The electricity use per unit volume of the cooling compartment was also similar to that in 1966. We calculated the electricity use of refrigerators per service unit (the cooling unit in the case of the refrigerator) by multiplying the volume by the difference between room temperature (18°C) and the cooling/freezing temperatures (5 and −12°C, respectively). Again, the electricity use per cooling unit shows a trend similar to that shown in *Figure 8.8* (the trends per cooling compartment volume and per service unit are not shown). After 1973 the electricity use of refrigerators per service unit declined steadily.

Figure 8.8 also shows the quality-corrected electricity use per service unit, which has also decreased steadily. Over the period considered, the electricity use of refrigerators decreased by 2.1% per year.

8.4.2. Freezers

Freezers can also be divided into three types: chest-type (the most common model in the tests), cabinet-size and wardrobe-type freezers (note that the freezer compartments of refrigerators are not considered here).

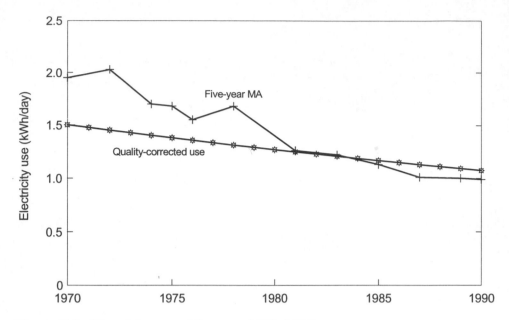

Figure 8.9. Electricity use of freezers, 1970–1990.

Figure 8.9 shows that between 1970 and 1990 the electricity use of freezers fell from about 2.0 to 1.0 kWh per day. We also calculated the electricity use per service unit (not shown). We defined a service unit (or freezing unit) as the volume multiplied by the difference between room temperature (18°C) and the desired freezing temperature (−12°C). The electricity use per freezing unit shows a trend similar to that shown in *Figure 8.9*. As with refrigerators, we also calculated the quality-corrected electricity use by estimating a hedonic price regression that relates the electricity use of freezers to their characteristics and a trend. *Figure 8.9* shows that the quality-corrected use is decreasing, as in the case of refrigerators.

8.4.3. Washing machines

In 1990, almost all (95%) households possessed a washing machine. We examined three models: a front-loader (including a spin dryer), a top-loader (without a spin dryer), and a twin-tub (top-loader with separate spin dryer). The electricity and water use of these models are shown in *Figures 8.10* and *8.11*. Efficiency improvements due to technological changes were not taken into account in these calculations.

Over the years the use of both electricity and water has declined. We used a hedonic regression to relate both electricity and water use to the characteristics of the washing machines as well as a time trend. These characteristics include the capacity (weight of dry laundry), the washing program temperature, the time per

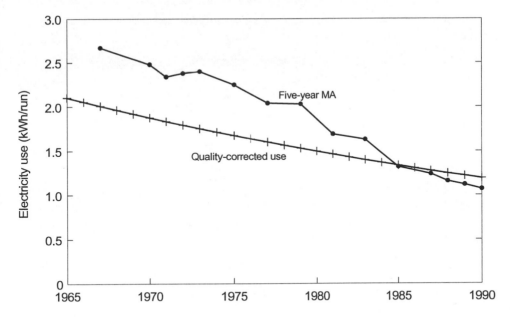

Figure 8.10. Electricity use of washing machines, 1967–1990.

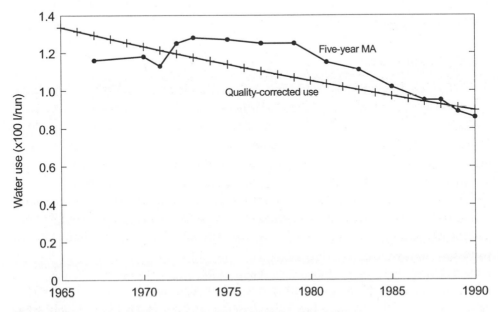

Figure 8.11. Water use of washing machines, 1967–1990.

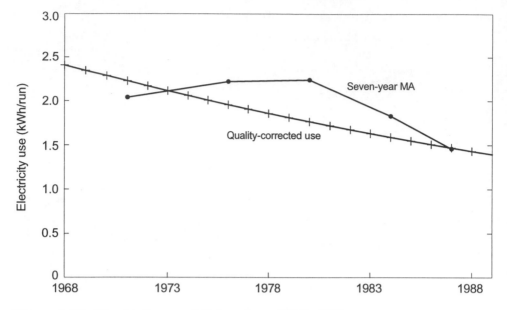

Figure 8.12. Electricity use of dishwashers, 1968–1989.

run, the presence of a prewash, and the type of machine. With the results of the regression we calculated the electricity and water use of the washing machines at a washing program temperature of 60°C and the average of the other characteristics. The results of the regression imply that electricity use declined by 2.3% per year, and water use by 1.6% per year.

8.4.4. Dishwashers

In 1990, only 11% of households in the Netherlands owned a dishwasher. It has also been the least tested appliance. The results of the first tests comparing three different types were published in 1968. The portable dishwasher, which could be placed wherever needed, was included only in the test in 1968. The other two types tested were the cabinet-sized top-loader and front-loader. The electricity and water use for our data set of 129 machines are presented in *Figures 8.12* and *8.13*.

To get a clear picture of the electricity and water use we corrected for quality changes. Electricity and water use were related to the characteristics, temperature, and the trend using a two-equation hedonic regression. The relevant characteristics were the capacity (number of baskets), the run time, the type of the model, the presence of an energy saving-program, and the option to add water softener. *Figures 8.12* and *8.13* show the quality-corrected (calculated) electricity and water use. The electricity use of dishwashers has fallen by an average of 2.6% per year, and water consumption by 3.6% per year.

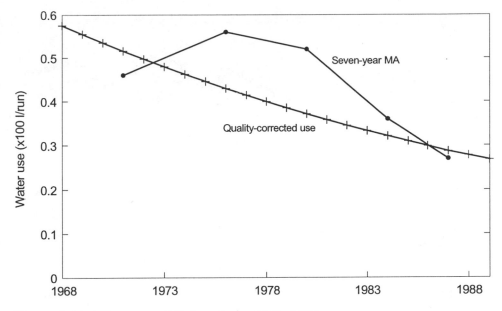

Figure 8.13. Water use of dishwashers, 1968–1989.

8.5. Household Waste

This section focuses on household waste, another important aspect of household metabolism. We summarize the changes in the amounts of household waste generated and the costs of collection per kilogram (in real terms).

Figure 8.14 shows the amounts of household waste collected by local authorities in the Netherlands in the period 1950–1993 (CBS, 1995a). The waste per capita almost tripled, from 140 kg in 1950, to 400 kg in 1988, and since then has remained constant. Society has an increasing concern for the reduction of waste, particularly household waste, which in 1991 accounted for 71% of all waste collected by local authorities (CBS, 1993). The Dutch government is now trying to stem the growth of the "waste mountain" by encouraging recycling (closing material and energy cycles). In the case of household waste, the main policy instrument has been the tax on waste, which is charged per capita (*Table 8.4*). The rate of this tax has increased steadily over the last 20 years, from Dfl 21 per capita in 1972, to Dfl 98 in 1993. Since 1988 the amount of waste has been roughly constant, so the revenue per kilogram of waste has almost doubled.

There were also changes in the tariff structures. In the past, the municipal taxes on domestic waste were charged per household, although the level of tax varied across the municipalities. With the introduction of the National Environmental Plan (Nationaal Milieubeleidsplan, NMP; see SER, 1989), the reduction and/or recycling of waste have been major policy goals. The price and the tariff structure

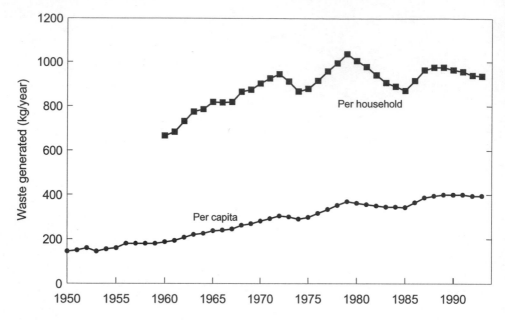

Figure 8.14. Household waste, 1960–1990. Source: CBS (1995a).

Table 8.4. (Real) taxes on household waste, 1972–1993.

Year	Waste tax (Dfl per capita)	Revenue (ct/kg)	Year	Waste tax (Dfl per capita)	Revenue (ct/kg)
1972	21.22	7.0	1983	43.32	12.6
1973	25.79	8.6	1984	44.23	12.8
1974	27.75	9.6	1985	44.05	12.8
1975	27.73	9.3	1986	45.74	12.5
1976	n.a.[a]	n.a.	1987	49.40	12.4
1977	29.91	9.0	1988	50.72	12.8
1978	30.94	8.8	1989	54.08	13.5
1979	36.58	9.9	1990	56.40	14.1
1980	36.60	10.1	1991	70.44	17.6
1981	38.98	10.9	1992	81.66	20.7
1982	41.66	11.9	1993	98.07	24.8

[a]Data not available.
Source: CBS (1995a).

are potentially important policy instruments for (local) governments, and there
have been a number of various experiments with financial instruments based on the
"polluter pays" principle, as adopted in the NMP. Some of these experiments have
attempted to find a more flexible tariff structure for waste (IPH, 1995), where the
costs depend on the container size, the frequency of collection, and the weight of
the waste.

The main purpose of tariff differentiation is to encourage households to separate their waste for recycling, and to reduce the volume of non-recyclable waste. In one experiment in the town of Oostzaan, for example, households were charged according to the amount of waste collected. The conditions of the scheme were that the cost of living should not rise (ensuring a fair distribution of the costs) and that negative effects, such as "waste tourism" (householders from outside the town coming to dump waste illegally in local woods or open water) would be controlled. Within the first year, the annual costs per household had fallen, and the amount of waste requiring collection fell by 38% (PME Consultancy, 1994).

8.6. Car Ownership and Use

The ownership and use of the car represent important components of household energy consumption, because high levels of car ownership indicate high fuel consumption. In the period 1962–1989, transport by car increased by 3.7% per year (Bennis *et al.*, 1991, p. 1). In this section we analyze passenger transport, including transport by private car, for which the population and thereby households are responsible. The share of transport by private car in the total passenger transport has grown steadily (see Chapter 2). Between 1960 and 1979, the number of cars per thousand households rose from 160 to 900, and then remained approximately constant (see *Figure 8.15*). Since 1994 the penetration rate has been more or less constant, with about 65% of households owning at least one car (CBS, 1995b).

A second aspect of transport by private car is the distance driven. This declined slightly over most of the period, but has increased again in recent years. It is important to distinguish between the use of the car for different purposes, because the costs to the consumer may differ; for example, if an employer reimburses the costs of traveling to work, then for the commuter the marginal costs of commuting are zero.

With the strong increase in car ownership, the private use of the car has increased sharply. The distance driven for private purposes is defined as the total distance driven, excluding business use, but including commuting. In 1963, 42% of the distance driven was for private purposes, but by 1993 this had doubled to about 81% (CBS, 1995a). However, growth has slowed in the last few years and there has even been a slight decline. *Figure 8.16* shows that between 1963 and 1993, the average distance driven for private purposes increased from 7800 to 13,600 km/year.

Figure 8.17 shows the changes in the real and nominal prices of fuel. Here, we focus on the real price of high-octane fuel ("super"); the fluctuations in the prices of other fuels, such as LPG and diesel, have been similar (for more details, see Chapter 2; Bennis *et al.*, 1991, p. 11). The lowest price, 156 ct/liter, was reached in 1969 and 1978, and the highest price, 203 ct/liter, in 1959 and 1981. De Wit

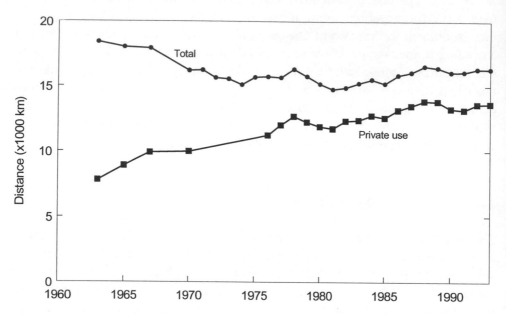

Figure 8.15. Car ownership: number of cars per 1000 households, 1960–1993. Source: CBS (1995a).

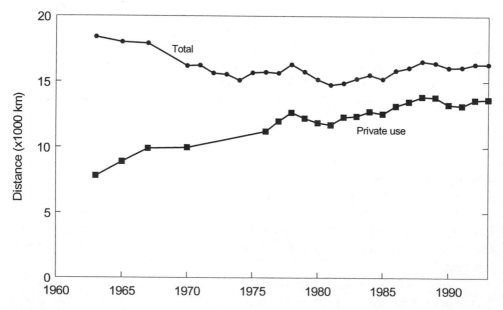

Figure 8.16. Car use: total distances driven per year, and shares for private use, 1963–1993. Source: CBS (1995a).

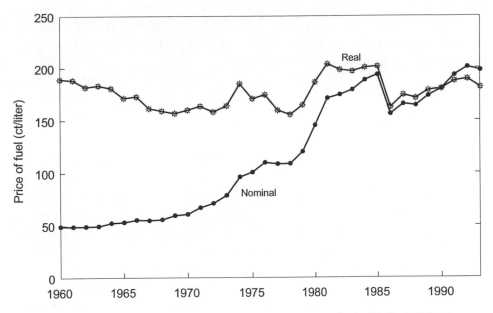

Figure 8.17. Real and nominal prices of high-octane fuel, 1960–1993. Source: CBS (1995a).

and van Gent (1986) calculated that the (short-term) price elasticities for fuel in the period 1955–1980 were approximately −0.1; they concluded that an increase in fuel prices would have a greater effect on car ownership than on the distances traveled by car. More recently, van Staalduinen and Rouwendal (1994), using monthly data, showed an elasticity of −1.0, so that a 1% increase in fuel prices would reduce monthly car use by 1%. De Jong (1990) found a fuel price elasticity of −0.65.

Finally, car fuel consumption has decreased over time. This was demonstrated in a case study of Bennis *et al.* (1991), who analyzed changes in fuel use and other characteristics of the Opel Kadett [4] in the period 1962–1990. From their data we have calculated the five-year moving averages of fuel use for the Kadett, from which we find that fuel use decreased slightly over time. The quality of the Kadett has improved, according to the study of Bennis *et al.* This quality index was calculated with the hedonic price regression. The quality improvement of the Opel Kadett indicates that the fuel use per service unit fell even more sharply.

Bennis *et al.* (1991) also analyzed the annual costs of running a car. These include the fixed costs (depreciation, insurance, taxes, loan interest, etc.), and variable costs, which depend on the distance driven (e.g., servicing, repairs, fuel). The fixed costs (in real prices) account for most of the total annual costs. According to Bennis *et al.* (p. 44), the costs fluctuated but did not increase much; every increase in cost was compensated in subsequent years. If the costs are corrected for efficiency improvements, the fluctuations were even stronger (p. 47). Note that cost fluctuations are due mainly to changes in fixed costs, so that in recent years, driving a car has not become more expensive.

8.7.   Conclusions

In this chapter we have focused on the prices and consumption of electricity, gas and water in the period 1950–1990. The government's growing concern for the environment has been reflected in its energy-saving measures and the use of price as a major policy instrument. The rates of VAT on energy, and of various taxes on energy and water consumption (the "ecotax") have been increased, and an extra tax (the MAP tax) has been introduced to finance environmental activities of the energy supply companies. Although all of these taxes increased nominal prices, the real prices fell in the period considered. In 1979, for example, electricity consumption per household was five times higher than in 1950, yet the real price fell from almost 60 to 20 ct/kWh. On the basis of the price elasticities reported in other studies we conclude that these declining prices contributed significantly to the increase in household metabolic flows.

The possession rates of a number of appliances have increased, as have their energy efficiency. However, the number of service units per appliance has increased. Thus the energy consumption per service unit declined, but the number of services per appliance and per household increased.

The government's concern for the environment has been reflected in policies aimed at reducing domestic waste and the use of the car. The sharp increases in charges for collecting waste, as with the waste taxes in the early 1990s, seem to have been effective in curbing the increase in the amount of domestic waste. The use of the car increased enormously between 1960 and 1990; the number of cars per household doubled between 1960 and 1980, while the real cost of fuel fell between 1954 and 1990. From the results of other studies we conclude that higher fuel prices have two effects: the distance driven falls, and consumers postpone the decision to purchase a new car or replace an old one.

We conclude that the falling real prices seem to have encouraged household metabolism in recent decades. It is therefore important to analyze the potential effectiveness of price instruments such as taxes and subsidies, as means of implementing and achieving government policy.

Summary

- The real prices of energy have fallen over the years, and are likely to have stimulated demand.
- The possession rates of many domestic appliances have increased. The energy use per service unit of appliances has declined, while the number of services per appliance has increased.
- The amount of household waste has increased steadily. The results of various experiments indicate that charging households for waste collection on the basis of weight will help to curb the increase in the amounts of waste.
- The use of the car has increased steadily, in terms of both the number of cars per household and the use of the car for private purposes. Real fuel prices have fluctuated but have barely increased despite the two oil crises.

Appendix A: Energy and water consumption of appliances

In this Appendix we summarize the results of comparative tests of domestic appliances conducted by the Dutch Corporation for Comparison Tests (Stichting Vergelijkend Warenonderzoek) in 1964–1992 (*Consumentengids*). These data sets were used to determine the changes in electricity and water use per service unit resulting from efficiency improvements, and provide a clear picture of the changing costs of the use of domestic appliances to the consumer.

Note that the washing machine and dishwasher (unlike the refrigerator and freezer) are not used constantly, so the variables are not measured per day, but per run. Thus the total amounts of electricity and water consumed are determined by both the amounts required per run, and by the number of runs.

Refrigerators

The results of the first comparative test of refrigerators were published in 1964. In our data set for 665 refrigerators for the period 1964–1991, we distinguished three types: cabinet-sized, two-door and combined refrigerators. Note that some cabinet-sized models contain a freezer compartment inside the fridge, and the two-door and combined fridges have separate freezer and cooling compartments.

Almost half of the refrigerators tested were cabinet-sized models, about 21% combined models, and the rest two-door models. *Table 8.A1* shows the relevant determinants of the refrigerator data set, and shows that 87% of the tested fridges also had freezer compartment. This implies that most cabinet-sized refrigerators have freezer compartments, with different capacities, ranked 0–4. The combined and two-door refrigerators had the highest capacity freezer compartments.

Our main interest is the electricity use of the fridges. The average electricity use per day was 1.23 kWh, measured at a room temperature of 21.5°C. The electricity

Table 8.A1. Summary statistics of the refrigerator data set.

Variables	Mean	SD	Min	Max	N
Price (Dfl)	866.00	427.60	185.00	2,600.00	662
Net volume (liters)	163.30	40.49	81.00	315.00	665
Quality of freezing	2.58	1.53	0.00	4.00	636
Volume of freezer compartment (liters)	40.20	37.70	0.00	137.00	665
Electricity use (kWh)	1.23	0.52	0.37	4.10	601
Year of test	1981	7.66	1964	1991	665
Number of doors	1.46	0.50	1.00	2.00	665
Dummies:					
Cabinet-sized refrigerator	0.50	0.50	0.00	1.00	665
Bottom-freezer refrigerator	0.21	0.41	0.00	1.00	665
Top-freezer refrigerator	0.29	0.45	0.00	1.00	665
Freezer compartment	0.87	0.34	0.00	1.00	665
Integrated into kitchen design	0.06	0.23	0.00	1.00	418
Environment temperature 18°C	0.45	0.50	0.00	1.00	665
Environment temperature 25°C	0.55	0.50	0.00	1.00	665

use was measured under different circumstances. In the first years of testing, a room temperature of 25°C was used, while more recent tests have used 18°C.

Freezers

The first comparative test of freezers appeared in 1970 and was repeated several times. By 1992, 350 freezers had been analyzed, including three models: cabinet-size, wardrobe-size, and chest-type. Note that the freezer compartments of refrigerators were not taken into account here, since these were accounted for in the data set of refrigerators. *Table 8.A2* summarizes some statistics of the freezer data set. The freezer volume varies considerably, depending on the model; the average was 198 liters. The capacity is the maximum weight of food that can be frozen at one time. The average electricity use of freezers is 1.25 kWh per day. As with refrigerators, the electricity use was measured at different temperatures. The average temperature was 22.5°C, and the measurement temperatures were 18, 20, or 25°C.

Washing Machines

We used the results of comparative tests on 660 washing machines (published in 1965–1992) of three types: front-loaders, top-loaders without a spin dryer, and twin-tub models (separate top-loader and spin dryer). *Table 8.A3* summarizes their characteristics, prices and electricity and water consumption. Washing machines are the most expensive to buy of the four domestic appliances we analyzed. The

Table 8.A2. Summary statistics of the freezer data set.

Variables	Mean	SD	Min	Max	N
Price (Dfl)	900.00	270.30	258	1,820	350
Net volume (liters)	198.00	88.60	19	495	350
Number of baskets	4.10	1.80	1	10	245
Freezer capacity (kg)	17.80	6.50	2	34	313
Electricity use (kWh)	1.25	0.50	1	4	346
Year of test	1985	8.20	1970	1992	350
Dummies:					
Cabinet-sized freezer	0.27	0.45	0	1	350
Wardrobe-sized freezer	0.30	0.46	0	1	350
Chest-type freezer	0.43	0.50	0	1	350
Environment temperature 18°C	0.24	0.43	0	1	350
Environment temperature 20°C	0.15	0.36	0	1	350
Environment temperature 25°C	0.61	0.48	0	1	350
Cabinet-sized freezer	0.17	0.37	0	1	350

Table 8.A3. Summary statistics of the washing machine data set.

Variables	Mean	SD	Min	Max	N
Price (Dfl)	1,237.00	409.30	398.0	3,300.0	660
Load (kg)	3.76	1.36	1.0	8.0	660
Water use (liters per run)	106.00	28.00	32.0	215.0	660
Electricity use (kWh per run)	1.66	0.88	0.3	4.9	660
Temperature of wash run (°C)	70.40	19.60	40.0	95.0	660
Time of a wash run (hours)	1.66	0.62	0.5	3.2	660
Maximum revolutions/minute	1,042.00	512.60	360.0	2,865.0	331
Year of test	1982	7.60	1965	1992	660
Dummies:					
Top-loader	0.12	0.32	0.0	1.0	660
Front-loader	0.77	0.42	0.0	1.0	660
Twin-tub	0.08	0.28	0.0	1.0	660
Program temperature 40°C	0.12	0.32	0.0	1.0	660
Program temperature 60°C	0.52	0.50	0.0	1.0	660
Program temperature 95°C	0.36	0.48	0.0	1.0	660
Synthetic program	0.30	0.45	0.0	1.0	660
Prewash	0.28	0.45	0.0	1.0	660

weight of the dry loads varied from 1 to 8 kg. Some machines (28%) were measured during a washing program including a prewash. There were four different programs with four wash temperatures: washing programs at 40 and 60°C; a special washing program at 95°C; and a special program for synthetics at 65°C.

Table 8.A4. Summary statistics of the dishwasher data set.

Variables	Mean	SD	Min	Max	N
Price (Dfl)	1,214.00	322.20	500.0	2,075.0	129
Volume of service unit (liters)	10.90	2.10	4.0	14.0	129
Water use (liters per run)	41.60	15.00	11.0	71.0	129
Electricity use (kWh per run)	1.90	0.60	0.6	3.2	129
Program temperature (°C)	62.40	5.30	35.0	70.0	129
Time of a run (hours)	1.30	0.30	0.5	2.0	125
Year of test	1979	7.10	1968	1989	129
Dummies:					
Portable dishwasher	0.05	0.21	0.0	1.0	129
Top loader	0.05	0.23	0.0	1.0	129
Integrated into kitchen design	0.57	0.52	0.0	1.0	109
Energy-saving program	0.02	0.15	0.0	1.0	129

Dishwashers

We gathered information on 129 dishwashers tested in the period 1968–1989. The first, in 1968, tested three models: a small portable dishwasher that could be installed near to the sink for waste water drainage, and two cabinet-sized models, one a top-loader and the other a front-loader. *Table 8.A4* summarizes the data set. Note that the volume of a dishwasher is not an accurate measure of its capacity, so we have used the number of baskets to represent the volume.

Appendix B: Hedonic regression

Technology generally improves over time. This also applies to domestic appliances; they have become more energy-efficient and perform a wider range of services. To compare the energy and water consumption of appliances over the years, we adjusted the data to take into account quality improvements using the hedonic regression technique introduced by Rosen (1974). The basic idea is to estimate a regression equation that describes the relationship between the electricity (or water) consumption of an appliance (on the left-hand side), and a number of characteristics, such as volume, freezing temperature, and a time variable (on the right-hand side). The estimated coefficient then indicates to what extent a change in a characteristic accounts for a change in electricity (or water) consumption.

In our study, we distinguished two cases: refrigerators and freezers, which use only electricity: and washing machines and dishwashers, which use both electricity and water. The (logarithms of the) inputs are related to the characteristics of the appliance and a trend. The equation is estimated by ordinary least squares. The estimated trend parameter reveals an annual decline in the quality-corrected use of

Table 8.B1. Estimation results of hedonic regressions (*t*-values in parentheses).

Variables	Refrigerator Elec.	Freezer Elec.	Washing machine Elec.	Washing machine Water	Dishwasher Elec.	Dishwasher Water
Constant	1.238	0.972	1.723	0.984	0.894	4.807
	(6.017)	(5.956)	(13.493)	(7.244)	(3.511)	(19.260)
Year of test	−0.021	−0.017	−0.023	−0.016	−0.026	−0.036
	(10.403)	(9.412)	(14.076)	(9.311)	(9.669)	(11.018)
Net volume of refrigerator	0.0004	–	–	–	–	–
	(0.919)					
Net volume of freezer compartment	0.004	0.002	–	–	–	–
	(5.063)	(13.062)				
Maximum load per run	–	–	0.038	0.086	0.044	–
			(4.122)	(8.735)	(4.185)	
Time per run	–	–	0.131	−0.007	0.639	0.549
			(6.956)	(0.337)	(8.639)	(6.031)
Program temperature	–	–	–	–	0.008	–
					(2.609)	
Dummies:						
Two-door refrigerator	0.527	–	–	–	–	–
	(10.569)					
Combined refrigerator	0.494	–	–	–	–	–
	(6.428)					
Freezer comp. cabinet sized model	0.265	–	–	–	–	–
	(6.439)					
Wardrobe-sized freezer	–	0.153	–	–	–	–
		(5.712)				
Cabinet-sized freezer	–	−0.371	–	–	–	–
		(13.656)				
Top-loader	–	–	–	–	−0.266	–
					(3.803)	
Environment temperature 20°C	–	0.122	–	–	–	–
		(3.771)				
Environment temperature 25°C	0.091	0.267	–	–	–	–
	(3.833)	(10.745)				
Prewash	–	–	0.118	0.096	–	–
			(4.259)	(3.245)		
Program temperature 40°C	–	–	−0.604	−0.039	–	–
			(0.948)	(1.262)		
Program temperature 95°C	–	–	0.471	−0.036	–	–
			(20.017)	(1.424)		
Energy-saving program	–	–	–	–	–	−0.263
						(2.082)
Softener	–	–	–	–	–	0.231
						(2.720)
R^2	0.61	0.75	0.86	0.38	0.73	0.69
Number of observations	601	346	660	660	125	125

energy and water for all four appliances; see *Table 8.B1*. These results were used to calculate the annual electricity and water consumption shown in *Figures 8.8–8.12*.

Notes

[1] 1 m^3 natural gas $\equiv 31.65$ MJ; 1 GJ $\equiv 31.60 \text{ m}^3$.
[2] This is not only the case for the Netherlands. Since the water companies in the UK were privatized in 1989, average household charges for water in England and Wales have shown substantial real increases. As pointed out by Rajah and Smith (1993), the debate over the level and structure of residential water charges is likely to continue, as the 1989 Water Act prohibits, after the end of the century, the current practice of levying water charges based on imputed market rental values of domestic properties.
[3] The average annual electricity use data here are five-year moving averages. For example, the average use in 1966 is based on data from 1964–1969.
[4] The Opel Kadett is known as the Vauxhall Astra in the UK.

References

Bennis, M.J., P. Hopstaken and F.M. Roest (1991) *De kosten van de auto en het openbaar vervoer vergeleken, 1962–90* (The costs of the car and public transportation compared), SEO Rep. 276, Amsterdam.

Booij, J.T., M.P. Klaassen and H.D. Webbink (1992) *Prijselasticiteit van het huishoudelijk energieverbruik* (Price elasticities of household energy consumption), SEO Rep. 279, Amsterdam.

CBS (1993) *Afvalstoffen: van gemeentewege ingezameld afval, 1991* (Waste: composition of municipal waste, 1991), SDU, The Hague.

CBS (1995a) *95 jaren statistiek in tijdreeksen* (95 years of statistics in time series), SDU, The Hague.

CBS (1995b) *Statistisch Jaarboek 1995* (Statistical yearbook of The Netherlands 1995), SDU, The Hague.

De Jong, G.C. (1990) An indirect utility model of car ownership and private car use, *European Economic Review*, **34**:971–985.

De Wit, J.G. and H.A. van Gent (1986) *Vervoers- en verkeerseconomie: theorie, praktijk en beleid* (Transport economics: theory, practice and policy), Stenfert Kroese, Leiden.

Consumentengids (several volumes), Consumentenbond, The Hague.

EnergieNed (several volumes) *Energiedistributie in Nederland* (Energy distribution in the Netherlands), EnergieNed, Arnhem.

Herrington, P. (1987) *Pricing of Water Services*, OECD, Paris.

IPH (1995) *Tariefdifferentiatie voor huishoudelijk afval* (Tariff differentiation for household waste), Informatiedocument IPH 95-03, Utrecht.

Kooreman, P. (1993) *De prijsgevoeligheid van huishoudelijk watergebruik* (The price sensitivity of residential water use), Economisch Statistische Berichten, vol. 78, pp. 181–183.

PME Consultancy (1994) *Afval voorkomen loont: Een gedifferentieerd tarief voor huishoudelijk afval gebaseerd op het gewicht in de praktijk gebracht* (Waste prevention pays: a practical example of the tariff differentiation for household waste based on weight), Zeist.

Rajah, N. and S. Smith (1993) Distributional aspects of household water charges, *Fiscal Policy*, **14**:86–108.

Rosen, S. (1974) Hedonic prices and implicit markets: product differentiations in pure competition, *Journal of Political Economy*, **82**:34–55.

SER (1989) *Nationaal Milieubeleidsplan* (National Environmental Policy Plan), SER Advies 89/17, The Hague.

Van Maanen, J.M.C. (1994) *Basisonderzoek elektriciteitsverbruik kleinverbruikers (BEK 93)* (Research on the electricity consumption of small users, 1993), EnergieNed, Arnhem.

Van Oortmarssen, G. (1991) *Beinvloeding van het tijdstip van elektriciteitverbruik door hiushouders* (Influencing the timing of electricity use of householders), thesis, University of Amsterdam.

Van Ours, J.C. (1986) *Gezinsconsumptie in Nederland, 1951–80* (Consumer demand in the Netherlands, 1951–80), thesis, Erasmus University Rotterdam.

Van Staalduinen, L. and J. Rouwendal (1994) *A Panel Data Analysis of Short Term Changes in Automobile Use*, Internal paper, Dept. of Household and Consumer Studies, Wageningen Agricultural University.

VEWIN (several volumes) *Tarievenoverzicht leidingwater* (Survey of tap water tariffs), Rijswijk.

Chapter 9

The Effects of Public Policies on Household Metabolism

J.J. Ligteringen

Abstract

Until now, the scope of most public policy evaluations has been limited to studying the impacts of policies specifically directed at certain fields. Most evaluations of environmental policies, for example, have concentrated on their impacts on the behavior of consumers and producers, even though this behavior is also influenced by policies in other fields. Policies related to the use of the car, energy for heating, and domestic appliances are often strongly interlinked: policy instruments in one field will often also influence the effects of others in other fields. Here we do not question the existence of such interlinkages; we present an overview of the actual interlinkages that can be observed in the case of policies that have affected household behavior, either intentionally or unintentionally. Overviews such as this are important because of the lessons that can be learned and taken into account in the design of more effective policies in the future.

9.1. Introduction

Since the 1980s there have been many studies of environmental policy, due mainly to the growing social awareness of environmental pollution and ways of dealing with it. Many of these studies have attempted to identify which policy instruments are the most effective in making individuals and businesses more aware of the environmental impacts of their behavior. Such policies include those specifically aimed at changing certain aspects of behavior, as well as those that were not specifically intended to do so. The side-effects of such policies unintentionally (and sometimes unknowingly) affect the behavior that other policy fields try to influence intentionally.

This kind of policy analysis can be usefully applied to the phenomenon of household metabolism. In this chapter we give an overview of public policies – specific and non-specific – that may have influenced household metabolism in the Netherlands since 1950. First, we deal with the unintentional effects of policies, and then the effects of specific policies.

9.2. Unintentional Policy Effects

Since the publication of the Environmental Policy Integration Plan (TK, 18 010, 1982–1983), the Netherlands government has consciously chosen a multifaceted approach: the environment should be taken into account in all policy fields. It is not surprising, therefore, that this goal has become closely interwoven in a wide range of public policies. Many recent studies have noted the existence of this interweaving of policy effects (Bouwer *et al.*, 1995; van Wee, 1993; ten Heuvelhof, 1994; VROM, 1992; Knoepfel, 1995; Naaijkens, 1989; OECD, 1995), where the effects of instruments in one policy field may be eliminated or weakened by those in another. This interweaving may explain the extent of target achievement in a field such as the environment. This chapter does not question the existence of this interweaving, but examines which policies have become interwoven in practice. Despite the frequent mention of "interweaving" as a general explanation of policy effects, few studies so far have dealt with this as a separate area of attention.

Studies of the interweaving of policies are important, in that lessons may be learned that can be taken into account in the design of policies in the future. Only by explaining concepts such as side-effects will we be able to use them (Drees, 1992). First, we examine *which* public policies may have indirectly influenced consumer behavior with regard to the use of the car, energy for heating, and domestic appliances (in this case, "white goods" such as refrigerators and washing machines).

There have been few systematic efforts to survey the policy fields that have influenced consumer behavior. The Ministry of Public Housing, Physical Planning and the Environment (VROM) did attempt to assess the side-effects of policies related to sustainable development by means of Action A-141 from the National Environmental Policy Plan (NMP; TK, 21 137, 1988–1989), but with meager results.

Policies in one field may have the intended effects in that field, as well as unintentional effects in other fields. In the case of the environment, such "side-effects" can be beneficial or harmful in terms of how they influence consumer behavior. Thus, if one policy has strong environmentally harmful side-effects, then the overall goals of environmental policy will be jeopardized. It is therefore important to determine which side-effects of other policies may influence the behavior of consumers with respect to the environment. One example of a policy field that has affected consumer behavior is that of physical planning policy. In the 1960s plans were drawn up to develop new residential areas some 25–50 km outside the major cities, in the hope that they would attract industries and jobs. Few jobs were created, however, and long-distance commuter traffic was not reduced. This was not the only policy that affected car use; an inventory of policies is given later in this chapter.

9.2.1. Problem definition and method

In this section we address the question:

> which policies in which fields have unintentionally influenced the rate of household metabolism with regard to the use of the car, energy for heating, and domestic appliances in the Netherlands since 1950?

Although in this survey we aimed to be as complete as possible, in the end almost all public policy fields appear to have influenced (albeit sometimes very indirectly) household metabolism, so that completeness is probably neither feasible nor desirable.

To answer this first question, we compiled inventories of both written and verbal information. We obtained written information on the relevant fields from the various ministries, and policy documents relevant to household metabolism. Then, for each field, we investigated whether the adopted policy instruments may actually have (intentionally or unintentionally) influenced household metabolism. As another source of written information, we gathered information on the policy fields and instruments related to sustainable development that resulted from the above mentioned NMP inventory, on the basis of which we examined the policies that may have influenced household metabolism. Finally, we interviewed government experts in the areas of the use of the car, energy for heating, and domestic appliances. We asked them to specify and comment on the list of side-effects, and for their reactions to the draft survey.

9.2.2. Results

The explanatory variables for the influence of policies on household behavior with regard to the use of the car, energy for heating, and domestic appliances were then classified. We found that policies related to four major areas could have indirectly influenced consumer behavior and thus household metabolism: demographics, sociocultural developments, economics, and physical/spatial developments.[1]

In addition to policies in these areas which may have indirectly affected household metabolism, we describe specific policies that were intended to influence behavior, such as energy-saving and environmental policies. However, it is difficult to make a clear distinction between the effects of different policy fields, because

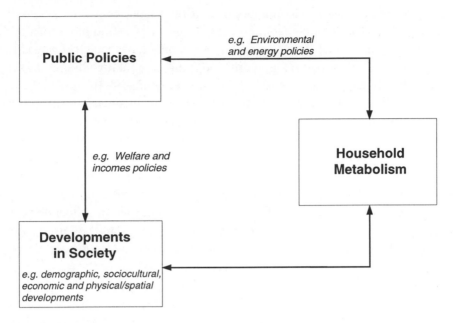

Figure 9.1. The influence of public policies on household metabolism.

environmental and other objectives sometimes coincide. For example, attempts to reduce car use may be in line with policies to reduce traffic congestion, as well as with environmental objectives. This mutual influence is depicted in *Figure 9.1*. In the following we describe the policy fields that have influenced each of these aspects of household metabolism.

Car Use

We first determine and operationalize the dependent variable, car use, which is defined as the total distance traveled by car per household per year. As noted in Chapter 2, both the number of cars and the distances traveled have grown significantly since 1950. Here, we discuss economic factors in terms of their effects on disposable incomes and expenditure patterns, and thus on the use of the car. Other factors include the availability and costs of various forms of transport, as well as socioeconomic development in general; the increase in prosperity has also led to increased disposable incomes. Hamerslag *et al.* (1988) found that as incomes rise, both car ownership and the distance traveled by car increase.

Incomes policy and socioeconomic policies in general have influenced car use. Until the mid-1960s incomes policy had a restraining influence on income, which may have reduced car use, but then incomes were allowed to rise and may have led to an increase in car use. Socioeconomic policies led to a reduction in working hours, providing consumers with more leisure time and the need for greater personal mobility. The number of part-time labor contracts increased, as did the number of holidays, enabling people to go on vacation more than once a year. The introduction of flexible working hours may have actually increased car use, however, since commuting to work, shopping, and taking children to school often involve three separate journeys (Leidelmeyer *et al.*, 1993).

Other policy fields that have influenced disposable incomes, and thus also car use indirectly, include *public housing policy*, which determines the levels of rent subsidies, and *social policy*, which sets welfare and child benefit levels.

Since 1950 fuel prices have influenced car use. Following the 1973 oil crisis, the sharp increases in prices had the temporary effect of reducing the distances traveled by car.[2] Research and experience have shown that a substantial increase in fuel prices initially causes a reduction in car use, but then the effect ebbs away. The long-term effect will be greater (Schrijnen, 1986, p. 42). The introduction of LPG reduced the costs of running a car. Since fuel prices also depend on policy with regard to fuel, *fuel policy* may also have influenced car use.

In the context of *fiscal policy*, charges include the motor vehicle tax and the Road Fund tax. The possibility to deduct traveling expenses (i.e., tax-deductible commuting expenses) intended to encourage mobility in the job market, is also part of fiscal policy.

Since the 1960s, *welfare policies* have also indirectly influenced mobility. In addition to policies to ensure equal opportunities for women,[3] the then Ministry of Welfare, Public Health and Culture introduced a number of subsidies, including the "Pass 65+", which provided cheap public transport for senior citizens.

Education policy may also have an impact on car use.[4] The Students' Public Transport Pass (1991) reduced the variable cost of using public transport for students to zero. However, encouraging students to use public transport now does not necessarily mean that they will always prefer it to the car. They may continue to want this freedom of travel, but using a car instead, thus increasing car ownership. On the other hand, some may become so used to using public transport that they would not want to use anything else.

Table 9.1 summarizes the public policies that have influenced the use of the car.

The Use of Energy for Heating

In this case, we adopt the use of energy for heating as the dependent variable; this is defined as the total energy used for space heating per household per year. The energy used for heating represents the largest proportion of household energy consumption (see Chapter 2). In the 1950s coal or oil stoves were usually used for domestic heating, but with the discovery of Dutch natural reserves in 1959, more households were connected to the gas mains and installed central heating systems. During the 1980s, the total consumption of natural gas for domestic heating fell,

Table 9.1. Public policies that have influenced car use in the Netherlands.

Non-specific policies with side-effects on car use	Explanatory factors	Policy fields influencing explanatory factors	Measures in indicated policy fields	Stimulating	Restraining
Through demographic developments	Population size and composition	Public health policy	Higher level of medical facilities and improved medication	x	
Through cultural developments	No. of households household activities	Welfare policy (emancipation)	Equal opportunities	x	
		Social security policy	Old age pensions	x	
		Public housing policy	Rent subsidies	x	
Through economic developments	Income development	Incomes policy	"Wage wave"	x	
		Socioeconomic policy	Reduction of working hours, part-time contracts, number of holidays, flexible working hours	x	
	Transport costs and facilities cost	Public housing policy	Rent subsidies	x	
		Social policy	Level of welfare and child benefits	x	
		Fuel policy	Fuel price policy	x	
		Welfare policy (elderly)	Pass 65+	x	
		Education policy	Students' public transport pass		x
		Fiscal policy	Motor vehicle tax, additional State Road Fund tax, deduction of traveling expenses		x
Through spatial developments	Travel distances local activities	Physical planning policy	Location policy (e.g., residential areas)	x	
	Transport system quality and facilities	Traffic and transport policy	Construction of roads and connections for various forms of transport, price of public transport	x	
		Educational policy	School enlargements of scale	x	
		Traffic safety policy	Car inspections, seatbelts, "wrinkling zones"	x	
		Technology policy	Technology subsidies	x	
		Public housing policy	Rise in house purchases due to rent increases and premiums on purchased homes	x	

due largely to the increased efficiency of domestic boilers and insulation (Groenen *et al.*, 1993).

Demographic changes in the Netherlands have influenced household energy consumption for heating. The population has grown, and so has the number of households (see Chapter 4), and the use of heating. The aging of the population has also increased the use of heating (Groenen *et al.*, 1993). Over the years, various policies have been introduced in response to demographic developments, and have indirectly increased the use of energy for heating. For example, *public health policies* have led to improved health care facilities, so that the average age of the population has increased, and *welfare policy* has made it possible for the elderly to live at home for longer.

Various spatial developments have influenced the locations of households, and the availability of facilities in or around the house. As part of *public housing policy*, the 1962 Housing Act required municipalities to draw up building regulations, including requirements for insulation. These insulation requirements can be seen as side-effects of public housing policy, but also as part of energy-saving policy; this is an example of "inter-policy cooperation". As the quality of the housing stock has been improved, houses have become smaller and better insulated, and older, usually badly insulated houses have been demolished. Due to the increasing demand for insulation (due mainly to rising energy prices), improved forms of insulation have been introduced and installed in existing dwellings.

In 1984 the Norm Cost System Bill ("normkostensysteem") was introduced to increase decentralization in the public housing sector. Financing and subsidies for new dwellings were based on new basic quality standards, as laid out in the Building Regulations. In 1993 the subsidy for low-emission and energy-saving heating boilers was abolished because these had found their way on to the market. In 1991 the new Housing Act was accompanied by a Building Decree, which also contained energy-saving requirements.

In 1995 there was a change in the system of financing housing construction, which had previously hindered the installation of energy-saving measures. Prior to 1995, all investments in social housing were charged to the state budget (de Maar, 1987), so in order not to exceed the budget, energy-saving measures were not included in new buildings, even though they would have been socially cost-effective. Under the new system, the extra costs of installing energy-saving measures are charged to the housing associations, who can recoup them through higher rents, and so are more likely to install them.

Another influencing factor is the availability of facilities in or around the home, such as connections to gas and electricity mains, or to district heating systems. We consider these facilities as being part of *facilitating fuel policy*. When the gas supply network was extended in the late 1960s, many households installed central heating systems (see Chapter 2), and so were able to heat more rooms to a higher average temperature. In the early 1970s this resulted in a rapid increase in the average gas consumption per household. When central heating was included in the building regulations, the percentage of dwellings equipped with individual central heating rose rapidly (Brezet, 1994, pp. 12, 13).

Subsidies provided under *technology policy* have meant that heating appliances have become more efficient and user-friendly over the years.[5] These measures (attributable partly to economic motives) may be seen as examples of the integration of environmental and other policies.

Physical planning policy may also have influenced the use of energy for domestic heating. In 1983 the Ministry of Economic Affairs emphasized the possibilities for municipalities to include energy-saving devices in their area development plans. Here again we see inter-policy cooperation between physical planning and energy policy.

Table 9.2 lists the public policies that have influenced the use of energy for domestic heating.

Domestic Appliances

Here we consider two aspects of the use of domestic appliances and their effects on the environment: the extent to which the use of electrical appliances determines the total energy consumption of households, and the qualitative or quantitative influence of these appliances in terms of the waste generated. As a dependent variable we may then choose between the consequences of the use of appliances for energy consumption, and the amounts of waste produced by households (see Former, 1995).

Various sociocultural developments have influenced the use of domestic appliances; here the number of households and the trend towards more independent lifestyles are used as explanatory factors. Since sociocultural developments have affected both household activities and the type of housing, policies in these areas may have an indirect influence on the use of appliances. For example, the population has grown, and the average household size has fallen (from 4.3 in 1947 to 2.4 in 1993; see Chapter 4). Thus the number of households, and the number of appliances, have increased more than proportionally to population growth. This process has also been partly responsible for the increase in purchases of electrical appliances.

Policy fields that have supported these developments, and have therefore influenced the use of domestic appliances include *public housing policy*, where the subsidy system enabled people to rent a property even if it was beyond their financial means, and thus to keep a separate household. *Social security policy* may also have helped more people to establish separate households, since many elderly and young people no longer found it necessary to live with their families for financial reasons.

Table 9.2. Public policies that have influenced the use of energy for heating and domestic appliances.

Non-specific policies with side-effects on the use of energy for heating and domestic appliances	Explanatory factors	Policy fields influencing explanatory factors	Measures in indicated policy fields	Stimulating	Restraining
Through demographic developments	Population size and composition	Public health policy	Higher level of facilities, improved medication	x	
		Welfare policy	Encouraging elderly to live at home	x	
Through cultural developments	No. of households	Welfare policy (emancipation)	Equal opportunities	x	
	Household activities	Social security policy	Old age pensions	x	
		Public housing policy	Rent subsidies	x	
Through economic developments	Income development	Incomes policy	"Wage wave"	x	
		Socioeconomic policy	Levels of welfare, child benefits, holiday allowances	x	
	Fuel and energy policy	Fuel and energy policy	Natural gas and energy prices	x	x
		Fiscal policy	Fuel tax		x
Through spatial developments	Location of residential areas and public facilities	Public housing policy	Massive housing construction, building regulations, building decree, "grossing" (*brutering*) operation		x
		Physical planning policy	Development area provisions, building decree		x
		Fuel and energy policy (facilitating)	Construction of and connection to the gas grid, central heating	x	
		Technology policy	Technology subsidies		x

In addition, the success of policies aiming at equal opportunities for women (as part of *welfare policy*) has meant that more women now have jobs, and there are more families in which both partners work. To resolve the problem of the lack of time for housework, labor-saving appliances such as dishwashers and washing machines are available. Other government measures that have encouraged more women to work may also have influenced the use of appliances in households (see *Table 9.2*).

Summary

The main social developments that have affected household metabolism over the years are demographics, sociocultural developments, economics, and spatial/physical planning (see *Tables 9.1* and *9.2*). In many cases it is difficult to quantify these effects on household metabolism because it is almost impossible to isolate the many factors involved.

It may seem obvious that these developments have influenced household metabolism, but this does not automatically mean that they also had the desired influence on these developments. For example, policies aiming at equal opportunities for women may have encouraged car use, but one could ask to what extent they have actually contributed to the emancipation process.

It appears that the use of the car and domestic appliances by households has been *stimulated* by the (unintentional) side-effects of policies in other fields. More policy side-effects have stimulated the use of these items than have restrained them. For the use of energy for heating, however, the situation is the reverse; the side-effects of policies in other fields appear to have *restrained* the use of heating far more than the use of the car and appliances.

In addition to non-specific policies that have influenced certain behavior through social developments, there are also policies that have intentionally aimed to influence behavior. However, it is impossible to distinguish between them because environmental objectives have now become integrated in all policy fields, to the extent that the objectives of policies in different fields are the same. For example, the objective of reducing car traffic is shared by both energy policy and environmental policy. Thus some of the effects of non-specific policies can hardly be regarded as unintentional side-effects, but as the consequence of "inter-policy cooperation" (Knoepfel, 1995). Here, we can make a second distinction between the use of cars and appliances on the one hand, and the use of energy for heating on the other. More (unintentional) side-effects of policies in other fields have influenced the use of cars and appliances, than those that have influenced the use of heating. In many cases, the use of energy for heating has been influenced by the integration of environmental objectives into other policies. Energy policy, for example, initially promoted the use of insulation for economic reasons, but soon environmental objectives were integrated.

    In this section we have shown how the interweaving of policies can allow
interactions between policy fields, and how this interaction may help in achieving
policy objectives. The instruments used to achieve the objectives of environmental
policy can be either strengthened, weakened, or even eliminated by the effects of
those in other fields. Thus, policies in other fields may have a major influence
on the environment. Recognizing such mutual influences is insufficient reason to
change policies in these fields. After all, the intended policy can also contribute to
the intended objectives, and thus can be evaluated in a positive way. Nevertheless,
it is important to be aware of specific cross-connections between policy fields. This
interweaving is generally recognized, but there have been few studies of which
policies in which fields affect behavior due to their side-effects. Future research is
therefore necessary to determine which policy fields are important in influencing
behavior.

9.3.   Specific Policy Effects

To obtain a fuller picture, we now look at specific policies that have influenced
household metabolism over the past 20 years. As noted above, it is often difficult
to distinguish between the effects of specific and non-specific policies on household metabolism, because their objectives may coincide (e.g., traffic/transport and
environmental policies), and because environmental objectives have increasingly
become integrated into most policy fields (e.g., public housing and environmental
policies). Here we discuss the objectives and instruments of these specific policies.

9.3.1.   Problem definition and method

In this section we focus on the question:

> what have been the objectives and the instruments of policies specifically
> aimed at influencing household metabolism with regard to the use of the
> car, energy for heating, and domestic appliances in the Netherlands since
> 1950?

To answer this question we studied various policy documents, research reports and
papers on environmental, energy, traffic/transport, and product policies relevant to
household metabolism. Information on specific policies were obtained from the
annual budgets of various ministries (Environment, Economic Affairs, Traffic and
Waterways), which provide surveys of the objectives and instruments of environmental, products, energy, and traffic and transport policies. Policy memoranda
from these ministries also outline the objectives in the various fields, but since
they usually do not state whether the intended instruments are actually used, they
were of little help. Information on the instruments that are used was obtained from

documents from the Second Chamber of the Dutch parliament (Tweede Kamer, TK), copies of the *Official Gazette* and newspaper articles.

9.3.2. Results

Environmental policy plays a central role in specific policies aimed at influencing household metabolism. The objectives of the current environmental policy originated in the early 1980s, when the National Environmental Policy Plans outlined policy strategy, the policy life cycle, and the priorities resulting from this, the planned approach, and the target group approach (Klaver, 1993). In the late 1980s the concept of "sustainable development", taking into account the environment's carrying capacity (WCED, 1987), was adopted as an objective of Dutch environmental policy, embodied in three principles:

1. closing material cycles within the chain of raw materials → production process → product → waste;
2. saving energy, in combination with increased efficiency, and the use of renewable sources of energy; and
3. stressing the quality rather than the quantity of products, production processes, raw materials, waste and environment, in order to ensure the use of materials within the economic cycle over a longer period.

High priority was given to raising public awareness of environmental issues. The Ministry of the Environment (VROM) launched a campaign, including TV advertisements with the slogan "a better environment begins with yourself". Since the government is less able to influence behavior now than in the past, it has to try to persuade other actors and citizens to cooperate. Here the pursuit of internal and external integration plays an important part. Preferred instruments are social regulation (communicative instruments) and economic instruments, as opposed to previous policy, where the focus was on legal regulation. In approaching the target groups, the government has chosen a consensus approach as an element of its policy, emphasizing the target groups' own responsibility to adjust their activities in an environmentally friendly way. The key concepts here are "internalization" and self-regulation (de Koning, 1994).

Car Use

Before the 1973 oil crisis car ownership was regarded as a basic need of the working class. The then prime minister Den Uyl stated that every worker was entitled to his or her own car. Since that time, the government has introduced measures to *limit* car use, focusing on the negative environmental impacts, the threatened depletion of fossil fuels, and increasing traffic congestion. In the following we describe a number of policies that were specifically intended to reduce the use of the car.

Since the 1980s, *environmental policy* has aimed to limit car use. The first National Environmental Policy Plan (NMP-1, 1989) tightened physical planning regulations by encouraging new businesses to locate in areas that were (or would be) well served by the public transportation system. Also, the NMP aimed to discourage facilities with a large workforce or many visitors to locate in areas that were easily accessible by car.

Another objective of NMP-1 was to intensify policies with regard to the Traffic and Transport Structure Scheme, so that any choice of passenger transport would result in minimal energy consumption and pollution. Public transport facilities were to be improved, and the use of the bicycle encouraged as an alternative to the car, particularly for commuting. Residential, industrial, commercial, shopping, and recreational areas were to be coordinated in such a way that the need for movement would be reduced to a minimum.

As part of *fiscal policy*, in 1988 the General Environmental Provisions Act (Wabm) introduced a general destination charge on fuel, but this charge was abolished in 1992 under the Environmentally Based Fuel Consumption Tax Act (Wvbm). In August 1990 tax reforms were implemented so that commuters could deduct the costs of commuting by public transport, making this more advantageous than traveling by car.

In 1991, the *duty on fuel* was raised by Dfl 0.25 to cover the government deficit. This increased the variable costs of running a car, and had the effect of temporarily limiting car use. However, while the duty on fuel and motor vehicle taxes were increased, incomes also continued to rise, so that traveling by car did not become more expensive.

There is a tariff differentiation for the use of diesel, petrol and LPG for passenger cars and other motor vehicles. In the 1990s, as a means of increasing public funds, the government raised the duties on diesel and increased the LPG surcharge in motor vehicle tax. Partly as a result of this, the market share of LPG for car fuels fell. The break-even point in the petrol/LPG relation shifted from an average of 16,500 to 25,000 km per year. The impact of this policy should not be overestimated, however. McKinsey (Ministry of Traffic and Waterways, 1986) estimated that doubling the motor vehicle tax would reduce car use (measured in terms of the number of cars) during peak hours in the west of the Netherlands by only 0.4%.

Car parking policy in the 1980s and 1990s favored higher parking tariffs, and thus may also have directly affected car use. Parking policy was intentionally used as a means of control under traffic and transport policy to reduce car use, since parking fees can be included in the variable costs of car use. During the 1970s many cities introduced parking fees in response to the increasing nuisance of excessive traffic. Parking policy also advocated limiting the amount parking space and other facilities for cars. In the Second Traffic and Transport Structure Scheme (SVV-II, TK 1989–1990, 20 922/15–16), parking policy was used as a means of limiting car use, but was difficult to implement. According to one respondent, local authorities wanted to safeguard competition and so implemented few of these measures. Thus, following the introduction of parking standards, the number of business parking spaces increased by 16% within three years. Nevertheless, in the late 1980s and 1990s parking permits were issued to inner city residents. In 1992, the Parking Policy Implementation Memorandum (TK, 1991–1992, 22 383/1) granted more power to municipalities to implement and enforce paid parking schemes.

In the context of *traffic and transport policy*, several efforts were made during the 1990s to encourage carpooling. The costs of traffic congestion and slow-moving traffic were – and still are – increasing every year. Thus one of the objectives of traffic and transport policy was to reduce the number and size of traffic jams. In the period 1983–1988 various awareness-raising campaigns were mounted to encourage carpooling, and a carpool register was introduced; the estimated savings were 24 million km per year. In 1990 the Second Traffic and Transport Structure Scheme introduced carpooling as a government target (until public transport could take over this task), and carpool parking spaces and separate carpool traffic lanes on highways were introduced. In 1993, 475,000 people made use of carpooling, 16,000 of whom had signed carpooling contracts that made them eligible for tax deductions. The government also encouraged business and industry to set up transport plans, on the basis of which it was possible to apply for small financial contributions in the form of subsidies. Partly due to the efforts of business and industry, and the Dutch Traffic Safety Association (ANWB) and others, the number of carpoolers rose to 555,000 in 1994, an increase of more than 10% on the previous year. The Second Traffic and Transport Structure Scheme also aimed to encourage teleworking: working at home or in collective offices.

Since 1974 the Dutch government has adopted various energy-saving policies, particularly in the traffic and transport sector. After the 1973 oil crisis two measures were introduced to prevent the depletion of domestic oil reserves. First, there were three "car-free Sundays", for which there was wide public support, and second, car owners were issued with coupons that could be exchanged for petrol. However, many gas stations boycotted the measure, so that many drivers were able to obtain petrol even without coupons. In the late 1980s the official speed limit on highways was increased from 100 to 120 km/hour in order to improve traffic flow, and because it was found to be difficult to enforce the lower limit. However, the 100 km/hour zones were soon reintroduced as an energy-saving measure and to reduce environmental impacts. The primary objective of *energy-saving policy* was to reduce fuel consumption, rather than to limit the use of the car as such, even though this has the same effect.

In summary, the main objectives of government measures to limit car use in the last 20 years were to reduce the negative environmental impacts of car use; to reduce the use of fossil fuels; and to reduce the negative economic effects of excessive car use (particularly traffic congestion). *Table 9.3* lists the instruments that were applied in the context of specific policies (environmental, parking, traffic

Table 9.3. Specific policies that have influenced car use in the Netherlands.

Specific policies to restrain car use	Measures in the given fields
Environmental policy	Choice of business locations
	Carpooling facilities
Parking policy	100 km/hour zones on highways
	Public awareness raising
Traffic and transport policy	Differentiation of motor vehicle taxes
	Fuel tax
Energy-saving policy	Deduction of traveling expenses
	Fuel charges
Physical planning policy	Parking fees
	Parking spaces

and transport, energy-saving, and physical planning policies) to reduce the use of the car.

Use of Energy for Heating

The main government measures that were introduced during the past 20 years specifically to *reduce* the use of energy for heating, were taken from the point of view of the environmental impacts, the threatened depletion of fossil fuels, and to reduce the dependency on foreign countries. In the following we describe the policies that specifically aimed to reduce the use of energy for heating.

Since 1974 the government has followed an *energy (saving) policy* with the aim of intentionally influencing household behavior with regard to heating (expressed in terms of the extent to which the use of heating determines household energy consumption). Prior to 1974 the focus was on controlling energy prices as an element of socioeconomic policy, and promoting dependable, continuous supplies of energy in the short and long terms. The government had followed a "demand-response" policy: whenever the demand for energy rose, the government responded with the required supply. The 1973 oil crisis caused considerable price rises, and the government issued a first memorandum aimed at saving energy, calling on the people to close their curtains earlier and to turn down the thermostat.

The main policy objectives were to reduce energy demand, to diversify (i.e., to spread energy consumption over carriers other than oil), and to develop and exploit new domestic energy sources as a means of reducing the dependency on foreign supplies. This first attempt to encourage energy saving was followed in 1979 by completely elaborated sets of instruments and legislation. However, the 1979 oil crisis again led to a rise in energy prices. In 1984 the Energy Policy Actualization Memorandum (TK, 1983–1984) brought this policy up to date on the basis of the new circumstances. By 1986 oil prices had returned to their previous level, so that the incentive to save energy because of the high oil prices disappeared again. Over the next few years energy policy was influenced by the Chernobyl nuclear reactor disaster and falling energy prices.

In the 1990s Dutch economic policy (of which energy policy is a part) has focused on maintaining environmental quality, so that economic objectives have been brought into line with those of the National Environmental Policy Plan (NMP). The equilibrium between energy and environmental objectives is now the main focus of energy policy. The government's current energy-saving policy aims especially at reducing household energy demand resulting from the use of heating, and to develop and install more energy-efficient heating devices.

Energy-saving measures are therefore part of energy policy, but are also used for environmental control. *Environmental policy* has therefore influenced the use of heating in households by encouraging energy savings. The NMP-1 (1989) has been the basis of a number of energy-saving measures in new and existing dwellings. In the Energy Saving Memorandum (TK, 1989–1990, 21 570) the Ministry of Economic Affairs elaborated the plans of the NMP-plus, and provided a separate action program for dwellings.

In 1974 the Energy Memorandum contained the first proposals for subsidies for insulating new and existing dwellings. In 1975 the Ministry of Economic Affairs issued an information leaflet with hints on saving energy in the home, and the insulation requirements contained in the Model Building Regulations of 1964 were tightened. The National Insulation Program resulting from the Energy Memorandum, initiated in 1978, contained plans for the insulation of 200,000 houses per year. Double glazing in living rooms and adjoining areas was made obligatory. The penetration of insulation in existing homes hardly increased during the early 1990s. The degree of insulation due to follow-up programs is still steadily increasing, but at a slower rate (TK, 1989–1990, 21 570).

As described earlier, *public housing policy* also played a part in improving the insulation of dwellings. Under the 1962 Housing Act municipalities were required to draw up building regulations, which could include requirements for insulation. Thus there were specific improvements in the housing stock; new houses were smaller and better insulated, while older, usually badly insulated dwellings were demolished. Due to increased demand, improved forms of insulation appeared on the market. The 1991 Housing Act and accompanying Building Regulations also included energy requirements.

Physical planning policy also played a part regarding the energy situation in the home and may have influenced the use of heating. In 1983 the Ministry of Economic Affairs required municipalities to include energy-saving measures in their development area plans. In 1984 the National Insulation Program introduced insulation standards for new buildings, and extended the subsidy schemes for insulating existing buildings. In 1987 the government issued stricter insulation regulations for houses under construction.

In 1993 the subsidy budget for saving energy in homes was increased substantially to improve insulation and the efficiency of heating appliances. The 1990
Energy Saving Memorandum allowed energy supply companies to levy an environmental surcharge on energy bills to finance their activities in the context of the
Environmental Action Plan (MAP). The MAP aimed to reduce energy consumption
by encouraging the installation of high-efficiency boilers, by means of information
campaigns, and subsidies. In 1993 the MAP was updated (MAP 1994).

In the period 1974–1985 the price of natural gas rose steadily, and the government mounted a major information campaign to encourage households to save
energy. The increase in natural gas prices was followed by a fall of 35% in
1986–1988.

Besides the charges on fuels introduced in connection with the General Environmental Provisions Act (Wabm) and the Environmentally Based Fuel Consumption Tax Act (Wvbm), the cabinet imposed a regulatory charge on domestic energy
bills, starting in January 1996.

The introduction of more efficient gas appliances also contributed to a fall in
gas consumption. In 1993 the subsidy on low-emissions, energy-efficient heating
appliances was abolished, because according to the Ministry of Economic Affairs
boilers of this type had found their way onto the market. In 1988, a subsidy was
granted on solar boilers (for heating water), but the budget in 1993 and 1994 was
apparently too low and was exhausted before the end of the year.

In summary, the main objectives of government measures to reduce the use
of energy for heating were: to reduce the environmental impacts of the use of
energy for heating; to reduce the use of fossil fuels; and to reduce the dependency
on foreign countries. *Table 9.4* lists the specific policies that were introduced to
reduce the use of energy for heating.

Use of Domestic Appliances

The main government measures that were introduced specifically to *reduce* energy
consumption due to the use of domestic appliances, and the associated waste, were
taken from the point of view of their environmental impacts and the threatened
depletion of fossil fuels. The government has so far done little to reduce household
electricity consumption. Although some appliances have become more energy-
efficient in recent years, more households are using more of them (Novem, 1989).
In the past, public policies focused on saving energy, but mainly by reducing the
use of heating.

We can distinguish various product-oriented policies. First, we look at the
materials from which the product is made (substance policy), emissions due to
the use of a product, energy consumption, the nature, composition, weight, and
volume of a product, the sound produced by appliances, how the products are
processed after they are discarded (processing policy), and waste policy itself. In

Table 9.4. Specific policies that have influenced the use of energy for domestic heating in the Netherlands.

Specific policies to restrain the use of energy for heating	Measures in the given fields
Energy-saving policy	Fuel surcharge
	Environmental Action Plan (leasing HR boilers,
Environmental policy	public awareness raising, personal consultations)
	Environmental surcharge on energy bills
Public housing policy	Subsidies for insulation
	Public awareness raising
Physical planning policy	Subsidies for HR boilers
	Building regulations
	Building Decree
	Development area provisions
	National insulation program
	Insulation regulations
	Energy Saving Appliances Act
	Subsidies for solar boilers

the past, little attention was paid to the environmental impacts of products, e.g., emissions during the use and waste stages, the use of finite energy sources and raw materials, and the amounts of waste generated. Until recently environmental policy focused on industrial emissions of harmful substances (industrial metabolism). In some cases the government entered into agreements with industry to reduce the environmental impacts of products (e.g., to reduce the mercury content of batteries and single-use packaging).

As noted above, in the context of the Environmental Action Plan (MAP), the 1990 Energy Saving Memorandum allowed energy supply companies to levy a surcharge on energy bills to finance their activities. According to the plan, 1.3 million energy-efficient refrigerators will be sold before the turn of the century. In March 1995 the cabinet imposed a charge on domestic energy use, starting January 1996. The first 800 kWh of natural gas is exempt from this charge, after which 3.5 ct/kWh is charged (see Chapter 8).

In late 1994, the European Commission introduced a standard for the energy use of domestic refrigerators and freezers, although the Netherlands had already implemented earlier (1978) EC guidelines. Under Article 6 of the Energy Saving Appliances Act (1986), information on energy consumption had to be provided in the labeling of all appliances. The Act was intended to reduce energy consumption, but the bill was severely curtailed in the course of its processing. However, in January 1995 the Decree on the Labeling of Energy Use by Refrigerators and Freezers (based on the Energy Saving Act), stipulated that all new domestic refrigerators and freezers had to carry an energy label.

In the context of *environmental policy*, facilities were set up to handle discarded refrigerators and to drain off their environmentally harmful CFCs. In 1993 50% of all discarded domestic refrigerators and freezers were collected (TK, 1993–1994, 23 400/2). Since 1994, under the Scheme for Environmentally Friendly and Energy-Efficient Refrigerators, energy companies have given a discount of Dfl 50 on all new, energy-efficient, ozone-friendly refrigerators or freezers if customers return their old models to an official collection point that guarantees the safe removal of the CFCs.

Policy fields that have influenced the handling of domestic appliances at the waste phase can be divided into those that focus on the consumer, and those that focus on the producers. Policies focusing on producers (*products policy*) are quite recent. The draft Products Act, first introduced in the late 1970s, would have required manufacturers to include environmental considerations in all their products, and to provide information on environmentally relevant aspects (van den Biggelaar *et al.*, 1989, p. 15), but this section was not included in the final version of the Act.

In 1990 the Ministry of Economic Affairs published the Energy Saving Memo-randum: Energy Saving and Flow Sources Policy Plan, which announced schemes to promote and develop new materials or products, and to ensure their use over the long term. The 1989 NMP also stressed the need for stronger policies with regard to the relation between products and the environment, at all stages in the product life cycle. The means to achieve this included consultations with target groups, industry, intermediate traders, and consumers; product research and assess-ments; and the standardization of the information provided in product labeling, in order to encourage citizens and industry to take responsibility for maintaining en-vironmental quality. The National Environmental Policy Plan-plus (NMP+, 1990) made a start, with the development of an integrated products policy, detailed in the Product and Environment Memorandum (VROM, 1993), under joint responsibility of the Ministries of VROM and Economic Affairs. This Memorandum aimed to encourage producers, dealers, and consumers to reduce the environmental impacts of products.

In summary, the main objectives of government measures that aimed specif-ically to reduce *energy consumption* and *waste production* due to domestic appli-ances were: to reduce the harmful environmental impacts due to the use of domestic appliances; and to reduce energy consumption. *Table 9.5* lists the specific policies introduced to influence the use of domestic appliances.

The government has tried to influence household metabolism in various pol-icy fields: environment, energy (saving), traffic and transport, parking, physical planning, public housing, and products policies. These specific policies always intentionally aimed to *limit* the environmental impacts of household metabolism, from the point of view of the threatened depletion of fossil fuels and to reduce traffic congestion.

Table 9.5. Specific policies that have influenced the use of domestic appliances in the Netherlands.

Specific policies to restrain the use of domestic appliances	Measures in the given fields
Environmental policy	Collection of refrigerators
	Environmental surcharge on energy bills
Products policy	Dfl 50 discount for old refrigerators
	European standard on the energy consumption
Energy-saving policy	of refrigerators and freezers
	Energy Saving Appliances Act
	Energy labeling of refrigerators and freezers

Tables 9.3–9.5 list the government measures to reduce the use of the car, energy for heating, and domestic appliances, respectively. Policies focusing on the car and domestic heating recognized these as subjects of government control more than 20 years ago; those focusing on reducing the use of domestic appliances are much more recent.

9.4. Conclusions

In this chapter we have looked at the influence of public policies on individual behavior. We have tried to identify policies that have intentionally tried to guide certain aspects of behavior, and those whose side-effects (intentional and/or unintentional) have affected behavior. However, it is often difficult or even impossible to make a clear distinction between the effects of particular policies because environmental objectives have now been integrated in other policy fields. It is also often not possible to define some of the effects of non-specific policies as unintentional side-effects; rather, they may be the consequence of "inter-policy cooperation" (Knoepfel, 1995).

To change behavior intentionally, it is first necessary to understand the factors that influence this behavior. Public policies can determine behavior, both intentionally and unintentionally. It is important to be aware of the side-effects of policies in other fields because they may weaken, enhance, or even eliminate the effects of others. By being aware of the relations between policies, one may attempt to prevent these effects, and possibly to try to utilize this interaction. However, recognizing such mutual influences is not sufficient reason to change policies, since the intended policy may contribute significantly to the objectives and as such may be judged positively. Nevertheless, it is important to be aware of the specific cross-connections between policy fields.

So far, there has been no systematic survey of which public policies affect particular aspects of behavior. Although the government does not have a complete picture of the relations between policies in various fields, behavior-influencing policies are being followed.

In the past, household behavior with regard to the use of the car, energy for heating, and domestic appliances was influenced mainly by policies that were not intended to do so. Examples of "non-specific" policies whose side-effects had a *stimulating* impact on consumer behavior include public housing, physical planning, and incomes policies. Only in the past 20 years has the government adopted policies that were intended to influence household metabolism, mainly in response to the growing social concerns about the environmental impacts of the car, particularly the depletion of fossil fuels and increasing traffic congestion. These specific policies were *limiting* in nature.

The first efforts to reduce the use of energy for heating were made in response to the threatened depletion of fossil fuels, but later the need to reduce other environmental impacts were also integrated in these efforts. These considerations were also important in efforts to reduce the use of the car, although the main objective was to reduce traffic congestion. The use of domestic appliances is a separate issue, because this has only recently been recognized as an area of government control. Measures were taken to reduce household electricity consumption because of the threatened depletion of fossil fuels, and later also its harmful environmental impacts. But specific attention to the energy consumption of some domestic appliances and the handling of old appliances once discarded as waste is relatively new. The main objectives of specific policies focusing on reducing household metabolism due to the use of the car, energy for heating, and domestic appliances were:

- to reduce the harmful environmental impacts of car use;
- to reduce the consumption of fossil fuels and energy; and
- to reduce the negative economic effects of excessive car use (particularly traffic congestion).

Since 1950, however, household metabolism has been stimulated as a result of the unintentional side-effects of other public policies. Only in the last 20 years have policies been adopted specifically to limit household metabolism. At first, the balance between unintentional and intentional public policies on household metabolism was largely on the side of unintentional public policy, but during the last two decades they have become more evenly balanced. However, an effective intentional public policy to reduce household metabolism is now needed, in order to prevail over the unintentional side-effects of other policies.

This chapter has illustrated the mutual relations between public policies and three aspects of household metabolism (the use of the car, energy for heating, and domestic appliances) since 1950. As expected, we found both policies which focused specifically on these aspects and policies whose side-effects appeared to influence household metabolism. *Tables 9.1–9.5* list the policy fields and government measures that have affected each of these aspects, all of which must be taken into account in policies aimed at changing household behavior. To control behavior, it is necessary to be aware of the interweaving of various policy fields, in order to prevent the weakening and/or elimination of the effects of policy measures that may result in optimum target achievement. Further research is necessary, therefore, to investigate which specific policy fields play a part in influencing other aspects of behavior.

Summary

- Over the period 1950–1995 household metabolism in the Netherlands has been stimulated by the side-effects of policies that were not intended to influence these aspects of behavior (non-specific policies).
- Only in the past 20 years has the Dutch government introduced policies aimed at *limiting* certain aspects of household metabolism, as opposed to relying on non-specific policies.
- The energy consumption of domestic appliances and their handling after disposal during the waste stage has been only recently been recognized as a subject of Dutch government control, whereas the use of the car and energy for heating have been subject of government control since the 1970s.
- For the future, an effective public policy is needed that focuses intentionally on reducing household metabolism, in order to prevail over the unintentional side-effects of other policies.

Acknowledgments

The author would like to thank Prof. dr. J.Th.A. Bressers for his support and comments on draft versions of this chapter.

Notes

[1] Technological developments are determined as physical/spatial developments, because of their facilitating character.
[2] It was not just the price that caused this reduction in car use. In 1973, in order to limit the depletion of the domestic oil reserves, the government announced three "car-free Sundays", and issued petrol coupons that could be exchanged for petrol.
[3] Although equal opportunities for women is part of welfare policy, this is not discussed here; we address only those elements of welfare policy that have influenced economic development.
[4] Here, education policy is only discussed to the extent that it has influenced economic developments.

[5] The increase in energy prices in the late 1970s, and the expectation that the replacement
     market for obsolete domestic heating boilers would expand considerably in the 1980s,
     contributed to these technical efficiency improvements (Brezet, 1994).

References

Bouwer, K., R. Groenenberg and P. Leroy (1995) Milieubeleid en ruimtelijk beleid (Envi-
    ronmental policy and land use policy), in: K. Bouwer and P. Leroy (Eds.), *Milieu en
    ruimte*, Boom, Meppel/Amsterdam.

Brezet, H. (1994) *Van prototype tot standaard: de diffusie van energiebesparende tech-
    nologie* (From prototype to standard: the diffusion of energy saving technology),
    Rotterdam.

De Koning, M.E.L. (1994) *In dienst van het milieu: enkele memoires van oud-directeur-
    generaal milieubeheer prof. ir. W.C. Reij* (In service of the environment: memoirs
    of the former director general of environmental administration, Prof. ir. W.C. Reij),
    Alphen aan den Rijn.

De Maar, H.G. (1987) *Energierecht* (Energy law), Alphen aan den Rijn.

Drees, W. (1992) Economie, milieu en overheid (Economy, environment and government),
    in: *Milieu: tijdschrift voor milieukunde*, 2:52–56.

Former, H. (1995) *Ontwikkelingen in huishoudelijk afval: Een beschouwing van de ho-
    eveelheid en samenstelling van huishoudelijk afval (waaronder witgoed) in Nederland,
    1950–2050* (Developments in domestic waste: A vision of quantity and composition
    of domestic waste (including white goods appliances) in the Netherlands, 1950–2050),
    Report No. 23, Center for Energy and Environmental Studies, University of Groningen.

Groenen, W., E. Pommer, M. Ras and J. Blank (1993) *Milieuheffingen en consument: de
    gevolgen van milieuheffingen voor de koopkracht en de consumptie van huishoudens*
    (Environmental charges and consumers: the effects of environmental charges on
    household purchasing power and consumption), Social-Cultural Planning Bureau,
    Rijswijk.

Hamerslag, R. B.H. Immers and W.H. Scheltens (1988) *Research on factors influencing
    car mobility in the Netherlands*, Dept. of Transportation, Planning and Highway En-
    gineering, Delft University of Technology.

Klaver, J.C.M. (1993) Milieubeleidsstrategie; een bijdrage aan de discussie (Environmen-
    tal policy strategy: a contribution to the discussion), in: *Milieu: tijdschrift voor
    milieukunde*, 2:71–77.

Knoepfel, P. (1995) New institutional arrangements for the next generation of environ-
    mental policy instruments: intra- and inter-policy cooperation, in: B. Dente (Ed.),
    Environmental Policy in Search of New Instruments, Kluwer, Dordrecht.

Leidelmeyer, K., F. van Wijk and A. Buys (1993) *Rondom mobiliteit: toekomst van de
    mobiliteit omgevingsverkenning* (About mobility: future of the study of the context of
    mobility), The Hague.

Ministry of Traffic and Waterways (1986) *Afrekenen met files* (Be finished with traffic
    congestion), McKinsey, The Hague.

Naaijkens, H.J.M. (1989) Integratieproblemen; theoretische en praktische inzichten (In-
    tegration problems: theoretical and practical visions), in: P. Glasbergen (Ed.), *Mi-
    lieubeleid: theorie en praktijk*, VUGA, The Hague.

Novem (1989) *De isolatiegolf: overzicht van 15 jaar energiebesparing in de woningbouw* (The insulation wave: an overview of 15 years of energy saving in housing), Delft.

OECD (1995) *OECD Environmental Performance Reviews: The Netherlands*, Organization for Economic Cooperation and Development, Paris.

Schrijnen, P.M. (1986) *Autobezit en autogebruik: een inventarisatie van invloedsfactoren en instrumenten, een studie ten behoeve van de milieubeweging* (Car ownership and car usage: an inventory of influencing factors and instruments, a study on behalf of the environmental movement), Amsterdam.

Ten Heuvelhof, E.F. (1994) Het vraagstuk van samenhang (The question of coherence), in: P. Glasbergen (Ed.), *Milieubeleid: een beleidswetenschappelijke inleiding* (Environmental policy: a policy science introduction), VUGA, The Hague.

TK (1982–1983) *Plan integratie milieubeleid* (Plan on integration of environmental policy), 18 010, Tweede Kamer, The Hague.

TK (1983–1984) *Actualisering energiebeleid: onderdeel van de memorie van toelichting op de rijksbegroting voor 1984* (Energy Policy Actualization Memorandum: Eplanatory Statement with the Government Budget for 1984), ch. XIII, no. 2, Tweede Kamer, The Hague.

TK (1988–1989) *Nationaal Milieubeleidsplan: kiezen of verliezen* (National Environmental Policy Plan: to choose or to lose), 21 137, nos. 1–2, Tweede Kamer, The Hague.

TK (1989–1990) *Nationaal Milieubeleidsplan plus* (National Environmental Policy Plan-Plus), 21 137, no. 20, Tweede Kamer, The Hague.

TK (1989–1990) *Nota energiebesparing: beleidsplan energiebesparing en stromingsbronnen* (Energy-Saving Memorandum: Energy-Saving and Flow Sources Policy Plan), 21 570, nos. 1–2, Tweede Kamer, The Hague.

TK (1989–1990) *Tweede structuurschema verkeer en vervoer* (Second Traffic and Transport Structure Scheme), 20 922, nos. 15ä16, Tweede Kamer, The Hague.

TK (1991–1992) *Uitvoeringsnotitie parkeerbeleid* (Parking Policy Implementation Memorandum), 22 383, no. 1, Tweede Kamer, The Hague.

TK (1993–1994) *Rijksbegroting volkshuisvesting, ruimtelijke ordening en milieubeheer* (Government Budget for Housing, Physical Planning and the Environment), 23 400, ch. XI, no. 2, Tweede Kamer, The Hague.

Van den Biggelaar, A.J.M., J.H. de Rijk and E. Tellegen (1989) *Consumentenbeleid en milieu: advies voor het integreren van milieu-aspecten in het consumentenbeleid* (Consumer policy and the environment: advice on the integration of environmental aspects in consumer policy), Amsterdam/Utrecht.

Van Wee, G.P. (1993) *Lokatiebeleid en ruimtelijke ordening: de effecten op verkeer en vervoer* (Location policy and physical planning: the effects on traffic and transport), RIVM, Bilthoven.

VROM (1993) *Nota produkt en milieu* (Product and Environment Memorandum), Ministry of Housing, Spatial Planning and Environmental Management, The Hague.

WCED (1987) *Our Common Future*, World Commission on Environment and Development, Oxford University Press, Oxford.

Chapter 10

Diagnosing and Evaluating Household Metabolism

K.J. Noorman and A.J.M. Schoot Uiterkamp

Abstract

In this chapter we summarize the main findings of the research carried out within the HOMES project so far. We briefly discuss the application of the household metabolism concept as a metaphor, and identify the most significant driving factors and counteracting factors underlying the changes in household consumption patterns in the past. We conclude with an evaluation of the outcome of this diagnostic research, taking into account the various views of sustainability as discussed in Chapter 1.

10.1. Introduction

In the last few decades environmental scientists have generally approached environmental issues from a supply side perspective, emphasizing industrial and agricultural production and their often adverse environmental impacts. In doing so, they have followed the traditional approaches of economic historians, who have tended to emphasize the importance of supply side issues and technological changes to explain the industrial revolution of the last century. In their view, the demand for products has increased as a result of rising incomes or lower prices for industrial goods, but increasingly this view is now being questioned (Schuurman, 1997). Following Thirsk (1978), McKendrick pointed out that the industrial revolution was only possible as a result of the increasing demand for consumer goods in eighteenth-century England (McKendrick, 1982), i.e., that changing consumption patterns were the driving force underlying the industrial revolution. More recently, however, based on a study of household inventories in coastal areas in the

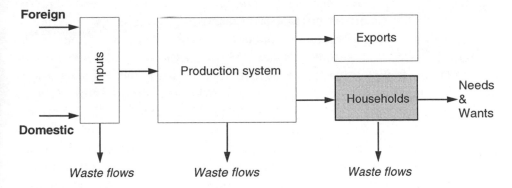

Figure 10.1. Households as an integral part of the economy.

Netherlands in the sixteenth and seventeenth centuries, de Vries (1993) concluded that people began to work harder in order to accumulate more consumer goods, rather than simply to escape poverty or famine. In all of these studies of cultural and economic history, households were found to have played an important role.

Recent sociological studies of consumption and the consumer society have emphasized either individual consumer behavior or institutional issues (Edgell *et al.*, 1996; Sulkunen *et al.*, 1997). We believe that the time is ripe for studies of past and present societies in terms of what they consumed rather than what they produced (Brewer and Porter, 1993). In the HOMES project, we have extended this idea by focusing not only on the past and present, but also on the future. Like all economic sectors, households directly or indirectly consume natural resources in many forms: energy, raw materials, water, food, and an almost innumerable, and still increasing, range of manufactured goods and services. These consumption activities result in the generation of waste, which ultimately ends up in the natural environment – in the air, water, soil, and in other living organisms.

The HOMES research team necessarily had to make choices regarding which disciplines should be included, which household characteristics would be studied, and both temporal and spatial limitations. For these reasons, important disciplines such as demography, sociology, history and technology assessment are not included in the present program, or only to a limited degree.

The HOMES research started from the notion that the significance of the household sector lies in both its *direct* and *indirect* demand for resources through the consumption of manufactured goods and services. As outlined in *Figure 10.1*, this view provides an appropriate framework for assessing the environmental impacts of all activities associated with household consumption. Households influence environmental conditions directly through the consumption of energy (mostly derived from fossil sources) for heating, transportation, etc., and for operating an increasing number of electrical appliances. Households also have a direct and mutual influence on their physical environment through the waste they generate, and the increasing spatial claims for housing or infrastructure. This is also reflected in a large body of research focusing on the direct resource demands of households. From the perspective of the direct demand for resources, the environmental impacts of household activities do not seem to be more significant than those of other sectors of the economy. For instance, the aggregated direct energy demand attributable to households in the Netherlands amounts to about 20% of the total indigenous direct energy demand. At the same time, however, the indirect impacts of household activities on the environment are quite significant; the use of an increasing range of goods and services influences industrial and service activities, and their related environmental impacts. The combined focus on supply and demand and the associated factors dominating physical flows throughout the whole economy justify the integrated and multidisciplinary approach adopted within the HOMES project.

The past, present and future patterns of household consumption, as well as individual consumer behavior, impact the environment. At the same time, the use of resources by households is influenced by many physical aspects such as climate conditions, the availability of resources, and spatial factors. Besides these mutual physical influences, both household consumption and its environmental effects are influenced by a variety of other technical, demographic, cultural, economic, behavioral, and institutional factors. Many of these aspects are dealt with elsewhere in this volume.

In the HOMES project the metabolism concept has been taken as a central metaphor to relate household consumption to the demand for natural resources, and the waste generated by the consumption of those resources. This diagnostic research has centered on the exploration of past and present characteristics and determinants of specific metabolic flows through Dutch households.

The IHAT formalism (Impact = Households * Affluence * Technology) adopted in HOMES is only used for descriptive purposes. We emphasize the need for a disaggregated classification of households, in which various characteristics simultaneously specify different household categories. This classification is necessary in order to explore satisfactorily the windows of opportunity for changing household consumption patterns in the future, taking into account sustainability and environmental quality objectives. Such characteristics include not only the types of housing, locations, household size, facilities inside the house, etc., but also the characteristics of individual members of the household and their interaction.

In this diagnostic phase of HOMES, research activities focused on two main research questions:

- What relevant trends in household metabolism in the Netherlands can be identified in recent decades, and what have been the impacts of household metabolism on environmental quality? To what extent have the observed trends been caused by changes in household consumption and/or by changes in the energy and material intensities of consumption, due to factors such as technological developments, economic, spatial, behavioral and social changes, or administrative policy measures?

- What conclusions about the future development of the use of resources for household consumption in the Netherlands can be derived by extrapolating these trends?

The preceding chapters have provided a substantial body of information on past patterns of household consumption in the Netherlands, and have attempted to explain the prevailing mechanisms and public policy measures underlying changes in household consumption patterns and related metabolic rates. In the remainder of this chapter we summarize and evaluate the various perspectives.

10.2. Evaluating the Metabolism Concept

The application of the concept of metabolism (which originated in the life sciences) within the context of the HOMES research has some limitations. In general terms, a metaphor can be used to describe a phenomenon in order to stimulate scientific thought, but can not be used to construct a theory. However, the metaphor has proved to be fruitful in linking consumer ends (increasing the quality of life) and means (the use of biophysical inputs and of manufactured goods and services). The metabolic models described in Chapter 1 also proved to be useful to relate the generation of waste to consumption activities (see also Noorman *et al.*, 1996).

The metabolism concept as used within HOMES emphasizes the mutual interdependence of structures and functions: functions take place or are performed within structures on which they are dependent, whereas structures change under the influence of functions (see *Figure 10.2*). Household functions are dynamically linked to physical and social structures. These links are characterized by time delays, different time horizons, and different spatial connections. For instance, the choice of a means of domestic heating (e.g., a coal-burning stove or a gas central heating system) is related to the availability of energy carriers and the necessary infrastructure. Changing social structures have also played a role; since the 1970s, for example, the growing differentiation between "home" and "work", as well as increased leisure time and incomes, have led to the greater demand for personal mobility. The explosive growth of communication services within the home provides another example of a rapidly changing structure that is now having a significant impact on the rate of household metabolism.

Researching a topic as broad as household metabolism requires access to a large range of data sets. Such data sets exist in the Netherlands, but are not always easily accessible, nor are the data always present in the required format. For example, data on direct energy and water consumption exist, but data on indirect energy and water consumption had to be extracted from diverse data sets that were often

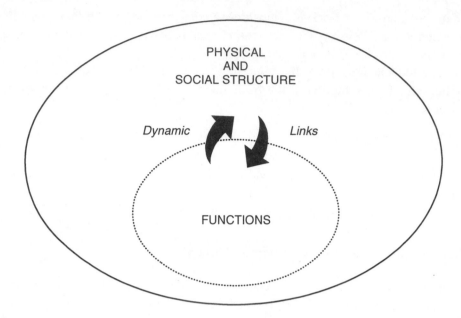

Figure 10.2. Structures and functions dynamically linked within the household metabolism concept.

collected for different purposes. Consumption data are often expressed on a per capita basis, so that for the HOMES research these data often had to be transformed to the household level. The collection of household-based statistics on a European scale has only just begun (Stanners and Bourdeau, 1995).

In using household metabolism as a metaphor, different normative aspects related to the debate on sustainability and environmental quality are important at two stages: in defining the goal of the metabolic model, and (more specifically) in evaluating the results. In the evaluation phase normative aspects are important when the observed trends in household consumption patterns and the related environmental impacts are set against sustainability and environmental quality goals. Different interpretations of sustainability and environmental quality yield different answers to the question of whether past and present household metabolism rates are in overall compliance with sustainability objectives. We discuss this topic later in this chapter.

The application of metabolic models does not mean that the aim of this type of research is to search for a state of equilibrium between social metabolism and natural metabolism. Here the analogy between the metabolism of a household and of living systems can be strengthened; living systems are not in equilibrium with their surroundings, but are in a constant state of flux, both adapting to changes in the physical environment as well as shaping it. The continuous process of evolution and change is often described in terms of adaptation, learning, creativity, and

Table 10.1. Factors underlying developments in household metabolism.

Driving forces	Counteracting forces
Demographic factors: *population growth, number of households, household size*	Technological improvements
Economic factors: *rising disposable income, declining prices*	Specific policy measures
Increasing opportunities and abilities	Public attitutes to environmental impacts of products and consumption activities.
Non-specific policy measures	

competition, descriptions that could also be applied to changing patterns of household metabolism. Transition paths towards the optimization of metabolic processes might be accompanied by the inefficient use of resources. This "squandering" of resources is often regarded as an inevitable feature of evolutionary processes.

10.3. Diagnosing Five Decades of Household Consumer Activities in the Netherlands

By integrating the outcomes of the projects described in this volume, we can obtain an overall retrospective diagnosis of the patterns of household metabolism in the Netherlands since World War II. *Table 10.1* lists the factors that have been most influential in changing both the rate of household metabolism and the related environmental impacts. We distinguish between factors that have had stimulating effects on household metabolism (i.e., driving forces), and those that have had limiting impacts (i.e., counteracting forces). Clearly, this list is incomplete (some other factors, including increasing leisure time, better education, and information campaigns, are dealt with in other chapters), which undoubtedly poses restrictions on the conclusions that can be drawn from the diagnostic phase of HOMES. The same holds for the spatial restriction to the Netherlands and the temporal restriction to the period 1950–1995. By focusing on households, other relevant organizational levels such as cities and states are also largely neglected.

10.3.1. Driving forces

Demographic Factors

Although in most European countries the growth in the number of households has exceeded population growth in the last 30 years, the Netherlands appears to be an extreme case in terms of changes in the number and composition of households.

The demographic structure of the Netherlands has changed significantly since World War II. In the early 1950s, with a population of about 10 million, the country could be characterized as one of emigration. Since then the population has increased steadily to about 15.5 million, and the Netherlands is now an immigration country. Between 1950 and 1994 the number of households increased from about 2.5 million to well over 6 million, and simultaneously, the average household size decreased from 4 to nearly 2.4 persons. As a result of this process, known as household dilution, about 65% of all households now consist of one or two people; this is now an important household category. In 1992 more than 30% of households consisted of just one person, i.e., about 12% of the total Dutch population now live alone.

The observed tendency towards more individual lifestyles in the last 50 years is also visible when considering the spatial claims of households. In dwelling design there has been a trend from limited, functionally undivided space inside the home, supported by shared facilities for common use outside, towards larger dwellings with greater functional divisions, and equipped with conveniences inside. The average area per person has increased, notably due to the decline in average household size.

Economic Factors

The disposable incomes of households increased substantially during this period. In real terms, the average income increased from about Dfl 20,000 in 1959 to nearly Dfl 35,000 in 1991 (1991 guilders), although the rate of increase has not been constant. Incomes policy had a restraining effect on incomes until the mid-1960s, but thereafter incomes began to rise. Although the nominal prices of energy and water increased due higher VAT and other taxes, the real prices declined as incomes rose. Although subject to fluctuations, the 1992 price levels of both natural gas and electricity were well below those of 1960 (in real terms). The combined effects of increasing real disposable incomes and decreasing real prices of important resources were manifest in increasing purchases of energy and water-using appliances, and rapidly rising private car ownership.

Opportunities and Abilities

Growing opportunities and abilities have resulted in increasing household con-sumption. Opportunity and ability factors themselves are a compilation of various factors; for example, the increased availability of many consumer goods to indi-vidual households is related to factors such as income, prices, advertising, leisure time, and the cognitive and physical capacity of individual consumers.

Non-specific Public Policy Measures

Household consumption has also been influenced by the unintentional side-effects of various non-specific public policies. Some aspects of household metabolism, notably the use of private cars and domestic appliances, have actually been stimulated by non-specific policies such as those relating to equal opportunities, incomes, and social welfare provision. On the other hand, such non-specific policies have untintentionally restrained the use of energy for domestic heating.

10.3.2.   Counteracting forces

Technological Improvements

Technological developments in both the production and household sectors have resulted in efficiency improvements in the use of energy and materials, which have generally had a restraining effect on household metabolism. The energy efficiency of many domestic appliances has improved significantly, so that the energy demand per service unit has declined throughout the period considered. Other factors such as the increasing number of services per appliance in the case of white goods, or the increasing weight of cars due to added features to improve comfort and safety, have worked in the opposite direction.

Specific Policy Measures

Many government policies have been specifically introduced to influence household metabolism. Policies in areas such as environmental protection, energy saving, traffic and transport, parking, physical planning, and public housing, have all aimed to limit household metabolic rates, in response to the need to reduce the rate of depletion of fossil fuels, harmful emissions, and traffic congestion.

10.4.   An Outline of the Overall Diagnosis

The analysis of past trends in some physical flows indicates that the use of energy, water, materials, and consumer goods have increased since 1950, although the rates of increase of natural resource use related to household consumption has not been constant. In our view, three periods can be distinguished. First, during the period of postwar reconstruction, 1950–1965, the emphasis was on rebuilding society, and low priority was given to the efficient use of resources or environmental protection. The second period, which began with the discovery of natural gas reserves in the Netherlands in the mid-1960s and ended with the second oil crisis (around 1980), was characterized by a rapid expansion of the welfare system. Households had easier access to resources such as energy and water due to large-scale investments in infrastructure, and many more consumer goods became available. In the third period (1980 to the present), there has been a decline in the explosive rate of growth in consumption seen in the previous period. The (temporary) oil price hikes and the associated concerns about future shortages of fossil fuels, the environment in general, and changing public attitudes about the environmental impacts of (the use of) products may have influenced this decline in growth. The penetration rates of many domestic appliances have also reached saturation. Nonetheless, new consumer goods are constantly being produced, incomes are still rising, and people have more leisure time, so that consumption and the related environmental impacts have also continued to grow.

We now discuss the patterns of use of energy and water to illustrate the changing rates of household metabolism. Until the mid-1960s, coal and oil were the main energy carriers used for domestic heating, but after the discovery of large natural gas reserves, natural gas became the major energy carrier for heating purposes. After the 1973 oil crisis, the demand for gas fell due to higher prices, successful energy-saving policies, and the implementation of energy-saving measures.

Between 1950 and 1979, the electricity demand per household increased by an average of 6.5% per year, from 500 kWh to 3055 kWh; it then fell to 2630 kWh in 1987, and rose again to 3030 kWh in 1995. Combining this pattern of electricity demand with the growing number of households, it can be concluded that, in contrast with the declining use of energy for heating in the last 20 years, the total residential electricity demand has risen steadily since the 1950s, and is likely to continue to rise in the future with the introduction of new electrical appliances, even if they are more energy efficient.

Along with the enormous growth in the use of the car, particularly for private use (the car fleet increased from 140,000 in 1950 to about 5.6 million at present), in 1995 energy demand for passenger transport (260 PJ) was almost six times higher than in 1960 (44 PJ). Analogous to energy consumption, residential water consumption has also increased steadily.

In order to understand these consumption patterns, we have investigated the underlying mechanisms, both at the level of the society as a whole and at the level of the individual household. Although it is difficult to assess their relative importance, at the societal level, technological, economic, demographic, institutional, and cultural developments have all influenced household consumption patterns. These factors have been discussed extensively elsewhere. Clearly, demographic factors (population growth, the increasing number of households and household dilution) have been important. Furthermore, the simultaneous rising disposable incomes and declining energy prices (in real terms) have not encouraged energy savings. In most cases, technological innovations have resulted in a decline in the energy demand per unit of service delivered.

The choices of households and individual consumers concerning the purchase and use of goods and how they run their households (i.e., differences in lifestyles) have a considerable influence on the environmental consequences of the household sector, as well as on the environmental impacts of activities in other sectors of the economy, such as industry, services, or transportation. The observed trends towards smaller households, larger and better equipped houses, increased car ownership,

Table 10.2. Schematic overview of some of the main developments in household consumption patterns in the Netherlands in the period 1950–1995.

Level 1	Level 2	1950–1995
Demographic developments	Population growth	++
	Number of households	+++
Resource use	Energy use	++
	Water use	0/+
	Spatial claims of households	+
Consumption growth	Possession of domestic appliances	+++
	Possession of cars	+++
	Passenger kilometers driven by car	+++
	Other consumer goods	++
Waste generation	Domestic waste	++

0 = no change; + = appreciable increase; ++ = strong increase; +++ = very strong increase.

etc., indicate changes in preferences towards more individual lifestyles in the last 50 years. These trends have also been influenced by a broad range of public policies. It is impossible to make a clear distinction between the effects of specific and non-specific policies, particularly in the case of environmental goals, which have gradually been integrated into all policy fields. However, it has become clear that the effects of many policies that specifically aimed to limit household metabolism have been weakened or even eliminated by the unintentional side-effects of other non-specific policies.

In summary, the direct and indirect consumption of resources such as energy and water, the increasing number of consumer goods used by households, as well as the waste generated by and the environmental impacts of these activities, have increased enormously over the last 50 years (see *Table 10.2*). This growth has been the result of a myriad of factors, some of which can be influenced relatively easily within short time horizons, and others that do not allow much interference that would be acceptable within current social settings.

10.5. Evaluating Household Consumption Patterns: Dealing with Uncertainties

Our diagnostic research on household consumption patterns in the past has yielded large data sets on the use of various natural resources, consumer goods and services, and the generation of waste. It has also provided helpful insights into the wide range of economic, technical, psychological, spatial, institutional, and cultural factors that have influenced household consumption. The key question now is to what extent this increasing consumption is threatening sustainability goals. In other words, are past trends in consumption (and the related production activities) in the Netherlands in overall compliance with sustainability objectives (taking into account environmental quality aspects) in the long run?

Clearly, the increasing use of consumer goods and services has coincided with rising demand for natural resources (energy, materials, water) and the related production of wastes that ultimately end up in the environment. Furthermore, in a densely populated country like the Netherlands, the spatial claims of households have resulted in conflicting demands for land. These past trends in natural resource use and their environmental impacts lead us to believe that current levels of consumption are not sustainable in the long run. This statement, however, presupposes that the environmental impacts of consumer activities are always negative – in the past, present, and in the (long-term) future.

When evaluating the outcomes of this research we touch upon the discord between the "hard" data collected, and the interpretation and use of these findings in formulating management strategies to redirect past household consumption patterns towards a "sustainable end level". This problem highlights the multi-interpretive and dynamic character of the concept of sustainability discussed in Chapter 1. The dynamics refer to time-related sets of norms and values that differ both within and among societies concerning human interactions with nature. Interpretations of events that happen in the "real world" are determined by the beliefs of the nature of the "reality" that is being explored. Different world views reflect different images of reality that deal with (social and environmental) risks and uncertainties in different ways. To answer the question of whether past consumption patterns are sustainable, and if not, what are the most suitable strategies (i.e., physically possible and socially acceptable) to achieve a sustainable situation, therefore requires insight into the patterns of uncertainty. In this context, the recurring question "Do we have sufficient knowledge to deal with the problems we are facing?" turns out to be crucial when dealing with either environmental concerns in general, or more specific problems such as global warming, or whether a consumer good or activity is environmentally friendly. Judging the answers to these questions depends on what factors are included in the judgment, and the relative weights given to each of them.

As mentioned in Chapter 1, the contributions of various sociocultural perspectives within the context of sustainable development and environmental quality are increasingly being recognized. To deal with the various norms and values when evaluating past consumer patterns and their environmental impacts in the Netherlands, we now recall briefly the cultural theory developed by Schwarz and Thompson (1990) to describe social and natural systems. They developed a four-fold typology (see Chapter 1) to investigate the beliefs in nature (or world views) that guide risk-taking decisions, by combining the typology of human nature with that of physical nature (the latter was derived from the work of ecologists such as

Holling (1979) and Timmerman (1986)). Holling stated that, when confronted by the need to make decisions even in the absence of sufficient information, (ecosystem) managers *assume* that nature behaves in certain ways (see also Adams, 1995). Holling proposed three "myths of nature" – nature benign, nature ephemeral, and nature perverse/tolerant – each of which can be associated with a different management style, and Schwarz and Thompson added a fourth – nature capricious – to combine these myths of nature with the typology of human nature. They distinguished four perspectives:

Individualists regard nature as benign. According to this myth nature is predictable, stable and forgiving. The management style associated with this myth is *laissez faire*. *Egalitarians* view nature as ephemeral, fragile and unforgiving, and to be protected from humans. The guiding management rule is the precautionary principle (tread lightly on the Earth). *Hierarchists* see nature as tolerant; nature is forgiving in most circumstances, but care must be taken not to tip the scales too far. The associated management style advocates control and regulation in order to prevent major excesses. *Fatalists* view nature as unpredictable, beyond human control, and one can only hope for the best. Therefore the most suitable management style is again *laissez faire*, in the sense that there is nothing to manage.

Returning to the question posed at the beginning of this section – are past and present consumption levels in compliance with sustainability objectives? – we cannot give a straightforward answer. Different myths of physical and human nature generate different answers and solutions. The participants in the debate do not dispute the fact that consumer activities have environmental consequences; the main question is whether the environment has been degraded beyond certain physical and ecological thresholds, and if so, whether these environmental consequences are a price worth paying for the benefits of increasing consumption levels. Since the representatives of the various perspectives argue from different premises, they naturally disagree about the appropriate (policy) response.

10.6. Evaluating Household Metabolism: Implementation of the Different Perspectives

In this section we evaluate past and present household metabolism from the perspectives of the individualist, the hierarchist, and the egalitarian. We do not deal with the fatalists' view of past household consumption patterns, since they see no point in participating in the debate. Nothing they will do will make a difference, and thus there is no need for them to learn from the past. For each of the three other perspectives, we present the general attitudes to economic growth, the role of government, technological developments, and nature (*Table 10.3*), and then evaluate household consumption patterns and their environmental impacts.

Table 10.3. Characteristics of three perspectives (partly based on Rotmans *et al.*, 1994; Janssen, 1996).

Notion	Individualist	Hierarchist	Egalitarian
Economic growth/ consumption growth	Preferred: creation of personal wealth	Preferred: creation of collective wealth	Not preferred
Driving force	Growth	Stability	Equity principles
Attitute towards government	Reject government regulation	Avocate government regulation	No externally imposed rules
Attitute towards technology	Developments autonomous	Regulating developments	Selective control
Attitute towards nature	*Laissez-faire*	Regulatory	Attentive
Attitute towards transition	Non-issue	Preferred within boundaries	Inevitable

The Individualist's View

Individualists tend to view economic growth, and along with it increasing consumption levels, as preferable. The generation of personal wealth is everyone's individual responsibility. Individualists believe in market forces and reject the regulatory role of the government. Technological innovation has led to the availability of an increasing number of consumer goods. Technology is also regarded as useful for overcoming the relatively small environmental side-effects of the generation of wealth. Since nature is regarded as robust and benign, environmental issues do not have high priority on the individualists' agenda: resources are abundant, nature's assimilative capacity is as yet infinite, and human-induced climate change may even open new possibilities for increasing levels of welfare in many parts of the world.

According to the individualists, the debate on a transition from the current unsustainable consumption patterns based on the use of fossil fuels, towards environmentally sound lifestyles, is premature and potentially hinders the aim of individual consumers to strive for increasing levels of wealth. They would argue that in all respects, much progress has been achieved in increasing the standards of living of Dutch consumers since the 1950s: a broad range of consumer goods that save time and increase comfort are now available; almost all households now possess a car, have higher disposable incomes, and have more leisure time. Clearly, these developments have been accompanied by rising levels of energy use and waste generation, but energy is now used more efficiently due to new technologies, and waste is controlled, managed and some of it is recycled. Although government regulation has been influential to a certain extent, the role of the market has been effective and accurate. Environmental problems such as the release of toxic substances have already been partly resolved (e.g., lead-free petrol is now available, and measures have been introduced to reduce acid depositions), and so far there are no signs that we cannot deal with similar problems in the future.

The Hierarchist's View

From the hierarchists' point of view, economic growth is also preferred, although they emphasize the benefits of collective rather than individual wealth generation. They believe in the equal distribution of wealth among households and advocate strong government regulation for the collective good (see also Adams, 1995). Rather than accepting technological developments as autonomous, hierarchists believe in regulating and controlling new technologies in order to achieve the optimal social benefit from these new technologies and to protect society from their undesirable negative side-effects.

If properly managed, nature is tolerant: most resources are available but some are becoming scarce, and nature's assimilative capacity is large although limited. The hierarchists regard anthropogenic climate change as a problem. The negative environmental side-effects of the growth in consumption in the past suggest that it is worthwhile to try to moderate economic activity in order to achieve economic growth patterns that are in balance with the environment's carrying capacity.

Although in the Netherlands much has been achieved in terms of increasing welfare levels, in terms of material standards of living and "well-being", it has also become clear that rising welfare levels have put pressure on the physical environment and caused other problems as well. For example, the continued use of fossil energy has led to serious levels of greenhouse gas emissions; the rising consumption of (ground)water, notably by the household and agricultural sectors, has caused falling water tables in many areas; and increased car ownership has led to traffic congestion, noise, and air pollution. To overcome these problems, strong policy initiatives (both national and international) and government regulations are necessary. The main challenge for the future is to achieve economic development while taking into account environmental thresholds.

The Egalitarian's View

Egalitarians believe that, in contrast with the current emphasis on economic growth, quantitative output growth is not preferable. Rather than measuring wealth creation in terms of the number of consumer goods and holidays that are now within the reach of individual consumers, egalitarians feel that quality of life depends strongly on non-material aspects of life. Egalitarians point out that history provides many examples of the potentially dangerous spin-offs of many new technologies (see Tenner, 1996), and advocate selective control of new technologies. Nature is viewed as fragile and precarious. Natural resources are scarce, and an increasing number of signs at all levels indicate that the interaction between humans and nature is not sustainable. In dealing with both environmental problems in general, and more specific problems such as global climate change, the precautionary principle has to be adopted. The need for a transition towards more sustainable lifestyles is not a subject for discussion. Routes toward sustainable lifestyles in which strong group loyalties and care for the environment are prominent issues, should be explored. With respect to the rising levels of consumption in the Netherlands, the increasing demand for resources such as energy, materials, water, and space, is alarming. History shows that these problems are beyond government control. Material welfare and other quality of life aspects have reached a state of imbalance, and these series of warnings should be at the basis of strategies aiming at environmentally sound lifestyles.

The boundaries between the various perspectives are rather vague, and elements of all perspectives can be found in designs for a sustainable future. This led Moll (1993) to propose a "paradigm-independent" perspective of the environmental physiologist. This perspective builds on the notion that communication between the various perspectives can to some extent be facilitated by the construction and application of integrated models that describe the interaction between social metabolism and that of nature. The environmental physiologist designs (formal) models that describe social and environmental metabolism, and evaluates the results in terms of their contributions to sustainable development within the domains of the different perspectives (see *Figure 1.5*). Such metabolic models might facilitate communication by exposing the differences and the similarities between the various perspectives.

This approach was the starting point of the diagnostic research within the HOMES project, and offers the possibility to evaluate past consumption trends in the Netherlands and the related environmental impacts. We have portrayed the various manifestations of household metabolism and have identified and examined the causal factors. The picture of household metabolism patterns since 1950 is by no means complete, nor is it intended to be. With reference to the outline of the diagnosis presented earlier in this chapter, we conclude that metabolic rates have increased rapidly since the 1950s. Considering the driving forces underlying these developments, there are no short-term signs that there have been any shifts towards sustainable household consumption patterns.

Returning to the question posed at the beginning of this chapter, our overall conclusion is that the evaluation of the diagnostic phase of the HOMES project shows that the future demand for resources due to household consumption will exceed the potential of the sustainable supply of resources within an acceptable level of environmental quality. These findings are supported by (environmental) policy responses, which can be regarded as the outcome of the ongoing debate within society in which, with the exception of the fatalist, representatives of all categories participate. This being so, "sustainable options" that aim to reduce household metabolic rates have to be (re)designed, and ways to implement them need to be identified. This conclusion yields a number of research questions for the *change* phase of HOMES:

- What are the possibilities for and constraints on achieving substantial reductions in the future use of resources by households? What technical, economic, spatial, behavioral and/or administrative policy options, instruments and methods could be used to achieve such reductions?
- What reductions in the use of resources by households can be (maximally) realized if the identified technical, behavioral, spatial, economic and administrative policy options, instruments and methods are (optimally) implemented?

To answer these questions, metabolic models will be designed and applied to explore possible routes for reducing the environmental impacts of consumption. By adopting the metaphor of household metabolism, we obtain a picture that relates the use of natural resources to the very reason for economic activity: consumption in households. The reorientation of consumption and production activities in the long term, under sustainable development strategies, can reasonably be expected to embrace the principles of closed-loop chain management of natural resources and of ensuring renewable supplies of these resources (Biesiot and Noorman, 1997). The HOMES research will proceed by constructing scenario variants that are consistent with the various perspectives, and describe the integrated metabolic flows of materials and energy related to the consumption of goods and services, and their associated environmental impacts. Although within each perspective there are different windows of opportunity for reducing the environmental impacts of consumption, the different scenario variants can be evaluated within the different perspectives.

Options that aim to reduce future household metabolic rates by lowering material consumption levels can generally be expected to be more difficult to implement and to meet more public resistance than those that aim to reduce future material and energy demands by increasing the efficiency in the delivery of services. This notion was also acknowledged in the *National Environmental Outlook 2* (RIVM, 1991):

> As production and consumption continue to increase, it will be continually necessary to adopt supplementary measures in order to stay within the environmental constraints. Such measures will require an increasing degree of sacrifice. If the technological options for adaptation become exhausted within the limited time available, then a fundamental revision of our expectations in regard to the nature and the extent of "economic" growth will be unavoidable.

The various types of households in the Netherlands, representing different consumer lifestyles, have different environmental impacts (as shown in Chapters 2, 3 and 7). These different household characteristics will be taken into account when designing scenario variants that aim to reduce metabolic rates. It is also important to note that any assessment of the amounts of energy and materials that will be available to households in the future touches upon the issue of global equity. A proportional and just distribution of available global resources will necessarily result in strong additional constraints on future rates of household metabolism.

The challenges posed by climate change and the desire for equity – important issues in the context of sustainable development – are formidable. It is clear that to achieve the reduction goals indicated above will require major changes in the metabolism of households and of production. Specific redesign rather than evolutionary change is essential, although this may appear to be at odds with the actual trend of ever-growing development, production, consumption, and disposal of products and services. This is especially true in areas where the fastest growth in consumption is in high energy intensity items (such as cars). This way of quantifying the issue of sustainable development shows the importance of interdisciplinary approaches; such redesign will require the involvement of many actors at different levels of society, the rearrangement of social institutions, the creation of new incentive structures, etc. Different disciplines will be required to investigate different aspects of household consumption patterns using specific sets of constraints, which will ultimately determine the potential for changing household metabolism along sustainability lines (Biesiot and Noorman, 1997). The similarities and differences between the results from various normative approaches will be explored further in the change phase of the HOMES project.

Acknowledgments

The authors gratefully acknowledge the help and comments on earlier drafts of this chapter of W. Biesiot, K.J. Kamminga, and H.C. Moll.

Notes

[1] We acknowledge that the cultural theory of Thompson and Schwarz (1990) has its limitations. In a critical examination, Boholm (1996) did not reject the theory as such, but noted the lack of empirical support.

References

Adams, J. (1995) *Risk*, UCL Press, London.
Biesiot, W. and K.J. Noorman (1997) Energy requirements of consumer lifestyles: A case study of the Netherlands (working title), *Ecological Economics* (submitted).
Boholm, Å. (1996) Risk perception and social anthropology: Critique of cultural theory, *Ethnos*, **61**(1–2):64–84.
Brewer, J. and R. Porter (Eds.) (1993) *Consumption and the World of Goods*, Routledge, London.

De Vries, J. (1993) Between purchasing power and the world of goods: Understanding the household economy in early modern Europe, in: J. Brewer and R. Porter (Eds.), *Consumption and the World of Goods*, Routledge, London, pp. 8/5–132.

Edgell, S., K. Hetherington and K. Warde (Eds.) (1996) *Consumption Matters*, Blackwell, Oxford.

Holling, C.S. (1979) Myths of ecological stability, in: G. Smart and W. Stanbury (Eds.), *Studies in Crisis Management*, Butterworth, Montreal.

Janssen, M. (1996) *Meeting Targets: Tools to Support Integrated Assessment Modelling of Global Change*, PhD thesis, University of Maastricht.

McKendrick, N. (1982) Commercialization and the economy, in: N. McKendrick, J. Brewer and J.H.P. Plumb (Eds.), *The Birth of a Consumer Society: The Commercialization of Eighteenth-Century England*, Europa, London.

Moll, H.C. (1993) *Energy Counts and Materials Matter in Models for Sustainable Development: Dynamic Life Cycle Modelling as a Tool for Design and Evaluation of Long-term Environmental Strategies*, PhD thesis, Groningen University.

Noorman, K.J., W. Biesiot and A.J.M. Schoot Uiterkamp (1996) Household metabolism: A new concept to investigate the society–environment interface, in: *Proc. Ecology Societé Economie Conf.*, Paris, May 1996.

Rotmans J., M.B.A. van Asselt, A.J. de Bruin, M.G.J den Elzen, J. de Greef, H. Hilderink, A.Y. Hoekstra, M.A. Janssen, H.W. Köster, W.J.M. Martens, J.W. Niessen and H.J.M. de Vries (1994) *Global Change and Sustainable Development: A Modelling Perspective for the Next Decade*, RIVM Report No. 461502004, Bilthoven.

RIVM (1991) *National Environmental Outlook 1990–2010 (2)*, National Institute for Public Health and Environmental Protection, Bilthoven

Schuurman, A. (1996) Aards geluk: consumptie en de moderne samenleving, in: A. Schuurman, J. de Vries and A. van der Woude (Eds.), *Aards Geluk*, Balans, Amsterdam, pp. 11–27.

Schwarz, M. and M. Thompson (1990) *Divided We Stand: Redefining Politics, Technology and Social Choice*, Harvester Wheatsheaf, Hemel Hempstead, UK.

Stanners, D. and Ph. Bourdeau (Eds.) (1995) *Europe's Environment*, European Environment Agency, Copenhagen, prepared by Earthscan, London, pp. 502–510.

Sulkunen, P., J. Holmwood, H. Radner and G. Schulze (Eds.) (1997) *Constructing the New Consumer Society*, Macmillan, London.

Thirsk, J. (1978) *Economic Policy and Projects: The Development of a Consumer Society in Early Modern England*, Clarendon Press, Oxford.

Timmerman, P. (1986) *Mythology and Surprise in the Sustainable Development of the Biosphere*, Cambridge University Press, Cambridge.

Tenner, E. (1996) *Why Things Bite Back: Predicting the Problems of Progress*, Fourth Estate, London.

Index